Big Pig, Little Pig

Big Pig, Little Pig

A Tale of Two Pigs in France

JACQUELINE YALLOP

FIG TREE
an imprint of
PENGUIN BOOKS

FIG TREE

UK | USA | Canada | Ireland | Australia
India | New Zealand | South Africa

Fig Tree is part of the Penguin Random House group of companies
whose addresses can be found at global.penguinrandomhouse.com

First published 2017
001

Set in 11.4/14.03 pt Bembo Book MT Std
Typeset in India by Thomson Digital Pvt Ltd, Noida, Delhi
Printed in Great Britain by Clays Ltd, St Ives plc

A CIP catalogue record for this book is available from the British Library

ISBN: 978–0–241–26141–5

www.greenpenguin.co.uk

MIX
Paper from
responsible sources
FSC® C018179

Penguin Random House is committed to a
sustainable future for our business, our readers
and our planet. This book is made from Forest
Stewardship Council® certified paper.

There is only one photograph of me on my fortieth birthday: January, a clear blue midwinter sky, sharp shadows. I'm wearing dark green overalls and wellies. The overalls are new, criss-crossed with pristine white zips, only a dusting of mud around the knees. I'm sitting on a pile of clean, fresh straw. Across the top of the picture, around head height, there's a long strip of old corrugated metal, some thick weathered tarpaulin and a couple of planks; another piece of metal is propped upright behind my shoulder. Beyond, in bright light, it's possible to make out the textures of a ragged stone wall and trails of ivy. I'm at the edge of a kind of den which recedes darkly behind me.

Later that day, before the sun drops too low, we have a celebratory barbecue. The front door to our house is on the first floor, approached by a broad flight of cracked stone steps; the top of the steps widens to create a concrete platform, a small square terrace by the door. This faces south: the sun pounds it all summer and even in January, on a fine day, it's sheltered and warm. We've eaten Christmas lunch here once or twice. And this is where I sit now, in a pool of faint warmth, while I open presents. Pork chops cook on the grill and Ed, my husband, pours wine. We talk about the odd construction we built that morning out of bits and pieces unearthed from the shed and garden: the main structure is cobbled together from a large plastic picnic table covered with the sheets of corrugated iron and secured with heavy planks. It has extra support at one end from two wooden pallets set upright and wedged against a tree stump; the other end is blocked off by another, smaller sheet of corrugated iron which is too holey to form any kind of roof but which encloses the space, in the same way a windbreak at the beach marks off a patch of sand. At various points, the slim trunks of young plum trees act as buttresses. Inside, it's high enough to crawl easily on your hands and knees, or to crouch. You can lie out flat, should you want to, nestling into the straw, with enough space for a friend to lie alongside you, although the end of your legs will poke out into the open.

This is our pig shelter. We've built it on a small piece of land about ten minutes' walk from our house, a disused orchard surrounded by ivied stone walls and accessed through a small wooden door. No one has paid any attention to this land for years. It's only around twenty paces wide and long – too small a patch to be of agricultural use – and, in addition, cut off from the fields around it by its walls. It's stuffed full with brambles, nettles and weak trees; the walls are crumbling in places, or completely fallen, the ivy roots pulling the stones apart. The door was once painted white, but now has a blueish-grey tone; the wood is rotten at the edges and along the bottom; you feel it give as you push it open. The first time I did this, fighting to open the door against the foliage beyond, catching my first glimpse of the enclosure within, full of skittering great tits and bramblings, snakes, no doubt, rabbits and mice, hidden things, I felt my heart in my throat; a secret-garden moment of discovery. And just as in *The Secret Garden*, this land does not belong to me; I have no rights over it. But it feels instantly special, intimate. It feels like my land, my patch, a hidden place. I'm already curious about its histories. Who planted the fruit trees? Why is such a small piece of land enclosed so carefully? Who tended this before me; who was it who came and pushed the little door, who whitewashed it?

In this derelict part of France there are plenty of such unanswered questions, glimpses of forgotten lives seen out of the corner of your eye: in every cluster of houses there are those which are dilapidated, sunken and ruined; between the neatly kept pastures, with fences and gates, there are frequently parcels of overgrown land with old or fallen trees, high, tangled weeds and crumbling walls through which deer and boar and badgers come and go. This is a long-peopled but empty land, a place of ancient dolmens, crumbling medieval villages half-lived-in, a network of old drystone huts, *caselles*, which once gave shelter to those working the fields or tending the animals – protection from the hot sun or the rain, an overnight bothy – and which are now crammed with bits and pieces of rusting farm equipment, or simply forgotten. The web of walled paths and tracks which divides the meadows one from the other and links each small hamlet with the next is unmarked and unreliable: here and there the tracks have been dug over and the stone taken away; others have been fenced off or blocked by tangles of brilliant-blue agricultural string; many are simply too overgrown to pass. This is the *département* known as the Aveyron, the rural heart of south-west France, a poor region on the edge of the massive, unforgiving limestone *causse*, a long way from motorways and TGV connections and urban centres, not well marked on tourist maps: the evidence of many pasts has been left to rot down here.

Our would-be pig enclosure is one of these abandoned remnants, too insignificant a plot for farmers to bother with, not worth the time and money required to salvage it. Our house has a large garden, almost an acre, mostly just a grassy field with a few patches of lavender and roses, hollyhocks and sweet william close to the house, a long wide strip given over to growing vegetables, some fruit and nut trees and a boggy pond that burps with frogs. But it's not ideal land for pigs: it's too open, bitty and irregular in shape, difficult to fence, making it almost impossible to keep livestock from encroaching on the house, the flower beds, the washing line. So we've borrowed this plot from some friends who have a portfolio of similar scraps of land, and who have agreed to lend us this one for a few months until the pigs outgrow it. It is accessible down a rutted track which turns off the lane which runs to our house; at one side there's a small barn; across the track a ruined farmhouse with sagging outbuildings and a charming circular tower, a *pigeonnier* once used to keep doves, a fairytale relic. This place, this hamlet, has a name, Mas de Maury, and a deep well which remains full except in the driest of summers; here and there you can see the broken outlines of other walls, buried and scrappy. *Mas* is the way of naming many of the hamlets here, the *lieu-dit*, the way a place is called; it's from Occitan, the local language, which borrows and lends to other languages in the area like Catalan and Provençal. *Mas* apparently comes from the Latin *mansum*, 'the place where one remains'. From the same root, modern French gets *manoir* and *maison*. The designation *Mas* was used through the Middle

Ages to mark a farmhouse of stature with dependent workers, a relatively wealthy place, a key player in the feudal system. What we see here are the remains of several families, or several clusters of the same family, a thriving enterprise, a community. There's a simple stone cross at the end of the track to the Mas de Maury, where it leaves the road; it's marked at the base with initials: I. B. A whisper of the family that lived and farmed here, nothing more. Now there's no one, except us.

We'd taken several days to clear the dense nettles and brambles. We had to cut our way through the door; cut our way into the door in the first place, hacking at the thick boughs of ivy that looped across it, and then inching it open, feeling the planks shudder, pushing it in the end just far enough to squeeze through. We borrowed a heavy-duty strimmer and worked painstakingly towards the centre of the land, disturbing all kinds of things with the noise and upheaval: a female kestrel that had settled in the barn and wheeled back and forth over our heads, flicking shadows; cormorants passing the winter in a huge ash tree by the lake a little further on; deer that bolted out of the hedges and bounced away, their white rumps bobbing. For a while, the skies and fields were skittish with anxiety and it felt as though we were intruding.

But the commotion, the disturbance, passes. The land gets cleared. The cormorants hunch again on the high branches, still and slightly sinister, and I trust that the deer return too, invisibly, lightly. Our comings and goings become part of this place. But I never lose the feeling that I'm being granted temporary leave to belong here; I become aware, all around me, of time, as though you can see it, as though it thickens the air, and I see quite clearly my smallness, my briefness, here, on this patch of land which other people, many other people over many centuries, have cleared and tended and abandoned, and which has allowed me to inhabit it for a while.

We've set up the shelter close to the highest of the stone walls for protection. Crawling in underneath, we push at the makeshift sides in the way we think a pig might. Nothing gives. We congratulate ourselves on its stability. When we lie in the straw, this feels like a cosy place, a den. I sense the primeval rush that comes from having made a safe shelter, the home-making impulse stripped bare: here among the fields that fold and stretch away on either side, the dense blocks of forest and the old tracks which join them, here is a square of land protected by a high wall, and inside this square is a new three-sided shack that will keep out the rain and wind and could be thought of as a 'house'.

Ten years earlier, when I turned thirty, I was working as an art gallery curator, indoors, in an immaculate, catalogued, climate-controlled environment. I did not own overalls or even wellies; I walked out at weekends on footpaths, and occasionally, at the end of a summer's day, I would lie back in the heather on the hills. But mostly I went shopping in my lunch hour, waited for buses and trains, accommodated myself to a townscape. To celebrate my thirtieth birthday, I met a few friends for a drink in Sheffield town centre; we ate burgers and ice cream in an American diner. The evening was drizzly and a bit grey. I don't remember much about it. It was pleasant enough, ordinary. But this, for my fortieth birthday, this is memorable; this now feels extraordinary. I wriggle in the straw; I lie out flat, staring at the metal roof above, pocked with holes through which the sky burns blue; I smell the rawness of this earth all around, laid newly bare, the freshness of the stalks of weeds that remain standing here and there, the damp dust of the old stone. I hear the silence of a cold winter morning when the air is crisp and pinkish with frost.

This is when the photo is taken: *click*: happy birthday.

It was Ed's idea, first, to get pigs. I'm not sure such a thing would ever have crossed my mind. We didn't move to France with any particular plans for self-sufficiency or a back-to-nature odyssey. We came more or less accidentally, on something of a whim, because we could, because our freelance writing work and the inexorable spread of the Internet made it possible to live anywhere and this seemed as good a place as any, a workaday, inelegant, unhurried place of distant horizons. Neither of us comes from farming or even rural families; neither of us had expressed a secret passion for a smallholding. I was a middle-class, suburban, only child, brought up in the cul-de-sacs of Birmingham and Manchester, in nice family streets where the gardens were taken up with lawns and flower beds and paddling pools, and everyone laughed at Tom and Barbara trying to keep livestock in the potting shed because that was the nature of *The Good Life*, a comedy, an eccentricity, not something real people did. I'd been taught to value the clean and orderly, the predictable. I didn't have a pet. But I did love being outside. At this point it couldn't be called anything as grand as a passion for nature, since I really only glimpsed nature by default in fleeting moments, disconnected from my daily life, but it was bright and auspicious, nonetheless: gathering conkers on a windy day, digging up worms in the garden, kicking through leaves on the way to school, summer picnics in country parks. There was a specialness about the outdoors, I realized that already. It had something to do with freedom and adventure, independence, courage; it also, somehow, touched on my interest in history and archaeology, in how people had lived and the things they left behind. But I didn't know where the connections were, or how to express them; I didn't know what it was that drew me to green places of moss and air, old trees, tatty urban fields, a mysterious outdoors where the sky and the land slipped away together in the distance, and layers of me peeled away, too, so that what was left was essential and unequivocal.

One of my clearest childhood memories comes from the summer when I was eleven. I went on holiday with my parents to the Yorkshire Dales. I went from a road in Birmingham, a busy commercial road with shops and petrol stations and traffic lights, to a cottage in Nidderdale. As soon as we arrived, while my parents unpacked, I ran up the hill, a distance of no more than a couple of hundred yards, and threw myself down in the shelter of a stone wall. Below me, the valley opened up, green and rolling and apparently without end; a few cottages here and there, a sweeping sky. I remember this, even now, with absolute clarity. I felt as though I had been tipped out of a box and fallen to this place, this utterly unexpected other world, and the landing had taken my breath away. I remember small things: a bee buzzing near my head, a beetle at my feet, the prickle of grass. I remember the wind, a gusty summer breeze, unlike any wind I'd known, smelling different, feeling different, and I remember the complete and absolute astonishment at such openness, such space, such powerful land.

I kept a secret diary, a tiny notebook with lilac pages, and in it I recorded the succession of marvels I continued to find breathtaking: crows lined up on a wire, flowers in a hedge, mist in the valleys, horizons. This was the first time I had really *seen* things; this was the moment when the world around me was not just *there*, like some kind of theatrical backdrop, but was alive and enveloping, irresistible. There are wilder places, of course, than the Dales and in time I discovered some of them. But the passion I felt at that moment, at eleven years old, was elemental and overwhelming; like a young gull launching from a cliff into the endless rise and fall of the thermals, I was sustained in a kind of euphoria until, a week later, we drove back home down the M6.

That emotional, instinctive, intense reaction to the nature of the land was to remain with me, become important to me, help decide who I am and where I should be. But I didn't think then that it would have anything to do with keeping pigs.

First came a dog, Mo, the summer after Ed and I moved to France, an indefatigable, scatty Dalmatian of imperfect spots. And around the same time, we started growing things. We'd come from a neat little terrace in Sheffield and a tiny garden of pebbles and paving to this old farmhouse with a sprawling piece of land, surrounded by woods and meadows. We hadn't been desperate to leave Britain; such a migration wasn't a lifelong dream for us as it is for some. But we already had a suspicion that we might like to stay; we were quickly seduced by the easy, free, sunny days, and we began to put down roots, literally, by making ourselves a garden. There wasn't a great deal to be done to the house. It's built to the local pattern: a straight-forward construction of two or three living rooms on the first floor, with stores and workrooms below. There's a small barn to one side and another (mostly ruined) outhouse to the other, enclosing a yard to the front. On all sides, the building is protected by trees so that it's sheltered from winds and shaded from sun and often seems to hide away, like a rabbit squatting in the undergrowth.

The house had all been knocked into a decent state by the previous owner and didn't need any real attention from us. But outdoors was a different matter: neglected and overgrown, the grass head-high and slithering with snakes, the trees packed too close, a droughty yellow, the soil jaded and stony. So we waded in to clear the field with strim-mer and scythes and shears, dug over the vegetable patch and extended it, cutting out a new piece of growing land. We retrieved the currant bushes from their cloaks of brambles and pruned the cherry trees; we planted a peach tree, too, and some vines. We began to spend more and more time outdoors, working on the flower beds at the front of the house and thinning the mass of plum and beech and oak that shaded them, planting herbs against the barn wall, learning how to germinate and bring on seeds. Tentatively, because they were new to us, we experimented with 'exotics' like aubergines and chillies that, to our delight, quickly flourished in the hot, dry conditions. We discovered that tomatoes don't have to be red, that black and green and white and orange varieties each have their own distinct flavour. A short while later, with great excitement, we brought home four black hens in cardboard boxes from the market, letting them wander freely in the garden and the adjoining fields, becoming accustomed to their friendly repertoire of squawks and discovering the daily tactile delight – and frustration – of searching for eggs among the straw in the woodshed, in leafy corners, alongside walls, in nettle beds – anywhere but in the neat little hen house.

But nearly all the local families dig vegetable gardens and have a few chickens; we were simply keeping up with the neighbours, fitting in. Whereas the raising of pigs was not a visible part of the lives around us. Next door, beyond the field beyond our garden, is a small farm, typical of the area, a muddle of old buildings in a patchwork of land. The old-fashioned farmer used the network of *caselles* as he walked his cattle about daily, moving them from one small patch of grazing to another, much as shepherds do, to be sure of the best pasture. The cows here are raised for young beef – *Le Veau d'Aveyron* – a deep-pink meat that has protected status, produced from cattle brought up in large, open spaces, kept alongside their mothers until they're stocky, muscly young adults. Traditionally, most herds were small – perhaps no more than ten or a dozen animals – and there's a photograph of our neighbour from twenty years ago driving his handful of buff-coloured cows beneath summer trees, his shoulders covered with an old sack, his smile sheepish beneath his beret. There was a pig at his farmhouse in those days and the days before – habitually, inevitably – just as there were chickens and rabbits in hutches and three large vegetable gardens. But shortly after we moved in, our neighbour was kicked by one of his horses and died in a field, a little over eighty years old. Now, there's no longer a pig. His widow, Solange, is relieved not to have to keep such an animal in the stall alongside the house; she prefers the smell of cows, she says.

The winter after we arrived here, just over twelve years ago, we walked across the fields to the next hamlet where we knew another farmer who lived in a modest, shabby 1970s bungalow with the old farmhouse abandoned alongside; on previous occasions we'd had a guided tour of the ancient tractor stock and the impressive woodpile. It was a day or so after New Year; it's good manners to make an effort to wish those around you '*Bonne Année*', one of those small undertakings which belies the isolation of those who live most of their lives alone with their families; it's a reinforcement of community which, in turn, means security and knowledge and variety. And so we intended to do the rounds of our neighbours and show that, even though we were odd English interlopers, we had at least some grasp of basic courtesies. We were met outside the garage by Sylvain, the teenage son. He was on edge; he did not greet us with the usual smile but looked up and down the deserted lane behind us, as though we might be trailing a gang of thugs in our wake. Something secret seemed to be happening. Something disreputable. He hesitated, and then anxiously ushered us into the workrooms under the house. 'Quiet,' he said, 'come quickly,' and he hurried us through a gap in the doors and closed them firmly behind us. Only when we were safely concealed in the basement did he stop and turn to shake our hands in greeting, and smile: *Bonne Année*.

The itinerant pig-killer had been, a man of brutal but inexpensive methods, who was just clearing away his tools. There were trestle tables covered with bits and pieces of flesh; there was a lot of blood, on the floors, on the tables, on hands and faces; there were buckets filled with a great deal more blood, and entrails; dogs were scavenging from one pile of meat to another. We watched for a while as the butchering progressed. Someone was grinding meat; someone else was doing something slippery with innards. I don't remember much detail. In the windowless basement, the light was dim and soupy, but that's not the reason my memory is hazy. It was a struggle to take all this in, the unexpected sight and sounds of dead animal in the winter cold, and the tense, exhausted excitement of the family. What I recall is a sense of the raw, hard, confused nature of what was going on, and shock at the knowledge that these neighbours had a pig at all – we had met them many times herding cattle from one pasture to another; their yard was filled with chickens, and often we came away with a bag of eggs; but I had no idea they kept a pig. This was an animal that had been locked in a small stone pen under an old barn by day and night, a pen without windows, without light, without air, stifling hot in summer, freezing in winter; it had been alone. It had been fattened without fuss and dispatched in secret. For the year or so of its pitiful life, it had been almost entirely invisible; more, it had been as though it did not really exist. I came away with a hearty but flabby roasting joint, and a feeling of having been witness to something shameful.

No one else we knew kept pigs. Even here, in the hidden pockets of *La France Profonde*, it was no longer a normal thing to do. Apparently, more hamlets and villages in France bear names referring to pigs and pig-keeping than to any other single activity – from the obvious *La Porcherie* (pig farm) to the more obscure *Suin*, derived from the root for swine – and yet this commonplace of country living is now not at all common. I couldn't have picked up the desire to keep pigs by wandering around the neighbourhood watching hearty old sows snuffle idyllically in gardens. Chickens scuffle in the lanes everywhere, ducks too, geese and noisy guineafowl; goats come and go around the houses, there are a few sheep – but no pigs. Animals that not very long ago would have been ubiquitous here have now disappeared. Keeping pigs would be a choice, not a habit.

We juggled the idea of our own pigs for a long time, back and forth between us, nothing much more than a 'what-if'. We came back to it time and again over months, even years, enjoying the whim. It didn't seem like it would ever really happen. But the more we talked about the possibility of pigs, the more it nudged its way to the front of our thinking, edging inexorably from a what-if to a must-have. Ed did some research, thorough and cautious. He began to drip-feed the information we needed to know: there was this piece of land we could borrow from neighbours; two pieces, in fact, the small enclosed old orchard for when the pigs were small and a larger field with sloping woodland for when they were older; pigs were ideally suited to forage among the oaks and could mostly fend for themselves; we would have to buy two pigs, because a pig needs company and should not be kept on its own. We looked at what pig-keeping might mean on a practical daily basis. There was, as always, the problem of money: Ed's journalism only paid essential bills; my novels only haphazardly brought in cash for extras; we were already scraping by, using up our savings to make ends meet. An investment in livestock would mean substantial costs – food, fencing and equipment, not to mention the price of the animals themselves – which would stretch us even further. But there were good things, too, about our situation: we both worked from home, so we could easily accommodate the routines of care and feeding, and we hoped not to have to go anywhere much for the next year or two, so we could guarantee being around to enjoy the pigs and, perhaps more importantly, the meat that followed.

And so, before we'd even really noticed, we had plans. I don't recall a particular moment of decision, just a momentum of wishing so that somehow it was agreed: we would have pigs. Two pigs. Our pigs. Even now, when I think of this, I feel a jump of excitement at the prospect, but in a sensible, responsible way we spent several more weeks discussing all the possible implications and making sure we had it all straight.

One other thing we discussed only briefly, because it seemed self-evident: our pigs would not be pets. They would be raised for meat. This was the whole point of it. Besides, we did not have the capacity to keep, or the money to feed, fully grown, adult pigs for any length of time – so we would have to kill them after we'd had them for around a year. This would give us two good-sized carcasses: enough to pack the freezer and to offset some of the expense. It would be good meat; we would know exactly its provenance and would be able to guarantee its quality.

That was the deal. Pigs as an investment. Without the final promise of bacon and loin steaks, chops, sausages and pâtés, the experiment was simply not possible. 'There is no savings bank for a labourer like a pig,' observed the agricultural writer Samuel Sidney in 1860: a pig-let bought for a sovereign in early summer, fed on household waste and fattened up on grains or fallen acorns and nuts in time for Christmas would not only provide a sumptuous feast but also 'hams [which] he can sell to buy another pig, and the rest will remain for his own consumption, without seeming to have cost anything.' The pig-killing, then, was a moment of reckoning, when the long months of nurture were turned to profit and the natural balance of the world properly poised. We were entering into the pig-keeping business with hard noses and clear heads; like nineteenth-century labourers, we needed a return on the expenses of rearing and husbandry.

That was agreed, then: we would kill them. It seemed simple enough. A straightforward calculation of investment and return; pigs as an old-fashioned 'savings bank'. We didn't know then, of course, what was to come. How could we? The pigs hadn't even arrived. There was no way of knowing what it might actually be like to raise a pig or how endearing they might be or how attached to them we might become. That was impossible to know. So we just went along with the basic tried-and-tested smallholding script: animals in, animals grown, animals slaughtered. That was how it would be, we thought. That was what we agreed, from the beginning.

Our pigs would be black. The *Gascon Noir*, or *Noir de Bigorre*, is an ancient, hardy breed of pig which can live outside all year round. It looks something like a wild boar, with thick, wiry black hair and a pointed face, but with long loped ears and a much bigger, heavier frame. These pigs have been part of family and farming life in the central Pyrenees and the surrounding regions since the Roman period: the nineteenth-century French veterinarian and zoologist, André Sanson, traced the *Noir de Bigorre* to a handful of original breeds that he considered 'pure', emerging from prehistoric Africa where it was domesticated by Iberian explorers, subsequently becoming widespread in Spain and southern France.

But it's a pig that takes a long time to mature, and so it's particularly unsuited to intensive farming methods. Many modern pigs are battery farmed: they are bred to grow quickly and can reach

a slaughter weight of 100kg in 24 weeks; often, they are killed
sooner – at four or five months – because smaller carcasses are easier
for abattoirs to handle. The meat is lean, pale, bland, cheap: popular
with shoppers. In France, the recovery from the Second World War
was linked to a push towards industrialization and more and more
intensive farming practices. No one wanted a pig which took two
years to 'grow', and which produced dark meat and dense layers of
rich fat. The *Noir de Bigorre* was out of fashion, an anachronism, too
expensive to rear and too distinctive for the modern marketplace.
Numbers fell so far in the post-war decades that by the 1980s there
were only two males and a handful of females remaining, hidden
away in small farms scattered around the Upper Pyrenees. A rescue
programme was launched to save the breed.

A few miles away from our house, we had bought meat from a
farmer called Benoît who had turned over acres and acres of oak
woodland to a herd of *Gascon Noir* pigs; several herds, really, num-
bering up to 120 animals at a time. We'd seen the pigs at a distance,
running into the trees at the sound of our car, and we'd been up close
in the enclosures where the sows farrowed and fed their piglets.
These were plain, stocky, beautiful animals, nothing frivolous about
them, not quite tame, no longer wild, still manipulated by humans,
anciently natural, as much a part of the dry, limestone landscape as
the prehistoric dolmens and medieval chapels that punctuate the
edges of forest paths. These were easy pigs to keep, genuinely and
habitually free range – and now famed for the quality of their meat.
In an age increasingly valuing slow food – a 'foodie' age of farmers'
markets and organic produce and strong flavours – the very characteristics which had once threatened the existence of these animals
were, ironically, their strongest assets.

We arranged with Benoît to sell us two weaners, piglets of around
twelve weeks of age. I suppose it had crossed my mind that we might
choose the ones we wanted, picking them from a litter like puppies.
Let's have that one, the cute one; let's have the one with the floppy ears; no,
that one. But then, then they would be pets, wouldn't they? And anyway, the idea clearly never occurred to Benoît who, in a businesslike
manner, simply took the order and asked whether we wanted him to

put rings through their noses, to prevent them from digging the ground. No, we said, no rings, and that was that.

In the days before the weaners are delivered I become obsessed by pigs. I've never touched a pig; I've only got vague memories of indeterminate piles of pink flesh in the barn at a children's farm; I've never been up close. I have no idea what to expect. What are they like? What do they 'do'? Do they smell?

I read as much as I can. The first thing I discover is that pigs are bright, capable, seriously intelligent. I have a vague sense that I knew this already, but it was information I'd never paid any attention to, and now I do. I look at studies. I marvel. Pigs, it turns out, are at least as clever and sociable as dogs, with a similar inclination to human company. This is good; I like dogs. I read about an experiment carried out at Cambridge University in 2009 which took four pairs of pigs and put mirrors in their pens with them for five hours. They could explore the mirrors in any way they wanted: at first they were cautious, but soon they were happy to press their noses close and watch their reflections; one pig charged at its reflection and broke the mirror; others looked behind, to try to work out what was going on. Each pig was then placed in a pen with an angled mirror and a partition, behind which were treats. (Apparently, pigs are partial to M&Ms; this, too, is a new discovery.) Seven of the eight pigs immediately understood what was happening with the reflections, looked behind the partition and found the food. A control group of pigs that had never seen a mirror before were suitably baffled and mistook the reflection for reality, rooting around behind the mirror in a fruitless attempt to track down the snacks. According to those who ran the experiment, this proves pigs have a high degree of 'assessment awareness', which is the ability to use memories and observations to assess a situation and act on it.

It's not yet clear whether pigs can actually recognize themselves in mirrors, a feat which would rank them alongside apes, dolphins and elephants in terms of intelligence, but they can certainly not be dismissed as dullard farmyard stock. Even though my research is hurried by the fact that there are pigs on the way, any day, I manage to unearth plenty of other cases which seem to prove the brilliance of pig cognition: apparently, pigs are among the quickest of any animals to learn new routines and are capable of jumping hoops, bowing, spinning, rolling out rugs, herding sheep and playing video games with joysticks, should you wish them to. They also have long memories.

Physically, too, there are interesting things about pigs. The pig genome and the human genome are closely related, large sections of both having been maintained in an unaltered state since the ancestors of hogs and humans diverged around 100 million years ago. Pig hearts are very like human hearts, metabolizing drugs in a similar way; pig teeth and human teeth are alike; pigs share a human propensity for laziness and so weight-gain and the diseases of sloth. Apparently, given the chance, they like to lie around, drinking, even smoking and watching TV. I wonder about the efficacy of the shelter we've built: no bar, no ashtray, no satellite feed.

Reading pig studies is fine. It gives me a sense of 'the pig' in a general way, allowing me to grasp facts and contexts. But it doesn't really seem to have much to do with my pigs, *the* pigs. Unexpectedly, it's shopping that makes it all immediate and authentic and certain; it's the discovery of a strange and uncharted array of goods and equipment that seems to say, yes, you'll soon be the owner of animals, livestock; you'll no longer be the person you were but a different person, one who knows what it is to keep a pig.

We live on the edge of an area known as the Rouergue, an ancient Occitan province bounded to the north by the mountainous Auvergne and to the south by the fruitful Languedoc, a region that was wealthy and powerful during the Middle Ages when wealth and power were largely determined by land and its produce. We briefly discovered the region on holiday but returned in less of a rush a few years later and chose this as a place to stay for good because we were drawn by its warmth and ordinariness, its food and history, and by the expanses of forest and field worked in a small personal way from one-man farms clustered in sparse hamlets. We didn't know a great deal more than the guidebooks told us but it was immediately evident that families and land here remained interdependent; you can't help being aware of the annual calendar of rural tasks: hedge-cutting, pollarding, ploughing, sowing, haymaking, harvest. But what has also become clear, as we've stayed longer, is how this is a place poised, teetering between one time and another, an old bundle of habits and a new one, a known, steady life and a fragile future. The depopulation of the post-war years has been halted, at least temporarily, by the influx of migrants like us – the British and the Dutch, principally – and the tenacious hold of a few young families, but even in the decade or so that we've lived here, our village has begun to loosen its grip on the land, farming giving way to short-term jobs of one kind or another with uncertain contracts: portering at the hospital, driving lorries, handing out publicity for the local radio station, care work. Gifted teenagers move away to university and rarely return; those who fail to pass the precious *Baccalauréat* struggle to find work of any kind and drift away anyway, barely hopeful. Very few local people here aspire to work from home in the way we do – what they really want is secure government posts with good pensions – and agricultural labour is seen for what it is: brutal and unrewarding. Small farms have been parcelled up and divided over and over again, from generation to generation, until they're tiny, the fields dotted around the neighbourhood, the scraps of forest unprofitable, the land barely providing a living for a single man, let alone a family.

This is a poor community, its fabric wearing thin, a place of widows. The obituary notices in the local press commonly announce the deaths of old women well over the age of ninety but men routinely die much earlier, and in the decades of widowhood, the picturesque rambling farms of leaking barns and tumbling walls are held together by the toil of women like Solange. Occasionally, they meet for an afternoon of gossip in someone's front room or, in hot weather, deep in the shade of the farmyard, but on most days they are alone, working their way through tough tedious chores, tending their gardens and bemoaning rising costs. It's not a life many young women, or men, aspire to these days. It can't go on. Solange has already rented out most of her land to another local farmer who's attempting to piece together enough fields to put together a sustainable business with several herds of cattle, but he's approaching late middle age himself, and when I look across the flowery meadows to Solange's farmhouse I wonder how this landscape will change, what will become of the old buildings and the old ways, how soon what I see now will become just another sediment of history here, buried and forgotten, hardly visible.

But for now, despite this growing sense of the precarious, our nearest town remains thoroughly and anciently agricultural. There is still a vibrant weekly produce market and a monthly cattle fair; it's easy enough to browse for what the pigs might need in one of the series of out-of-town suppliers that line the main road. But it's baffling. There's a whole new language to be learned which helps define the different stages of animal growth, the technicalities of feeding and watering, dietary nuances and medical needs. What's more, this stuff is really expensive. We have to spend a serious amount of time picking through the detail to find out what is absolutely necessary and what might be considered optional, or even a frippery. It comes as a surprise to learn that local farmers can be tempted into buying all kinds of apparently unnecessary equipment, from decorated feeding trays to state-of-the-art vehicles, until I remember that the toy shop further along the road, wedged between the supermarket and the timber yard, has aisles and aisles dedicated to toy tractors of all models and colours, harvesters, trailers and livestock pens: children here are taught from an early age that objects of desire are to be found around the farm.

We don't buy very much: some green plastic poles and some metallic string which we can connect to a battery and make into a basic electric fence; a black bucket, also plastic; overalls and some new wellies. This is the most basic of pig-keeping starter kits, but even this makes me feel as though we've properly begun. It heralds a life change; it makes it clear that something is on the way. It's exciting and memorable, like buying your first record, your first make-up, your first bra. It feels like a rite of passage; it feels as though something astounding is about to happen.

Some things we look at but don't buy: things for the end, for killing a pig, for managing a carcass. We've not yet got the weaners; there's no hurry to equip ourselves for their last days. But it's in our minds, nonetheless. I look into the cost of buying an additional freezer so that none of the meat is wasted. And I begin to read about abattoir conventions and what it takes to slaughter a pig. Ed works out carcass weights and processing costs. We make an effort to face up to the details of death and we start to edge towards a significant deci- sion: we don't want our pigs to be subjected to the trauma of an abattoir slaughter; we want to have some control over the act; we want to do the best by them. We read and we talk and we make a promise: when the time comes to kill the pigs, we will kill them our- selves and we will do it here, at home.

But we don't really know what such a promise means, of course. How many comfortable, middle-class, western European people like us know, these days, what it means to kill a pig? And even now, at the back of my mind, there are doubts. I don't mention them to Ed, and mostly I ignore them. But every now and again I wonder if I'm really the person to do this, to slaughter an animal; I wonder if I'll be able to face up to such a task in the end. In an abstract way it seems a reasonable decision, ensuring the most humane end for the pigs, keeping everything close to home, following tradition. But I'm not a nineteenth-century French farmer. I'm a twenty-first-century writer who spends much of the day in front of a laptop and who gets upset when small birds fly into the windows and break their necks. How, then, will I manage with a fully grown pig at my mercy? Do I grasp – really grasp – what that would be like?

Of course I don't. Not yet. It's no more than a landmark in the far distance, just about perceptible but unapproachable, indistinct. It's true that in my reading there are plenty of warnings about taking on the task of killing a pig at home: 'To kill a hog nicely is so much of a profession,' wrote William Cobbett in *Cottage Economy* in 1828, for example, 'that it is better to pay a shilling for having it done, than to stab and hack and tear the carcass about.' But it's hard to make such advice from the past *matter*. It's easy to think we know better. After all, we don't mean to stab and hack and tear. We mean to be simple and compassionate. It seems right that we should take responsibility for the end of the pigs, as much as for the cute beginning. We'll have done all the raising ourselves; we'll be eating all the meat ourselves. It seems logical to take charge of the slaughter as well.

So then: simple and humane. And perhaps a little adventurous. And perhaps, too, with half an eye on our place here in this land of many people's pasts. Other families have killed a pig here in this house, in this hamlet; so can we. So *should* we? We've been in France now a good handful of years; we have friends, attachments, habits. But there is no way you can come to a different country to live without viewing things for a long time as an outsider and without *being* an outsider – and the need to belong is powerful and seductive. Is there something, right at the back of my mind, that tells me killing pigs at home will somehow bind me irrevocably to the past, to the place, root my life here so that it seems less transient? Do I hope that this act of slaughter – this sacrifice? – will somehow appease the grumpy old gods who pester us with bills we can't pay and threaten us with a return to the drizzle of British cities and proper jobs? Much more than simply a means of stocking the larder, killing a pig is traditionally a landmark, a rite, one of those events which acquire resonance through repetition from one generation to the next. Being present at a pig-killing is a mark of respect: to the animal which provides so much, to the family who own it, and to the customs and practices of the neighbourhood. Killing a pig is an act of belonging. Just at the moment, this seems important.

But I don't agree on the home slaughter with any of these thoughts clear in my mind. I agree to it because I honestly think it will be best for the animals. And it seems sensible to make the decision now, at the beginning, so that we can make proper preparations and so that we can know, from the start, what the end will be. If we go into the process now with our final intentions clear, then there can be no mistake, no doubt.

And it doesn't occur to me at all that we might change our minds. I don't really consider that a decision taken in the cool good faith of planning and preparation might be upended by the plain, tangible reality of the pigs themselves. At this point all the reading and discussion seem to make things perfectly clear; we've been thorough and pragmatic. It all appears straightforward. Emotion simply doesn't seem to come into it.

After all, how difficult can it be to kill a pig?

★

Here they come. The van is bouncing down the track; the trailer bouncing behind. Standing by the low wooden door into the orchard, I watch Benoît manoeuvre deftly across the ruts and tufts to bring the back of the vehicle close. It's an open trailer and I can see both of the weaners, side by side, their noses raised. They are stocky, about the size of a smallish Labrador, with wide backs and small bright eyes; their ears flap forward and the underside is a soft, leathery greyish-brown. They look about them, tussle and nudge, look again, curious and eager; they keep up a quiet chorus of grunts and chatters, but don't seem particularly put out by their journey across the main road.

Benoît leans over the side of the trailer and grabs the first weaner by the hind legs, swings it above the bars, tucks it under his arm and carries it through the door, stepping over the string for the electric fence and placing it inside. It squeals energetically, as you would expect a pig to, and squeals more mournfully when it's left momentarily alone while the whole operation is repeated with the second weaner. But as soon as they're together, they become quieter, just chattering together in their low grunts. They stand still on a little patch of soil and ivy between slender tree trunks, puzzled and wary, looking about them. They don't like to move, that's clear. They don't trust this place, this ground.

Benoît, too, looks about. He's a lean, strong man with deep wrinkles and big hands, a slow smile. He tests the solidity of the electric fence, walks the length of it, pushing at posts and wires. He suggests that we put in some additional posts to strengthen it at the corners. They'll push, he explains, and test all the boundaries. Coming inside, he smiles at the shelter, slaps the plastic table legs hard and says much the same thing: they'll have this down, in time. He is methodical, businesslike. There's no chit-chat or pig pleasantry: he checks the pigs will be secure, fed, warm, that's all.

Then he leaves. The weaners listen hard to the sound of the van and trailer driving away. Still they move only their heads; their trotters are planted. They don't risk even a step.

We take a close look at what we've got. These are beautiful animals. They have a thick dark hide like an elephant's, with long black hairs which lie flat on their rump and shoulders but which come together in a kind of bristly mane along the length of their backs; they have a fluffy fringe on their brows which sweeps rakishly between the ears. Their skin seems too big for them; it gathers into loose wrinkles around their necks and shoulders, as though they're wearing a new jumper a few sizes too big. They have squat soft snouts, wrinkled too, leathery to the touch, knobbly knees and wonderfully smooth tensile tails, strong and active, always on the move; sometimes held straight like a rat's, sometimes curled. The tails of the two pigs are different: one coils more readily and more tightly than the other.

We put down some grain for them, directly on to the ground among the trails of ivy leaves which have survived the clearing. It's a couple of yards from where they're standing, and so now they have to move if they want to eat. They sniff, hesitate. Yes, they want grain, but in this strange place with these strange people the smells in the air are confusing and foreign, new sounds come unexpectedly, there are risks. They look at us, weighing us up, their faces apparently unchanging, and yet somehow full of expression. In the slight dip of their heads and their intense black stare, in the twitch of their ears, they give away their reluctance to move, their astonishment at the way the morning is unfolding, their bewilderment. For long minutes they watch us uneasily, making no noise. But they sniff again, their noses working hard, taking in the comforting cereal smell of the dry grain. And pigs + food is a reliable equation. In the end, they can't resist. One of them takes a step, and then another step, quickly now, desperate to be first. In an instant, the diffidence has vanished: all of a sudden this pig seems to have made up his mind; all of a sudden this is a competitive pig, active and hungry and focused. And before he's even reached the pile of food, the other responds. They're barging and tussling. They each head for the same side and splash their noses through the grain, bringing them up white and floury like old-fashioned Sherbet Dabs. They wrangle for the best spot, push their heads hard together, flick their tails, and finally come to some quiet agreement, settling to serious feeding side by side. The strangeness and menace of arrival seem completely forgotten in the familiar delight of eating together, shoulder to shoulder.

They seem quite content. They eat peacefully and methodically, snuffing up the dry husks with their noses so that it winnows away. There's no more than a few handfuls of food, but they're diligent in finding every last speck, truffling into the soil with their noses and nuzzling under leaves and twigs. In this way, with their heads down and their ears flapping over their eyes, they edge gradually away.

Now they're on the move. All at once mealtime is over and they begin to explore. They trot towards the clump of trees at the far end of the enclosure; they catch the scent of something and begin to dig with their noses; one of them comes back to us, his snout raised and muddy, the other finds the water tray and drinks a little before standing in it and sloshing around. They are inquisitive and confident, and never still: they wrestle with the flapping fabric of my overalls; tip over the plastic bucket and roll it, examine it from all angles as though it was the subject of some experiment; they go back to where the grain was scattered and check nothing has been missed; they sniff the air and listen. They listen a lot, to our voices and to each other and to occasional sounds from outside: cars passing on the distant lane, or tractors; the church bells striking the hour. They briefly examine their shelter but at the moment they don't show much interest in this: they want to be outside under the bright blue sky, scampering from one thing to the next. I get the sense they are sizing things up: the scope of the enclosure, the strength of the stone walls, the efficacy of the fence, the sweeping possibilities of open land which lie beyond.

It's not easy to tell them apart. There's the difference in their tails, but this can be deceptive, since both spring and wiggle so constantly. One weaner's head is a little longer and narrower than the other, and their frames, too, are slightly different: one is broader, shorter, lower to the ground. As they grow, these variations in build will become more evident – in the months to come we will discover that the pigs have contrasting characters, too – but these two small black animals foraging in front of us have a long way to go, and for now you could be forgiven for thinking they are identical.

We give them names. We need to be able to identify them, one from the other, so that we can know which pig is doing what, which pig is fattening better, which pig is sick or lost. It's a pragmatic decision and we're very careful: we don't give them pet names or indulge in anything fanciful. We don't want to make them cute or lovable; we simply want to be able to tell them apart. We look them over and decide the minor variation in physique will be enough to define them, so we just call them 'Big Pig' and 'Little Pig'. Big Pig: Little Pig. Epithets chosen simply on the basis of a slight physical difference, without emotional implications or associations, without any kind of anthropomorphism. Big Pig: Little Pig. It doesn't seem like much of a concession to sentimentality. How can the name 'big' or 'little' inspire affection? It's just a recognition of size, nothing more. But language is a slippery thing and we're not to know, just yet, how much complex and unique identity can be bundled up in the name 'Big Pig', or how much fondness can be implied in the way 'Little Pig' becomes the butt of jokes.

At the moment, watching the weaners scrum and squabble on the damp earth of nearly-spring, there's no way of knowing this.

★

The pigs are an attraction. Word spreads. Later, when I go down the track with a bucket of food, I find someone has pushed open the wooden door, and I can hear voices from within the enclosure. An elderly couple have walked from one of the nearby hamlets with their toddler grandson and they are standing together just outside the electric fence; the weaners are performing admirably, edging as close as they can, squealing and snuffling and then skittering away. I have no idea how these people knew so soon that the pigs were here.

They appraise the quality of our livestock and judge them to be fine. They inquire, in detail, about what food I'm using. They have plenty of advice. In particular, we should be careful, apparently, of boar who will charge the fence, either in an attempt to free their long-lost kin or to mate with them. I point out that both our pigs are male.

When I come to feed the pigs at the end of the afternoon, new visitors have arrived. These are from further afield, making the journey on an orange tractor; I don't know them and have never spoken to them, but recognize the woman vaguely as a local farmer. She's with her father, who looks the pigs over with a practised eye for a long time before agreeing with the earlier assessment that they're fine stock. Again, there's a boy, older this time, about ten years old perhaps, old enough to climb over the fence into the enclosure; the pigs snort with delight and bustle happily with their new playmate.

Over the following weeks, most of our neighbours come to see the weaners. Some of them come regularly. Pig-watching, I soon realize, is something everyone seems to enjoy. And I find I, too, spend a long time over the small daily tasks that need doing. For the first few minutes the pigs pay attention to me. They greet me with lively grunts and skip to the fence; they come close, push against me, claim me, and seem to want to rediscover me each time. But once the food has gone down, they pretty much ignore me. They're quickly busy instead with other things – and yet I stay, and I watch them. I like seeing them rearrange the straw in their bedding, or snout around for grubs, or grumble and tussle. They are entertaining. Their constant activity is somehow uplifting and there's something soothing about the sight of their elephantine haunches.

This fascination I share with my neighbours doesn't just seem to be a local quirk. When I go back to my reading I find that people everywhere have been obsessed by pigs for ever. The pig is pervasive in our cultural history, a recurring motif, a touchstone. Which seems a remarkable achievement for a creature that lacks the mystery of, say, a soaring eagle or the beauty of a fine horse or the nobility of a tiger, for an animal that is ordinary and ubiquitous and plump. And of course on the one hand, it's the ordinariness and plumpness which preoccupy us: the pig is associated with filth, pollution and brutishness, a metaphor for greed and grossness. Think about the common use of words such as 'hog', 'swinish' or 'porky'; or phrases like 'pig-headed', all of which have connotations of hostility and disgust – here the pig stands for the uncouth and the uncivilized. Quite often, moral judgement is also implied. In the Bible, pigs are often presented as lowly creatures representing deplorable conditions and poor moral choices: 'As a jewel of gold in a swine's snout, so is a fair woman which is without discretion' (Proverbs 11: 22). Centuries later, in a letter of 1749, the Earl of Chesterfield urged his son to discern between acceptable and unacceptable pleasures, between 'the elegant pleasures of a rational being, and [. . .] the brutal ones of the swine'.

But running alongside this bad press there's also an enduring connection to the pig which reads like affection, or perhaps even love: the pig as companion, entertainer, provider. Many accounts emphasize the pig as sage and loyal, as an expression of community and well-being and sufficiency. Pig-like creatures appear as valuable members of society in ancient cave paintings: the oldest known representation of another species, painted over 35,000 years ago, survives in a cave on the Indonesian island of Sulawesi, east of Borneo. The reddish ochre drawing shows a babirusa, a strange, rotund beast with thin legs and a pointed nose; its hairy coat is painted with energetic lines and splashes. This is an early form of pig, a deer-pig, and this is what these early people chose to paint, the animal that meant most to them.

By the first century AD, Plutarch was experimenting with a philosophical pig who enters into long conversations with Odysseus: he tells the lively story of a sailor, Gryllus, who is transformed into a pig by the sorceress Circe. Gryllus finds that he prefers life as a pig and makes a strong case for being raised above humans because of his new capacity for virtue, bravery and pleasure: he finds he delights now in simple things, rather than the poisonous pursuit of wealth and fame. Pigs, suggests Plutarch, know what's what; they are honest, worthy, dependable.

And so it goes on. For all the stories of filthy pigs and coarse, swinish behaviour, there are others of the pig as bright and capable. In a medieval manuscript from fifteenth-century France, a row of fearless pigs is shown leading soldiers into battle against a herd of odd, squat monsters which, from their tusks and trunks, appear to be elephants. The fortified town of Carcassonne, under Saracen rule, is said by legend to have been saved from a devastating five-year siege by Charlemagne's forces when a fattened pig was thrown from the highest tower, bursting on the troops gathered below in such a shower of grain that they were fooled into thinking the residents were still well stocked with provisions, and so went away, leaving the starving town to recover and sing the praises of its noble pig-martyr. In the eighteenth century, Erasmus Darwin remarked, 'I have observed great sagacity in swine,' while artist George Morland painted flattering portraits of prize pigs, raising them to celebrity status and asserting their beauty. Accounts by farmers and naturalists dwelt on marvellous stories of pigs which could open gates, shake apples from the best trees in the orchard, act as hunting 'dogs' by pointing out game, and even 'tell the hour of the day by the bare inspection of the watch'.

By the twentieth century, pigs had become increasingly viewed as quick-witted and warm-natured: in the 1910s and 1920s there was a sudden fashion for postcards and greetings cards using pictures of bouncy, smiling pigs to convey good luck and kind wishes. A few years later, the huge bulk of a Berkshire sow, the 'Empress of Blandings', attracted the obsessive affection of P. G. Wodehouse and her owner, Lord Emsworth; while it was the intelligent pigs in Orwell's *Animal Farm* which led the rebellious farmyard. After the Second World War, Winston Churchill – whose face and rotund form, you have to admit, had certain porcine qualities – apparently

praised the pig for its honesty and openness, its tendency to 'look
you in the eye' as an equal.

Amidst this historical mishmash of pig stories, I become interested in
one in particular; or rather, one that becomes several, and in multi-
plying becomes legendary. It's an eighteenth-century story of
spectacle and gullibility, of get-rich-quick schemes and fashionable
foolishness, but also, ultimately, of sadness, even tragedy. I become
interested in it, first, because it's about a black pig, exactly like my
pigs, and briefly I imagine myself back in the days of wigs and licen-
tiousness and philosophy, in a vaguely rural, slightly lawless world, a
cross between Henry Fielding's *Joseph Andrews* and Samuel Johnson's
Scotland. But after that initial moment of imaginary displacement,
the story still fascinates me. I read more; I find pictures and hand-
bills, cartoons of black pigs in the British Library. The eighteenth
century squeezes into the nineteenth, and still there is a black pig
making a mark. I realize that this story is not so much about a single
pig but about humans and pigs, how we get on together, what we
see in each other. And so it's about me and my pigs. It might give me
clues about what to expect from these weaners and, more importantly, from myself. It might help me understand how I feel about
my pigs.

The story begins, the first time, with a man called Samuel Bisset.

Bisset is born into a modest household in Perth, Scotland, in 1721.
He's the youngest of three brothers. Reports I find in early Scottish
newspapers suggest that he began his working life as a journeyman
shoemaker, but he's clearly ambitious and restless and when the
chance comes to marry a wealthy young woman, he grabs at it and
her, and moves to London to set up in business as a broker. I find
nothing about Mrs Bisset. I don't know where she comes from, or
how she's acquired her wealth. And it's not clear at all what happens
to her after the wedding. Having provided a hefty dowry, she disappears from record, which is perhaps convenient for Samuel, or
perhaps a great sadness. All I know for certain is that by early middle
age, Samuel is alone again and his eye is caught by a report of a 'thinking horse' which has been performing to marvellous acclaim at a

country fair. With tricks and flourishes, this astonishing animal astounds spectators with its cleverness and guile. Following in the footsteps of other performing horses from as early as the 1580s, it can play dead or urinate on command; it can distinguish between colours or between virgins and harlots; it can bow to distinguished guests and count the money they throw into the ring. Overcome with enthusiasm, Bisset runs to the markets of eighteenth-century London and buys a horse of his own, plus a dog and two monkeys, and he begins a new life as an animal trainer.

Bisset has a knack with animals. His methods are a secret but his enthusiasm and dedication are clear for all to see, and within months one of his monkeys is dancing merrily on a tightrope while the other has learned to play the barrel organ. The monkeys do well. They perform diligently and attract some attention. But there are performing monkeys all over London, all over the land in fact, all doing much the same routine. This is dull, hackneyed: Bisset knows he has to do better. What is it the voguish populace craves? What brings out the crowds? What is new and exciting? This is the 1750s. These are the years of famous castrato celebrity singers, of extravagant musical spectacles and rousing scores. Handel's operas are being performed across Europe, Rameau's opera-ballets are in fashion in France. And so the ambitious Samuel Bisset goes in search of opera stars and returns home with three kittens, heritage unknown.

In the fifteenth century, the French Abbot of Baigne, 'a man of great wit', entertained Louis XI by setting up a velvet pavilion and filling it with pigs, 'a great number of hogs of several ages', from piglets to ageing sows. The animals performed together to produce 'a concert of swine voices' which the Abbott conducted with the help of an ingenious instrument 'which pricked the hogs' as he pressed the keys. He apparently made them 'cry in such order and consonance, as highly delighted the king and all his company', winning himself some fame and much favour in royal circles. But Bisset doesn't think of pigs; not yet. And it is his kittens which form a choir instead, learning to play the dulcimer, banging small drums and accompanying the music with 'squalling [. . .] in different keys or notes'. Bisset is quietly hopeful about the kittens' future, and his own. He hires a room near the Haymarket, at the centre of stylish London society, and he announces the first public performance of his Cats' Opera.

Scottish newspapers proudly announce the success of their countryman, 'The Sensation of London'. The Cats' Opera adds several more nights to the run and still tickets sell out. The gentry, the dilettanti and the curious flock to see what Bisset has achieved, and by the end of the week he has £1,000 in his pocket, a fortune. He's the talk of the town, the man of the moment. Buoyed by his triumph, and anxious to expand his repertoire, Bisset turns his attention to other animals: he teaches a hare to beat military drum marches with its hind legs; he exhibits linnets and sparrows and canaries that can spell people's names; he trains six turkey cocks to step out the perfect country dance and he finds a turtle that can fetch and carry like a dog. But London audiences are fickle and demanding, and these new acts don't tempt them. Bisset finds he cannot repeat the glory days of the Cats' Opera. His name fades; eyes turn to other attractions – a mermaid on display on the Strand, giants and midgets, a cockfight, the fountain of mirrors in the pleasure gardens. Exasperated, disappointed, he turns his back on the capital and crosses to Ireland to join his brothers, who have emigrated to set up home in Belfast. He's determined to give up the anxieties of performance and concern himself no longer with the caprices of the fashionable crowd. He buys a quiet public house where he can settle as landlord and for almost thirty years he leads a different life – but he can't quite throw off his old ways, and when trade is slow he tries a series of experiments on a goldfish 'which', notes *The Lady's Magazine*, 'he did not despair of making perfectly tractable'.

And so we come to the pig. Bisset is set a challenge: a pig, someone tells him one evening in idle bar-room conversation, is too stubborn to be trained. You can do nothing with a pig. But Bisset is a man who still believes in his natural talent as an animal handler; he has faith in himself; he can do what no one else has ever done, he is sure. Even in his advancing middle age, even after so many years of retirement and resignation, he's determined to prove that he can tame any animal to his will: at the next opportunity he takes a trip to Dublin market and he invests three shillings in a young black male pig.

For six months, Bisset battles with his pig. He repeats exactly the methods which have led to such success with dogs and monkeys, turtles and hares. He devotes hours to training and practice; he is at turns firm and at turns kind. At the end of half a year, Bisset's black pig is sturdy and lean and energetic, but untamed. It will, when it wants to, respond to a command to lie down under Bisset's stool, and remain there while he works at the bar, but it will perform no further; it does not seem to want to do tricks. Bisset admits to being despairing. He's tried everything he knows and still the pig resists. But he cannot quite bring himself to give the animal away or have it butchered for bacon, and he begins to work on new methods. They are just as secret as the first, but perhaps more unconventional. A neighbour who watches his efforts reports later to the poet Robert Southey that he never once sees Bisset beat his pupil 'but that, if he did not perform his lessons well, he used to threaten to take off his red waistcoat – for the pig was proud of his dress'.

After a further sixteen months of sartorial bargaining with his pig, Bisset has proved the doubters wrong and emerges as the proud owner of 'the most tractable and docile' of creatures, 'as pliant and good natured as a spaniel'. There is no evidence that this is the same pig as the stubborn one which refused to learn its tricks. There is nothing to prove that Bisset has not been dining on ham while training up a new pig, more amenable and compliant. But the pig looks the same, it's black and the right age, and the papers claim that it's absolutely the same. I'm happy to believe that Bisset has triumphed. Why spoil a good story? All my research suggests that his guile and effort have overcome the pig's reluctance and created a performer. And the local crowds believe it, too. Word spreads: suddenly customers flock to the dingy rooms of this ordinary Belfast boozer; people tell tales of a marvellous magical hog; fairs and celebrations press for an appearance by Bisset's black pig.

Naturally, Bisset is jubilant. In a flurry of excitement he sells his inn and takes to the road again, this time with his pig for company. He is over sixty years old: this is an act of faith in himself and his animal, and a final chance to recapture something of those glorious few days at the Haymarket three decades earlier. He believes he has the best act of his life; he anticipates great things for his pig. And so he heads to Dublin, putting on a show for two nights at Ranelagh, just outside the city, and then, with the permission of the chief magistrate, moving to a more central venue in Dame Street, a busy thoroughfare packed with theatres, playhouses and assembly rooms. The black pig performs. Without any apparent prompting, it spells the names of those watching; it adds up sums and tells the time, correct to the second. It kneels to those of status in the room, and accurately distinguishes the married from the unmarried. Most astoundingly, the pig displays the capacity to read minds: when a member of the audience is asked to think of a word, Bisset's pig miraculously divines the word and spells it.

This is August 1783. It's a summer that oscillates between heatwaves and extreme cold. The American Revolution has recently ended. Europe is suffering famine and deadly acid rain caused by the eruption of the massive volcano Laki, in Iceland. An unexplained and alarming 'great meteor' is seen flashing through the clear skies over Britain. A few doors further along Dame Street in Dublin, the celebrated Sarah Siddons performs the lead role in *The Grecian Daughter*, a tragedy. And yet here is a stout black pig who could be said to be hogging the limelight; here is a black pig, just like mine, about to take the world by storm.

So then, patience. Determination. Observation. I don't want to train a pig, and I certainly don't want to put my weaners on the stage, but I'm interested in what Bisset's story seems to suggest: that his pig has a character, a personality, and that he manages to establish what we would define, in human terms, as a 'relationship'. He works to understand his pig, and in return, his pig does what it can to please him. They have what you might call a friendship.

'Each pig you come across has an individual character of its own; even members of the same family or litter have their own individual characteristics,' noticed Robert Morrison, a farm manager, in 1926. 'They will get to recognize the tone of your voice and know their name.' Although he was writing about practical matters of breeding and husbandry, Morrison was so impressed by the relationships people struck up with their pigs, by the 'feeling of faith, trust, and good fellowship between man and beast', that he felt compelled to mention this, too; he noticed how the pigs came to rely so much upon this fellowship that a pig left alone would 'pine for sympathy and company'.

Pigs, then, by all accounts, are 'individual characters', each one unique and different. Pigs need company and sympathy to flourish. Bisset's story shows that it's possible to strike up such a close under-standing with your pig that it will respond to your every move, to the slightest hint and signal. At the moment, as I stand in the enclosure with Big Pig and Little Pig, this kind of rapport seems unlikely. They like me being there – they certainly relish the companionship – but they're boisterous and blunt, responding to shoves and bulging buckets rather than anything more subtle. And for my part, I can hardly tell my weaners apart. What I see are two black pigs, a jostle of hair and snout, that's all.

But it is fun to think of getting to know them. There's delight in anticipating some kind of 'fellowship between [wo]man and beast' of the kind that impressed Robert Morrison. I'm pleased when they rush to the fence to welcome me, closing in on me so that I can't find room to step over the wire; I'm amused by them. Isn't that, after all, why Ed and I liked the idea of keeping pigs in the first place, rather than sheep, say, or rabbits – because they would respond to us on a personal level, with intelligence and character?

Whenever I can, I go down to the orchard and I watch Big Pig and Little Pig. I like them already, a lot. They're bright and entertaining. They're very young still, so there's something of the sameness of the litter about them, but I can already see how Bisset might have become so attached to his particular pig that he dedicated years of his life to understanding, coaxing and training it, and years more to an exuber-ant adventure alongside it. But of course there's a doubt in all this, a question. Since pigs are clearly so likeable and characterful, so com-panionable, so bonded to their human friends – what does this mean for me, when in just under a year I fully intend to kill the two I have here? Do I realize what I've taken on? Is there a moment, even now, watching these little weaners scrummage through the ivy on the wall, their tails swishing, when I think about what it might be like to kill them, and whether I'll be able to do it? What if we just let them go on being pigs instead – would it really matter if we didn't finally bring them to slaughter? I feel myself catch my breath, look away. I don't think I'm ready to test my resolve.

Big Pig and Little Pig are settling in. They test the electric fence, which shocks them just enough to elicit a squeal. I only see each of them receive a single shock; they learn quickly and seem to decide that what lies beyond the fence will have to stay out of reach for now.

They are comfortable in their shelter and, with extreme care, they've moved the straw around to their own liking. Whenever I take a new bagful to refresh the bed they spend a great deal of time nosing it into place, working it into the corners of the shelter and creating mini windbreaks against the draughts. I realize that they're better at such housekeeping than I am, and after a few days, instead of interfering, I get into the habit of leaving the straw in a pile just outside the shelter. When I return later, every scrap is gathered up and tucked away. The shape of two small pigs is still worn into the bed, but the new straw has been piled up around the dents: day by day they create a deeper, softer nest for themselves, shaped to their form as perfectly as any memory-foam mattress. They are scrupulously clean, and keep their bedding clean, too: they make sure to excrete as far away as they can, designating an agreed toilet area in one corner of the enclosure, close to the wall.

They find a favourite scratching post. At first this is one of the slender tree trunks to one side of the shelter, but for some reason this becomes unpopular, and after a few days they prefer rubbing up against one of the table legs. They rub a lot. They are already strong, solid. Their haunches and shoulders, which is where they mostly rub, are impressively firm to the touch and the musculature well defined. The table begins to wobble. It's already an old table, discarded from its use in the garden; there's a creaking in the plastic joints. I remember the way Benoît had smiled at our shelter contraption; it had never occurred to me that such small pigs could be so powerful.

As well as neighbours and well-wishers, Big Pig and Little Pig meet our dog, Mo. Mo has been part of the preparations; he's been there while we've been clearing the land and building the shelter; he's used to running in and out of the enclosure and hopping over the fences. But this time he comes with us and finds two pigs. They're not as large as he is but they're stronger, probably, and in partnership. He sees them from the open door, pauses, stunned at this new discovery, and then bolts away into the lane. The pigs, too, scatter. They rush to the far end of the pen and hold out there together, side by side, glaring. We can hear Mo shuffling in the long grass on the other side of the track; Big Pig and Little Pig mumble. A stand-off.

But after a while, Mo makes his way back. He comes to the door, feet firmly planted outside, but leaning in as far as he can, watching the two strange interlopers. He's disgruntled but curious; after a minute or so he gathers his courage and comes towards the wire, edging towards the pigs, staring. In turn, Big Pig and Little Pig are equally curious. They shuffle a step or two and then make their way towards him in a wide circle, closing in slowly. They hesitate for a moment with the shelter between them, a line of defence, and then, finally, they sneak to the fence, together, side by side; they come as close as they can without their snouts touching the wire. Mo is at the fence too now, on his side, also close, his nose also more or less up against the wire. Big Pig: Little Pig: Dog. They all stand nose-to-nose, regarding each other quietly but intently. Noses twitch, much sniffing goes on. And in time, somehow, something is agreed: this is all right, they concede, this is acceptable. Immediately and silently an affinity is asserted and everything is settled. All part of the same pack.

And this is probably the first time I really become aware of the pigs as different to each other. This is when the pair of black weaners becomes clearly and intriguingly two black pigs. Big Pig: Little Pig. It's not only their size, I realize, that defines them. It's not *even* their size. The variation in stature, in fact, is the least different thing about them. What really sets them apart, one from the other, is the way they react to things. They do, it's true, have characters. It's Little Pig, I notice, who runs further when Mo makes his entrance; it's Little Pig who trembles and makes more noise. He's a scaredy-cat and per-haps also something of an exhibitionist, a drama queen. Big Pig is calmer. He has a steadier gaze; he is wary and surprised, but reason-ably unflustered. Big Pig is the brave one.

But then Little Pig gathers his courage and returns to his position at the wire and while Big Pig moves away, going back to his rum-maging through the ivy, Little Pig stays. Big Pig turns his back in some apparent disdain and sets his mind to truffling out insects from the layers of soft earth, but Little Pig is interested in Mo. Not just curious, although there's plenty of curiosity, but interested. It's as though he wants to make friends with Mo. He wants to be sociable. There's an affability about him; he's open to the idea of another com-panion, charmed by another potential playmate. It's only the fear that Big Pig has unearthed a secret cache of tasty bugs somewhere on the other side of the shelter that finally pulls him away.

So then, already, Big Pig is not just Big; Little Pig is other than Little. We've got an extrovert and an introvert. I'm taken with the discovery. It makes me want to know more about each of them. It fuels my obsession with watching them. But at the time, this revela-tion that the weaners have character is just amusing and fascinating, a talking point. Little more. After all, dogs are much the same: each new puppy has a different character from the last. Horses, too, I suppose, although I've never kept a horse. Perhaps even hamsters, for all I know – I've never kept a hamster, either. But if you're raising an animal for slaughter there are implications, of course. There's a difference – isn't there? – between the thought of killing an unidentified, unidentifiable pig, just another animal, and the prospect of killing a particular pig, Big Pig, say, or Little Pig, an animal which you recognize by its actions and reactions, by its character, an animal which you could pick out from a scrum of other similar animals because you *know* it.

But I don't think of this. Not yet. The plan's going well. Big Pig and Little Pig have adapted quickly to their new home and seem healthy and contented. We know they are already growing. Weighing a weaner on any kind of scales is a tricky task; weighing a fully grown pig is more or less impossible. But we need to keep track of their growth every couple of weeks in order to know how they're doing and when they'll be 'ready' with good meat, so we loop a piece of string under each pig in turn to measure the girth – the 'heart girth' – just behind the front legs. Then we measure the length of each from the base of its ears to the base of its tail – we square the heart girth and multiply this by the length, then multiply the final figure by 69.3. There's some fumbling with string and wriggling of pig, some bumping and barging and miscalculation, but in the end we have it: the weight of each weaner. And yes, just as we already guessed, Big Pig is big, and Little Pig is little: the difference is not enormous but it is significant. Big Pig weighs 24.5kg; Little Pig is almost exactly two kilograms lighter.

This is what I think of: weights and measure, practicalities. Not pig character, or the nature of the individual. After all, we resisted the temptation to give the pigs pet names, because we didn't want to become too attached to them. We wanted to be businesslike about this, disciplined. It's like planting seeds in the vegetable garden: a pleasure, of course, but only worthwhile, only possible, because we have half an eye on the end product, on harvest and yield. So, Big Pig and Little Pig, putting on poundage, a crop, an intention, a purpose; that's all.

★

Winter days are quiet, slow; winter evenings shut-up and chill. We don't see much of the neighbours unless we bump into them coming and going to the pigs. There's only really one social event of the season: the *quine* (Bingo) run by the parents' association at the school to raise funds. There are just over thirty children at the school, aged from two to eleven, taught in two classes with a *maternelle* for the infants, and they've outgrown the cramped stone schoolhouse nestling in the centre of the village, just below the church steps. The intention is to convert a larger building into a new school, with a yard for playing games and space for project work. Several years ago, the last nuns were moved out of the tall grey convent which sits in a dip alongside the stream, the stone wash house on one side and the land rising to the old well on the other. The move disturbed the settled landscape of the village – a disruption I took as inspiration for a novel – and now it's this ugly place of draughty corridors that's been earmarked for the new school. So money needs to be raised; plenty of money. But most likely there would be a *quine* anyway – all the local villages have them through the winter, whether or not they need a new school. For a long time, the *quine* has been an important way of keeping in touch during those months when life closes in on itself.

We go along on the Sunday after the pigs arrive and take our seats at one of the long trestle tables that stretch the length of the village hall, the *salle des fêtes*. We never quite know how long we might be able to sustain our lives in this place. Sometimes it seems as though we might be here for ever – already the silver birch behind the garden pond, which were pale saplings when we arrived, are taller than the house; the pines have matured and drop huge cones; we can mark our time in the growth of things, and it's easy enough to imagine being present each autumn when the walnuts fall, for every spring planting, trampling footprints in every snowfall. But work continues to be precarious, our income meagre and unreliable. We've made our plans to stay at least for the life of the pigs, and the freezer full of meat afterwards, but sometimes even this seems too ambitious; we find ourselves treading gingerly from week to week and month to month, pausing in amazement to find ourselves still here. We want to belong. We want this place to be home, with all its connotations of intimacy and constancy and comfort, but for now everything feels uncertain, a bit rickety, and more than ever it seems important to take part, to *be* part, while we can. And so we're here in the chilly old hall, on hard benches, on a Sunday afternoon playing a game of Bingo; we're here, and many people we hardly recognize nod at us in solemn approval.

Two girls come and sell us a packet of bright yellow plastic counters; their mums follow along a while later with the bingo cards. The hall is packed. There is much chatter and long greetings – this is a three-kiss part of France and it can take some time to work your way round a table of friends, three kisses at a time – but in the end the numbers start to roll: French numbers, tumbling, spiky with local accent, tricky. *Quatre-vingt-douze. Soixante-dix.* We play for a while without winning. When we think of taking a break, our language skills losing their nimbleness in this torrent of figures, we're pressed on by those to either side of us who point at lines on our cards or flip yellow counters in our direction. No time off, no let-up – this is *quine* played intensely, energetically, with determination.

After several hours there is a pause. The fire is stoked with logs and the bingo caller climbs down from the blocks which have been set up at one end as a stage. Outside the long windows, dusk is falling. Players shift, stretch, move around. More cards are sold. And two burly young men parade the star of the afternoon: a *jambon de pays*, a local ham, aged, we're told, for nine months. Glossy in the lights, solid, the surface mottled dark, the ham is hoisted from table to table by its trotter and we're encouraged to guess its weight in order to win it. It's not an enormous ham – I guess at just over six and a half kilos – but it's a good round shape and the meat has the deep tone of old wood, and it becomes clear over the next few minutes that some people have come to the *quine* solely with the intention of winning it. Playing the numbers was fun – winning trinkets, biscuits or bottles for lines and 'houses' kept the afternoon ticking along – but this, this *jambon*, this is the reason our elderly neighbours have put on their best coats and hats and left the comfort of their cosy *séjours* to spend hours in the bare, draughty *salle des fêtes*. This is competitive now:

weights are whispered, tried out on the tongue. It's not permitted to touch or lift the ham, so this is a test of an experienced eye. Squint, peer: turn the ham. Time is taken, a long time; the ham moves only slowly from group to group, from table to table. Even when it's moved on, some ponder their assessment, not yet putting their guess down on the list, waiting, reflecting. This leg of aged meat is such a luxury, such a delight, that it's worth any amount of time and trouble: the bingo caller is ready again at the microphone, all the cards have been sold, the children are back in their seats, but still the ham is on parade.

This is an expensive prize. A *jambon* of this size and quality would cost at least €100 to buy in the shops and I can't imagine any of my neighbours ever having bought one. But it's not just about the financial value. A whole ham is a mark of plenty, of indulgence; it's a mini, self-contained store cupboard against the threat of lean times; it's meat to share with friends and family as an act of generosity. This is a prize worth winning because it *means* something: in a village where older residents still talk frequently and with horror about the deprivations and starvation of the years of occupation during the Second World War, this ham is a guarantee of one of the finest and most comforting pleasures in life: a full table.

Eventually, the ham has done the rounds, all the guesses are recorded, the men haul the prize on to the stage – and the weight is announced. Much applause, some grumbling. *Is that right? That can't be right! Let's see them weigh it.* The delighted winner – a short, very old man in a black beret and a brightly patterned jumper – more or less leaps on to the stage in his excitement, grabs hold of the shiny trotter and stands with his trophy like a Formula 1 Grand Prix winner with his magnum of champagne. Eyes down: the numbers are beginning again. But there's still the faint rich whiff of ham circulating among the players, and for some time our neighbours are distracted by the thought of the prize lost.

And with the scent of ham in our nostrils, talk turns to pigs. Our pigs. Big Pig and Little Pig. The sight of fine *jambon* has got everyone reminiscing: ham as it used to be; pigs raised in the old way; sturdy, hardy, family pigs. Between the jumble of numbers, we're asked a lot of practical questions. What do we feed them? How will we fatten them? How much do they weigh? When will we kill them? This is what people want to know. No one asks us if we like having pigs or how we feel about them; no one asks us what we've called them. They assume, I suppose, that they don't have names at all. Practical, not sentimental. This is how we want it, of course; it's how we expected it would be. Everyone here appreciates that these are animals raised for meat. But Big Pig and Little Pig: I notice that we talk about them with pride already, and with enthusiasm. With fondness.

The weaners have lice. When I tease aside the thicker hair on the ridge along their backs I spot small clusters of whitish-grey eggs glued near the skin; where they've knitted together they've formed a yellowy crust. I look closer. There are more eggs, around the folds of the neck and the ears, on the flanks, too. And now there are adult lice, crawling, each one about the size of a ladybird but more unpleasant, with grasping, scuttling legs and an odd transparent sheen, a tiny alien.

The lice are not our fault. It's nothing to do with the shelter we've built or the rickety old picnic table or the scruffy patch of land. They must have been endemic in the herd and were probably passed on from the sow, or from the scramble of older pigs at the food troughs. It explains the energetic rubbing. Just like in humans, lice are an irritant: if they're left untreated, the pigs might eventually rub so hard and so long that they scour patches of bare skin; if they go on rubbing even then, they will open up flesh wounds which may fail to heal under the constant attrition. A severe infestation might prove so stressful that the weaners would fail to grow properly.

And so Big Pig and Little Pig are shampooed.

It's not yet February. The weather is cold, and we don't want them to be chilled, so we choose a sunny day and make sure there's enough time for them to dry before dusk falls. The church bells have just rung out the angelus, twelve noon, into a high blue sky; the sound reaches us already, echoing. In all but the most shaded of ditches the frost has melted, and there's the gentle crackling of leaves from the row of old oaks along the lane. The trees turn a charred bronze at the end of the autumn and their leaves remain stubbornly attached through much of the winter, providing some extra shelter for small birds; during a heavy midwinter hoar frost, the ice clings in crystals to the edge of each leaf, sparkling repetitions of silver and gold, stretching out for miles and miles across the *causse*.

It is quiet; silent. It can be silent here, sometimes, really, truly silent. In the heavy heat of summer or at night. The absolute absence of noise. At other times, sound springs and bucks and elongates and you can hear someone clicking a door latch half a mile away. Today, when the bells cease ringing, there is nothing for a moment or two, longer: no cars, no breeze, no voices. A family of long-eared owls has set up home in a copse of hazels just beyond the ruined barn, and they watch us, sleepily, but they, too, are silent; their watching only serves to thicken the sense of quiet. The light comes and goes on their dappled plumage and on the thin branches clustered around them, so that they sharpen and then fade and then sharpen again, their wide surprised faces sometimes seeming close and vigilant, sometimes becoming invisible.

But such peace cannot go on. There are pigs to be deloused. And washing weaners is a messy, splashy, wriggly affair – and noisy. They're taken by surprise by the sudden flurry of wet sponges, and they're indignant; they squeal and chunter and shy away, flustered. Pigs like to be snug and warm; they dislike draughts and are careful to keep out of the rain. It goes against the grain for them to be slooshed in this way. They kick up a fuss, and the owls, in response, flap away, swooping through the trees to quieter perches.

We can only deal with one weaner at a time. I straddle Big Pig and try to keep him still between my knees, holding him as gently as I can so that he can be doused all over with the mixture. He's resigned; after the initial protests, he stands placidly enough and allows us to work the treatment through the coarse hair and on to the skin. Even when we let him go, he does not move far away but loiters to watch us repeat the process with Little Pig, to offer moral support perhaps, or to gloat. And Little Pig, too, is well behaved. He stands and sniffs at the air, the mixture, the sponge. He nibbles the zips on my overalls, and then the fabric. He grunts and snuffles to the touch. And I realize that after their initial chagrin the pigs are enjoying their baths: they allow us to sponge them all over, their stomachs and their heads, behind their ears. The bottom part of their legs, towards the trotters, is stiff and bony, lice free, but we tackle around their tails, their eyes, their snouts. I marvel again at the feel of their hide: soft, elastic, coarse, warm, dry like old paper; something you might want to stroke, just for the satisfaction.

This is in part a getting-to-know-you game, an indulgence perhaps. But there are more serious matters to consider. If conditions in the breeding herd have allowed for the lice infestation then other parasites may also have thrived. We worry, in particular, about worms: worms in a young pig can cause severe illness; they can even be fatal. Worms can burrow into the internal organs and even the flesh; they might still be there, much later, when you come to butcher the pig or eat the meat. It would be a waste of time and money to raise a worm-infested pig: a shame, in the fullest sense of the word.

The pigs seem fine. There's been no hint of any symptoms – coughing or vomiting; stiff movement – but we want to be sure. We do our research on the Internet and discover that there are laboratories that will analyse faeces and send us a report detailing any anomalies or infestations. This seems sensible, scientific; responsible. But for some reason, no longer quite clear, we decide we prefer the look of a UK-based service. I can't recall the exact reasoning. Perhaps similar services don't exist in France; more likely, they're more expensive. Perhaps we doubted our ability to adequately translate the technicalities of faeces analysis. But while I don't remember how the decision came about, nor the apparent logic which drove it, I do remember the consequence. A few days later I have a meeting in London with my agent. I take the pig poo with me, wrapped in a freezer bag. Pig faeces are dense and dark and sticky; in the case of our pigs, the remains of their grain diet is evident. The lump I have in my hand luggage is not unlike a dollop of good-quality haggis, black and oaty. The Customs officers at Gatwick Airport show no interest; there's no telltale smell on the Tube; my agent displays only moderate surprise, and no distaste, when I explain what I've brought with me. I keep the pig poo with me while I go about my meetings, in and out of the shops along High Holborn, hurrying through the respectable, pristine gardens of the Inns of Court on my way to the station, and at the end of the day I finally send off a special plastic envelope to the laboratory. This is twenty-first-century London, largely pig free. But the city, like every other, was once a place of animals, as well as people – from commonplace pigs, dogs and horses to exotic birds and reptiles supplied by popular menageries. It was once a place of pig poo and horse manure and general stench. So it seems quite fitting, a nod to the past, to bring this tiny piece of Big Pig and Little Pig with me into the heart of modern commerce. And by the time I return home, a couple of days later, the laboratory has sent back the results: the pigs are worm free. Worth a small celebration.

2.

In the hot, slow summer of 1783, the second night in Dublin goes even better than the first, and so for a third consecutive night the room is booked and the posters hurriedly printed. After decades of drudgery and disappointment, of swilling out his bar room, man-handling mute drunkards and sloshing wet sawdust into the street, Samuel Bisset has been thrust again into the dazzling limelight because his animal is a star; people love the black pig. And why not? It's a good-looking beast, sturdy at the neck and haunches but not overgrown or flabby; it's like the pigs everyone has at home but per-haps sleeker, with a better sheen to its hair and a nice sharp clip-clop to its trot as it crosses the boards of the stage. And it has a look in its eye that they haven't noticed in their backyard animals: a glitter, a knowing gleam; an intimation, surely, of sagacity. This, they agree, is a once-in-a-lifetime pig, a prodigy of its race, some miracle of nature that they are blessed to witness. 'Wonderful and extraordinary' proclaim the newspapers.

Bit by bit, I unearth more details of Samuel Bisset and his twisting story. As I get to know Big Pig and Little Pig, as they preoccupy more and more of my time, so I become increasingly fascinated by this other pig, this black pig from a long time ago, wrenched from animal anonymity to a bizarre stardom. The act is simple enough. A series of alphabet or number cards are laid in a circle and when Bisset asks the pig a question, he points, letter by letter, or number by num-ber, to the answer. Some questions are straightforward – what is the name of the fair lady in the blue dress, for example – but others demand apparent reasoning or calculation, or even telepathy: how many of the gathered company have debts of £500, or what's the gentleman with the stick thinking at this very moment? There are no stooges or confederates planted around the room. Bisset and his pig work alone – that much is clear – and audiences can find no evidence of cheating or sleight of hand: Bisset makes no obvious signals, he doesn't whistle or squeak or stamp or sneeze. People are puzzled by what they see, it's true, mystified by such a clever pig, but they're entranced, too, and quickly won over by its confident performance. No one seems to doubt that it's the pig's marvellous intelligence allowing it to pull off such feats, an intelligence honed by nothing more than Bisset's careful training.

Offstage Bisset is very quiet, perhaps gathering his thoughts: I can find out very little about how he lives during these Dublin days, or what he does when he's not performing. Most likely, he's taken aback by his sudden fame. He has sustained himself for so many years on the thought of those heady days long ago in London that the memories would have worn thin and faint, and he could be forgiven for being overwhelmed by the bright bluster and noise of a new success. I imagine him in the relative peace of a rented room, pleased to have the pig alongside him, the familiar tart smell of dung in his nostrils and the pleasant feel of rough skin against his hand as he caresses his new star, flips his ears, mutters this and that about the day. And I wonder about the pig, thrust into a strange and raucous new world, a place of disconcerting commotion. I hear it chuntering, like my pigs chunter, snuffling the dust that's packed into the cracks in the floorboards. Together, no doubt, they pass the hours between one performance and the next shut away in the gloom of their lodgings, inseparable: the pig needs to rest and eat, keep its strength and its spirits up; Bisset feels himself floating in the heat, not quite sure how it's come to this again, his thoughts fermenting like yeast in beer, his dreams of the future vivid. He reaches out to pat the rump of his animal, to keep calm.

I find I revel in time spent with Big Pig and Little Pig, just watching, touching. There's something calming about the way they go about things, their rhythmic, unruffled search for food, their confidence in finding it; there's a pleasure in watching these sturdy, shapely beasts ambling between the trees. They are continually busy, in a slow way, perpetually occupied, moving steadily, covering ground. I always knew that animals required space to properly thrive and I've always bought free-range pork and poultry when I can. But watching the pigs shuffle and dig and grub, seeing the constant activity which occupies their day, has brought home to me how miserable it is to confine a pig, any pig, so that it has no room to move, nothing to do, nowhere to go. Pigs need land to roam, soil to turn, work to do, as much as they need the basics of food and water. I can't imagine Big Pig and Little Pig in a cage.

As the days lengthen and the sun has more warmth, we bring down an old plastic chair and set it up inside the enclosure. Sometimes I come to sit and watch; sometimes Ed does. We come one at a time, alone. It is quiet, respectful, a fellowship of sorts, a way of sharing the day together. I begin to know the little habits of the pigs' behaviour, their choreographed tussle over food, the way one will follow the other, their incessant curiosity for what lies just below the next layer of sticky soil. I enjoy seeing them dig or catching them sprawled and dozing, a lazy huddle. I laugh at the many ways weaners take fright, bolting in absolute terror at a sudden noise – a stick falling from the tree they're shoving, a donkey braying, the bin lorry – while in the next moment they're calm again, such a terrible ordeal completely forgotten.

And so, slowly and quietly, I get to know Big Pig and Little Pig. Before my eyes they grow. And as I watch them, inevitably, I sometimes think about their deaths. Ed and I rarely talk about killing the pigs. I know Ed is quite happy with the arrangements; he understands that we'll need to slaughter them. That there will be no choice. And I understand that, too – but I also find myself imagining what it would be like to take a knife in my hand, to pull one pig aside, here and now, and slit its throat.

I couldn't do it. I know that. If I was asked, now, to drag one of my weaners – Little Pig, say – out of the enclosure, squealing and writhing, and drive a knife through the soft black skin, I couldn't do it. I shy away even from the thought of it; let my mind run on only so far; look away from the close-up view. But that doesn't matter, surely. Because we don't want to kill the pigs yet. There are six months or more of life to go. And by then it will be the proper time and so it will seem the proper thing to do. By then I will be prepared and it will all happen as it should. Everything in its season.

And so I construct a rational argument that suggests matters are perfectly in order. But there's a part of me, the less rational part, that recoils from the prospect of the slaughter and I begin to wonder whether, in the end, rationality might not be enough. I begin to wonder whether the pigs might just trample logic and sensible husbandry as they trample the most robust and gnarled of roots. Which will leave just soft things: the feeling of me and them, the time we've spent together, our shared place on the land. It will leave me with the bare emotion of animals to kill. And I'm not at all sure what that might be like.

But Ed, I know, is steadily determined, his mind on practical matters of meat, and I don't talk about my qualms. Instead I bury them, for now, in a smallholder's matter-of-fact preoccupations. And as we watch the pigs together with increasing familiarity and fondness, we become more and more like Bisset in our determination to get the best from our animals. His eye was on performance, of course, on tricks and bravura, on the money that might be made, but our daily discussions about how to do this thing well, how to keep pigs well, how to have them in the very best of health, starts to have the same obsessive focus on detail, the same sense of scrutiny and expectation: how are the pigs looking? What's their weight now? When should we move them to new ground? How do we move them? Are they happy? The pigs are already more than just a routine of daily feeding and cleaning: they're a form of entertainment; they're a responsibility, a connection to this place, a philosophical conundrum; they're a precious investment. So I probably didn't need to take pig poo to a publishing meeting; the anxiety about worms was probably an overreaction. But I've never kept pigs before and I marvel, like Bisset, that such remarkable animals are in my care and, like him, I'm eager not to let this opportunity slip through my fingers.

And sitting in the enclosure on a March morning, with the mist still drifting up from the lake and lingering in the nooks of the ruins behind me, with Big Pig and Little Pig standing in the sun so that the ridge of hair on their backs glitters with dew and the hide beneath transforms to a rich, shifting, storm-cloud grey, I continue to remind myself, as I must, that these animals are here for a reason. Even though they distract me from tedious worries, they're not here for my distraction; even though I'm learning a great many interesting things about livestock and husbandry and wondrous performing pigs, their purpose is not an educational one. All such things are nothing more than a pleasant by-product: the product is meat. When we measure the pigs now with our length of string and make the calculation, we find that they've put on 20kg each – in fact Little Pig has outstripped Big Pig with something of a growth spurt and has added nearly 22kg of bulk since he arrived. When we track the measurements on a graph, the rise of a blue and a red line – blue for Big Pig; red for Little Pig – indicates a sure, inexorable progress towards the moment when these two live animals become only a weight of meat. Pigs for meat, that's what I remind myself. Special pigs but not pet pigs. Lovable pigs that must not be loved. Or not too much. Because too much would mean I could never kill them, and what would happen then?

The hedgerows and verges are clotted with violets and cowslips, the scrappy land beyond the pig orchard is spiked with grape hyacinths and clusters of early purple orchids. On fine days, there are butterflies now flitting across the enclosure – orange tips and the occasional swooping swallowtail – and we can hear the stags baying in the woods during the rut. The place shimmers green: the grass, the hedges, the new leaves are all a luminous, unreal shade like unmixed gouache, the fields filled with sturdy calves lying curled alongside their mothers: several mornings in a row, when I walk with Mo, we come across a newborn calf in a slither of placenta being licked clean and trying, shakily, to stand.

With the settling in of warmer, drier weather, we have to collect water for the pigs more often from the *fontaine* in the village. This requires a short journey in the car: the steep slope back to the enclosure is too difficult to attempt on foot or bicycle loaded with sloshing containers. But it's a free supply of natural spring water – the house has a meter to measure consumption – which makes it worth the journey. The *fontaine* sits in a dip of land opposite the *mairie* and

the church, alongside the old convent building, with a large pale
weeping willow to one side and a stately pine to the other. There's a
stone wash house fed by the source, a low, open-sided building with
an ornate tiled roof, not unlike some kind of monastery cloister.
Inside, the water pools; around the basin there are wide washing
plinths, poised like open missals. This is where the women used to
come and do their laundry together. Today everyone has a washing
machine, although Solange, my neighbour, prefers to bring her laundry outside in a bucket and scrub it on a similar washing plinth set by
a sink alongside the garage wall and fed from rainwater collected
from the guttering. I doubt she's alone in resisting or ignoring modern changes. On a misty winter's morning, with smoke rising from
all the chimneys and the tiled roofs shimmering with frost, the view
of the village from the brow of the hill must be much the same as it
was very many years ago. There's an occasional parked car by the
wash house but little other evidence that this is, apparently, a twenty-
first-century community. It seems as though it might be asleep, Rip
Van Winkle-like, so old and settled that it's simply waiting for the
past to catch up with it.

But this, of course, is an illusion. Change here is slow – it sidles
quietly under the more obvious alterations of the season – but even
in the years we have been here, the nature of this place has shifted in
small but significant ways. The *boulangerie* has moved from premises
in the heart of the village to a purpose-built shop on the main road,
with new ovens and a car park to allow lorries to pull in. The other
businesses that were once here – a *charcuterie*, a butcher's, hardware
stores, garages, cafes – have all long since closed, leaving only the
intimation of commercial life in remnants of wide display windows
or ornate doorways or fading painted advertisements on roadside
walls. We live in a *commune* of four villages but there's no way of getting between them without a car, and only the *boulangerie* and a small
tabac survive to serve the daily needs of the six hundred or so residents. Even the parish priest, recently such an important figurehead
in the village, now has charge of twelve churches and takes the
opportunity provided by weddings to complain to the congregation
about poor attendances. Our French village is no different to rural

villages across Europe – a place of incremental loss, unromantic
hardship, isolation.

But for now it manages to cling on, just about. In the face of all the
evidence that suggests this should long ago have ceased to be a viable,
animated place of any kind, this is a village that comes together for
fêtes and funerals and to clear the footpaths each spring, where neighbours keep in touch despite the expanse of fallow fields between
them, and where very old rivalries and jealousies still prosper. And
as some sort of metaphor for the tenacity of such a community, the
spring that feeds the *fontaine* bubbles on, lively and reliable, in all seasons and weathers. It's drawn from deep under the *causse*, from the
meandering system of streams and caverns that tickle the limestone
belly of the land. On one side of the wash house, under the shade of
the willow, it's piped out at shoulder height and falls into a long deep
trough, a massive stone sarcophagus that runs the length of the building. The overflow seeps away to sustain the modest village rose
garden. All the local farmers take advantage of this free, natural supply and bring hefty metal tanks on trailers, like the bodies of old
steam engines, and fill them with water, taking them directly into the
fields for the cattle. All I've got are three white plastic containers,
each holding about twenty litres, but I stack them up on the top
of the trough and flip the length of pipe like an old hand and lean
against the wall while they fill.

The first time I came with my *bidons* I felt a fraud. I thought I
sensed everyone in the village watching me, peering from behind
their shutters and tutting at the temerity of this strange Englishwoman
stealing their water. I was awkward; I fumbled the pipe and the containers, soaked myself and sloshed the paving, struggled to heave the
filled canisters into the boot of the car. It was a simple act: collecting
water for animals. But coming here to the *fontaine* felt completely different to filling a bowl from the tap for Mo. This felt like a moment
of significance, like stepping into the shadows of the past. It was not
just the watching eyes of the present but the glances of a receding
history that I felt over my shoulder: this source had rescued liveli-
hoods during the wretched drought of 2003, preventing the death of
whole herds; here the resistance *Maquis* had gathered during the

occupation of the Second World War and talked in low voices as they filled their pitchers; during the long identical summers of the eighteenth and nineteenth centuries, children came to the source to cool off after toiling, hungry, in the fields for hours; in the distant, unknowable past of the Middle Ages this source had spirited a village to life.

I could have drawn comparisons, I suppose, with other watery rites of passage drenched in ancient ritual, like baptism. But this wasn't a religious experience.

'I hear you've got pigs,' a middle-aged man said, pausing on his way to the school.

We talked for a while; the water overflowed the container.

'We always used to have a pig,' he said.

I nodded. That's what everyone says: we *used* to have a pig.

He went on: 'And I'll tell you a good story. You know you starve a pig before you kill it, so you have nice clean guts?'

I'd been reading about this so, yes, I knew that for the day or so before slaughter you weren't supposed to feed your pig.

'Well, you see, when she came to kill it, my mother put the pig in a pen next to the chicken run the night before. It was round the side of the house, out of the way. But the pig, well, you know what they're like –'

I'm getting to know, I wanted to say; *I really am.* But I let him speak; he seemed to be enjoying his story.

'– and so, of course, the old pig got hungry and when my mother went back the next morning, it had got through into the chickens and eaten one.'

I said I'd never heard of a pig eating a chicken. I wondered how a pig would even catch a chicken.

He shrugged, smiled. 'No, well, the thing is: when they came to split it open, its insides were full of feathers. Stuck everywhere, on all the intestines, everywhere. Full of feathers. My mother was furious. How were they supposed to make sausages with that?'

Pigs. That was enough. People understood, approved; they treasured the connection to their own history, their family, this place. Pigs, I'm coming to understand, have the ability to provoke an odd nostalgia; they romp through memories of all kinds of pasts, both real and imagined. So here at the *fontaine* taking care of my pigs, I was not intruding, not overstepping. Quite the opposite – I began to realize just how much my pigs were helping me consolidate my place here. Drawing water from the village source, I was reiterating old gestures and old connections and in so doing becoming part of the community. And I felt a pang, a stab of melancholy, because just at the moment when I grasped that precious sense of belonging, we were talking, again, about leaving: Ed's journalism work, the slender backbone of our domestic economy, was drying up and in the faltering freelance marketplace, there was nothing much to succeed it. We'd managed to find a few hours' work each month making 'secret shopper' calls in French to high-end hotels around the world, testing their booking services and customer care. We were already adept at arranging phantom reservations for bespoke meeting rooms with buffet lunches, video projectors and scribbler pads. But while this was a good way of honing our language skills, it was, in the end, like all such jobs, poorly paid, tedious and insecure. It would not do for very long.

'You'll enjoy your pigs. There'll be good eating,' the man said. He laughed, shook his head, and went away smiling.

But I was left with my heavy *bidons* slopping water down my legs and over my feet, and the niggling anxiety that we might not have the chance to enjoy our pigs, after all; that it might all be taken away from us just as we were getting used to it.

When I take the water to the enclosure, the pigs have knocked down the shelter, just as Benoît foretold. There's a heap of green plastic and metal roofing and planks. Because of the upheaval, the pigs have not noticed my approach; I poke my head through the doorway and in the moment before I'm rumbled I see Little Pig nosing the debris energetically, even frantically, as if in the hope of a resurrection, and Big Pig eyeing the disaster with indignation. It's raining lightly, and it's quite obvious that they resent having to stand outside in the damp when they could be flopped side by side in the nice dry straw.

As soon as they sense me, they rush to the fence, clamouring; each time I move to one side of them to step over the top wire, they move with me. It's some kind of country dance, and it takes me a while to find enough space for my wellies and my bucket among the flurry of pig. They're always delighted to see someone with food; in fact, they're delighted by visitors of any kind. But this greeting has extra urgency to it: *Look what's happened. What are we going to do? It fell down, just fell down. What are you going to do?*

Grain in the trough takes their minds off the calamity. It sticks to their wet hair, coating their noses and trotters, dusting them around the eyes. They tussle and squabble, as they always do. Big Pig never manages to maintain his dominance at feeding time, or to make his larger frame count: Little Pig's greed is a relentless force. My chickens have a pecking order, to keep mealtimes nice and tidy, to enforce hierarchy and order; everyone knows where they are. My pigs pile in, head to head or shoulder to shoulder; they barge and bite, kick and butt, not with any kind of vehemence or enmity – in fact, usually with a fraternal good nature – but with a single-minded determination to be first to the food, and to eat the most. It's easy to see why pigs have long been synonymous with poor table manners: 'Don't fall on your food like a pig, snorting and smacking your lips,' Erasmus warned the youth of the early sixteenth century.

On this occasion, though, I'm grateful for the pigs' enthusiasm. While they're trotter-deep in grain, I take the opportunity to examine the damage to the shelter. It's clear what's happened. The rain has softened the soil and the scratching-post table leg has finally given way with the constant nudge of growing pig, bringing down the roof and the supporting walls. It needs a complete rebuild. And as I begin the process of balancing and buttressing I understand two things. Firstly, the pigs are much bigger, already, than when they came. I know this, in a factual way, from our piece of measuring string and the graph of their growth: over 50kg a pig now, more than double the weight they were when they arrived. But the statistics come to life in a real sense when I examine the shelter carefully – where they used to snuggle into a corner, they now fill almost the entire thing and so roll and push against it at all sides. What had seemed perfectly adequate for two weaners back in January now suddenly seems rather mean and cramped. And secondly, this makeshift affair of garden and household rag-and-bone is not the solution to pig housing that I once imagined. I now know how rumbustious Little Pig can be and with what vehemence he makes his feelings clear; I realize how powerful and heavy Big Pig has become. In view of all this, the shelter appears flimsy and ragged and a bit hopeless. I've become so used to the routine of the pigs that I've not really noticed how much they've flourished. It's like one of those spring mornings when you stroll out and discover that the trees are in leaf, full and green, as if all of a sudden: you know it's been happening – you've even seen the buds swelling – but still it comes as something of a surprise. And so it is with the pigs. I'm startled to see how large they are; as I run my hand along their backs, I'm impressed by the solidity of them; I've been caught out by their evident maturity. As if overnight, they've outgrown their shelter. Big Pig and Little Pig – both big pigs.

Over the following few weeks the rain continues to fall and so does the shelter. I prop it up; it slips. I wedge the dodgy table leg; it sinks lower and collapses the roof. I try a new arrangement with the corrugated metal; the pigs take umbrage and knock it down. They're very protective of their home and don't like it to change. They like to arrange the bed of straw as it's always been. They prefer to consolidate what's already there, rather than risk an unfamiliar setup. But it's getting to the point where making do, bodging, just won't work any more – and the pigs are quick enough to show their fury if the roof is leaking or the rain is running down one of the tree trunks and on to their straw.

It's not only inside the enclosure that the wet weather is causing problems. The lane that leads to the Mas de Maury is little more than a dirt track; one of the farmers has been driving a heavy tractor along twice a day to see to cattle in a field up beside the lake, bringing straw sometimes in a trailer, cutting through the mud with massive tyres. Deep, pooled ruts have formed; when Ed tries to drive the car down with containers of water it gets wedged in the mire, its undercarriage clamped against the stony ground and its wheels disappearing. In the rain we stuff sticks and stones under the tyres and try to ease the car forward far enough to turn on to more solid ground, but it's well and truly stuck. We can hear Big Pig and Little Pig grunting and squealing further down the track, behind their high wall, listening to our endeavours, calling out for their bucket. They always recognize the sound of the engine and know that if we've brought the car to the enclosure it usually means a new delivery of grain. But they're going to be disappointed. Supper has to wait until we've managed to unstick ourselves.

Ed and Mo walk across the fields to Paul's house: Paul is an Englishman with a garage full of useful tools and a barn packed with all kinds of unlikely equipment. He's come to our rescue in the past: once to solder closed a hot-water pipe when we'd sawn through it; several times to lend us an ancient rotavator to plough the garden; many times with curious-sized spanners and specialist wrenches and air compressors and all manner of things you never think you'll need. Now he drives round slowly in his weighty old Peugeot, loops a long tow rope to our car and hauls us out. 'I'll come down and see the pigs,' he says.

With the rain, the growing season is suddenly upon us. The climate here is testing but predictable: hot dry summers punctuated with ferocious storms of thunder and hail; long soft autumns, turning foggy around Armistice; freezing winters of bright skies and brittle cold; and then these wet, mild days when everything bursts into life. Birds are busy everywhere: swallows gliding into Solange's open barn; sparrows and tits and redstarts nesting in the walls of our house; the hens turning broody. Mornings are suddenly bouncing with rabbits. New growth pings through the soil in the pig enclosure, luring them with the promise of nettle shoots and succulent roots, and we need to turn our attention to digging the garden and getting seeds planted. No time now to sit and contemplate the mysteries of pig behaviour. All around us field hedges are being trimmed, cattle brought out to pasture, land ploughed; on a small scale we do the same. We dig and hoe and weed, get in the early crops like potatoes and peas, sow summer seeds like courgettes and cucumbers in layers of wet tissue and hang them in the fireplace to germinate.

And we talk about moving day. The Mas de Maury enclosure is already showing the strain of three months' stomping and grazing and digging by growing pigs; we don't want to exhaust the ground.

It's time for Big Pig and Little Pig to go to a new home, to the bigger patch of oak woodland and scruffy meadow that will tide them through the rest of their lives. They will have shade there for the summer, a water supply, good sources of wild food; they will clear the land and rejuvenate it. Early April, we calculate, would be the perfect time to move them on and get them settled before the weather turns warm.

But it's a distance of perhaps a mile from the Mas de Maury to the new land, and we already have over 100kg of animal: boisterous, spirited, independent. This is too much pig to fit in our car, and we don't have a trailer. We've always intended moving Big Pig and Little Pig – the orchard was only ever meant as a nursery pen for weaners – but we haven't really given much thought as to how we might actually get them from one enclosure to another. Now we have to.

We will walk the pigs. It sounds simple: we'll lead them from the patch of orchard, along the rutted track to the stone cross, over the lane, down a grassy path to the edge of the next hamlet, turning by the fig tree and another stone cross, over another lane and through a field to the new terrain. It's a walk I often do with Mo, early in the morning, a walk full of rabbits and foxes, partridge scuttling from the undergrowth. It's lined most of the way with big old oak and walnut trees; the path is banked with plum trees, too, and brambles, and I collect fruit here in bucketfuls, but if you're not pausing to gather produce and you go on at a good pace then it takes no more than twenty minutes.

But it's notoriously difficult to walk a pig. They tend to move slowly, but they can also show a surprising and sudden turn of speed if they feel they want to; their enthusiasm for nuts and berries, insects and leaves means there's always something tempting just a sniff away; their curiosity about new things lures them off track; their tendency to take fright at sudden noises can have them veering aside in a panic. They don't follow a herding instinct, like cattle or sheep, and if you slip a rope around their necks, dog-lead fashion, they protest noisily and are likely to haul you away or simply refuse to move. If you watch pigs in the ring at agricultural shows, they're often shuffled in front of the judges by a handler wielding a stick and a large board which is supposed to keep them moving steadily and prevent distraction, rather like blinkers on horses. Quite often it doesn't work. Quite often the pigs find their way into the crowd.

In the past, the pig drovers who plied back and forth on the old routes from farm to market were skilled animal handlers, and patient men. Pigs rarely managed to travel more than about six miles a day. There are remarkable stories of great 'hog drives' in America before the age of rail, walking thousands of animals with resounding 'soo-eeys' across the Appalachians, or out of Kentucky through the Cumberland Gap, or along the Kanawha River in West Virginia – in 1855, more than 83,000 pigs were recorded on the trail through Mount Airy in North Carolina – but in Britain most of the droving was on a reasonably small scale. Nonetheless, walking pigs to market was not an easy undertaking. Drovers set off from the remote farms of Wales or Cornwall to the pig market at Bristol with the prospect of at least a hundred miles' slow progress ahead of them: that's over two weeks of pig walking, all day, every day. From Wales there was also a journey by boat to contend with, linking Sully, near Cardiff, to Bridgwater near the Somerset coast, a short cut, but a noisy, stinking, chaotic affair.

In an attempt to make the task more manageable, drovers often muzzled the animals, or those of them with a more fiery temperament. The Victorian travel writer George Borrow also noted on a visit to Llangollen Fair that handlers there had a nifty routine for managing each pig, 'keeping the left arm round the body of the swine and with the right hand fast grasping the ear'. This kind of hands-on approach highlights just how valuable these animals were, and so how much effort went in to keeping them in good condition. Here's one of my favourite pig facts, for example: because pigs' trotters are not as robust as horses' or cattle's hooves and not as well suited to covering long distances, they were sometimes fitted with little woollen boots with leather soles to protect them on their travels.

A pig in boots. Since Samuel Bisset dressed his pig in a gorgeous red waistcoat, I like to think he prepared for their trip to Dublin by acquiring, or making, some equally rakish boots. After all, this was the age of the dandy, the self-made man of refined habits and elaborate costume, and Bisset was a lover of spectacle and rumbustious display. I can find no evidence of boots, but I like to imagine the two of them on the road, ambling along side by side between high hedges, a flash of brilliant colour and fine linen in the thick greens of summer.

Boots or no boots, Bisset was still faced with the task of walking his pig from their old home at the inn in Belfast to their new rooms near the theatre in Dame Street in Dublin, a hundred miles of man-and-beast negotiation. This is not the same as a performance, which can be practised, perfected, choreographed; this is not like running through a routine in the pub's backyard. This is an expedition, a journey into the unknown, a test of togetherness. Even if they manage to walk ten miles a day, they still have to find many places to overnight, and Bisset would not want his special pig shut in some putrid sty or mixing with more lowly beasts or teased by village children. During this hot August, the nights were fine and short; it would have been easy to find a place to settle out in the open, away from the main turnpike roads and the clatter of passing coaches, and no doubt they slept comfortably together, tucked under trees. But they could not avoid calling at inns for food for Bisset and water for the pig; they could not skirt all the villages. It was not such an unusual sight, a man walking a pig, but when a stranger appeared with a stout, sleek black pig (possibly in boots) it was still an attraction, a diversion from the grind of daily life, and it must have taken all of Bisset's 'unwearied patience' to keep this most precious of animals in his sights and out of the clutches of curious housewives, measuring its rump for bacon, or unscrupulous landlords who would steal his livelihood from under his nose.

There are few details of the route they took or the journey they made. All I know is that Bisset kept the pig constantly with him, sleeping, dining, walking. One hand on the pig, one hand on his stick. Through the undulating lands of the north, down close to the coast, crossing rivers and farms. And by the time the two of them arrived at their destination, their partnership was well and truly consolidated. They'd walked together from Belfast to Dublin; a crowd of expectant pleasure seekers was nothing after that. They could begin again with what they knew, their learned routines. And I take heart from the thought of Bisset's journey. I find I'm enjoying the prospect of walking the pigs. People have done this thing for generations: eighteenth-century impresarios, French *paysans*, drovers, farmers, children earning a penny. I have some confidence in Big Pig. He'll be sensible, as far as a pig can be, and prudent. Little Pig I'm less sure of. He's naturally more scatty, more susceptible to panic. The expedition might test his mettle. But his greed is surely in our favour: he'll do anything for food, even for the prospect of food; the whiff of a treat should, surely, be enough to secure his attention.

And so we set a date for the following week. This gives us time to prepare the new enclosure. The move is on.

The blackthorn bursts into flower, all the hedges breaking out white against the tired browns of winter. The moon rises full in the morning – white, too, in a blue sky – and hangs through the afternoon in the high bare twigs. Blackbirds sing loudly in the trees in front of our house until, a few days later, the first of the nightingales arrive and

bully them with their louder torrent of song. The days seem to lengthen all at once; the light is suddenly, impossibly bright. In the garden pond the frogs begin to croak in chorus, harsh and discordant; the frogs at the lake by the Mas de Maury call back until the air rings with echoes. Every day I come across cars pulled up in odd places, precarious on verges or jutting into the road: a few yards from each, inevitably, someone will be bent over, picking, a carrier bag in one hand and a bouquet of floppy green stalks in the other. This is the first harvest of the year, *rapountchou*, the early tendrils of a climbing plant, a wild asparagus. Although it's strong and bitter, an acquired taste, it's a local obsession, gathered in bundles and salted or pickled in jars, but it's eaten fresh, too, the first new growth of the season, traditionally a vitamin boost after a long winter surviving on conserves.

The pigs are also gorging on shoots and new leaves. They're delighted by the arrival of spring. I find them lolling in the sunshine; they've pulled some of the straw out of their shelter so that it catches the early warmth of the day and they lie here in a snug muddle of dark flanks, one half on top of the other, eyes sleepy, limbs lazy. They have the thick, coarse hair of adult pigs now, bristling after the winter, matting over the paler elephantine shade of their skin so that they are well and truly black. They fill the shelter. They're about six months old, the age at which many commercial pigs are slaughtered. They're hefty, muscular, meaty: as they sprawl and stretch, it's easy to see the way their bodies are constructed, and some of the butchery cuts that correspond – there's the shoulder, of course, and a nice row of ribs, Little Pig's good-looking belly, Big Pig's shapely haunch for a fine ham. When I look at them objectively in this way – as poster boys for the meat trade – I wonder whether I'm losing my misgivings about my ability to kill them when the time comes. Perhaps I'm toughening up. Perhaps I'm learning enough about what it takes to be a smallholder (a small smallholder) to be able to set aside my sensitivities.

But then I look at them again – two lovely hairy pigs cuddled together in a jumble of straw and black limbs – and I think, perhaps, I'm kidding myself.

I leave them sunbathing and go to work on the new piece of land. It's at the edge of the neighbouring hamlet, La Graudie, which perches on the edge of an escarpment, the last outpost of the high *causse* before it plunges down to softer, lusher ground and the river. There's a field, bumpy and overgrown, long fallow, surrounded by untidy hedges of blackthorn, spindle and brambles; this is where the shelter can go, under the shade of a big old ash tree. At one side, the field becomes woodland, a steep bank of oak that finally opens up just short of the *fontaine*; a path along the boundary runs directly into the village. The woods are overgrown, unmanaged; there are fallen trees, sick trees, ancient trees with gnarled massive girths. It's perfect land for pigs: interesting, fruitful, a playground; they can work their way through all this mess, tidying up as they go, exploring and eating what they find.

But first we have to nudge and wrestle a way through the under-growth with the trail of wire for the electric fence. We've got a container of small black plastic eyelets to screw into strategic trunks, a bundle of posts to fill any gaps, and over half a kilometre of wire coiled on a bobbin. Slowly I work my way from tree to tree, trying to find the easiest route for setting a fence. I start at the top of the slope, precarious, and slide down from one point to the next on the dry, leafy soil, securing the eyelet, passing through the wire. It feels like some kind of giant knitting, weaving the thread through the trees, passing it around trunks: knit one, purl one. Ed is working on the other side of the woods, bringing the fence in the opposite direction. I can't see him or hear him unless he whistles, which he sometimes does; Mo runs wildly back and forth between us, ecstatic about this new game in a new place.

Like the walled patch at the Mas de Maury this is abandoned land, neglected and forgotten. It feels as though no one has set foot here for very many years. But these precious woods were once tended for timber and grazing; there may well have been other pigs here, cattle certainly. Working alone in the quiet, I have something of the same feeling I had at the *fontaine*, a sense of repetition, perhaps even communion. In the spring warmth, I catch glimpses of the church spire through the greening trees; the bobbing calls of tits collide with the steady old toll of the bells. For a moment it seems as though I've been here, part of this, for a very long time. But in the quiet euphoria of such a feeling there's already, instantly, a sadness, too, because here in this elusive glimpse of shared lives and continuity there's also a nagging sense of rupture and disappointment and ending. We still haven't managed to find a solution to our work troubles; reluctantly, we're beginning to talk about the possibility of heading back to the UK; we're keeping an eye on job adverts in the newspapers. As I knit myself through the trees, binding myself into a labyrinth with a coil of twine, there are questions pricking in my head: will we have to move now? Where would we go, and to do what? Can't we just squeeze a bit more time here, a few months more? Can't we have the summer at least so that we can see the fruit of all this work; so that we can follow the smallholding experiment through to the very end? I slip down the slope to the cluster of smaller trees near the boundary – hawthorn and rowan, spindle and hazel – and I decide that all I can do is place my hope in the pigs; trust them to keep us here. Big Pig and Little Pig securing us to this little plot of land and all its many ghosts; Big Pig and Little Pig compelling us to stay.

The pigs' new enclosure is next to a farmhouse, the last building in La Graudie, sitting on the edge of the hamlet where it peters into rocky fields, the woods opening out beyond. Jean-Claude lives here with his wife, Camille. They've never farmed – he used to be the district postman – but every year they have an immaculate vegetable garden; they have a busy flock of chickens and ducks, some goats, a woodpile of sculptural beauty. If I walk past with the dog in the misty dawn, they are working in their garden. If I pass again in the settling dusk, they're still working in their garden. They grow beans and peas in weedless straight lines; their strawberries tumble over the drills in handfuls; their artichokes thrust high and straight. They dig and tend, cultivating order, precision, abundance; putting the rest of us to shame.

Pigs are disorderly and untidy, noisy, unpredictable. But Jean-Claude and Camille insist they like the idea of having Big Pig and Little Pig as neighbours: they've agreed to let us run a hose over the wall from their outside tap so that we can have access to plenty of water as the weather warms up, and they come to the top of the woods to watch as we put the finishing touches to the fence. Camille remembers when all the hamlets around here had pigs; there were pigs everywhere, she says, in the lanes and foraging in the tracks, or lazing on the warm stones by the farmhouse steps. Everyone had a pig. As a child she used to take turns with neighbours' children to look after them, sitting with them after school, trying to keep them out of the way of the grown-ups doing their chores. She liked it best when she was allowed to ride the big old sows, sitting astride as you would a squat pony, trotting down the shady paths. Her younger sisters whooped and hollered alongside, driving them on, giggling. She talks fondly, with energy. Pigs and childhood. Pigs and family. Pigs and home.

According to Camille – and supported by other material I've read – things changed not long after her childhood years, sometime in the late 1960s and early 1970s, when the directives of the Common Agricultural Policy took effect even in these old farming heartlands: pigs started to become a crop like any other, raised on an industrial scale, economically and in bulk. The village pig started to disappear. What had once been a symbol of a thriving homestead, of good husbandry and a healthy family, became indiscriminate cheap meat. Even at the beginning of the twentieth century, popular French art was bemoaning the loss of the traditional pig to the forces of modernization: a series of belle-époque postcards, for example, shows a variety of unfortunate pigs being run over by cars, bicycles or trains; one shows a bosomy peasant in a long skirt gazing at the rear end of a pig that's been trapped under a steam train, railing in traditional patois against *lai valaine invention*, 'the nasty invention'. By the time the new laws came into force the pig was already a potent symbol of a life lost to mechanization and speedy living, a reminder of the way of the *paysan*, a connection to land and community, to *le terroir*.

Big Pig and Little Pig are a hint of an unrecoverable past; they're welcomed because they are already almost familiar – with the slippery, defective memory of nostalgia, our neighbours connect themselves to our pigs, trace old associations that don't really exist, make our animals part of their own histories. And so it seems fitting that Big Pig and Little Pig should mature here, as part of a hamlet community, reviving, if only for a few months, an old tradition, an historic intimacy. They'll have Jean-Claude and Camille's grandchildren playing on the other side of the wall; they'll have the scruffy collection of hamlet dogs coming and going through the patch of field; they'll be lullabied by the steady thrum of tractors and chainsaws, strimmers and rotavators, the particular low-note muzak of daily life.

Many of Camille's stories are about thrift and old-fashioned housekeeping skills. Pigs were largely animals of the active poor. Not just here but across Europe, the wealthy hunted for game, raised beef cattle, and could afford to buy meat, if necessary, from the market; they could have a fresh supply more or less whenever they wanted it. But the working classes had to make do with their pig – a single pig, usually – for a whole year. A pig was a promise that they would not starve.

During both wars, when thrift was a matter of patriotism, local councils in Britain urged people to join pig clubs, grouping together to share the cost of feed and scraps from the kitchen in return for some precious pork. There were almost a thousand pig clubs by the time war broke out in 1914 – encouraging discipline, respectability and good behaviour as well as frugality – and during the Second World War, the Ministry of Food was giving the pig responsibility for the future of the Empire:

> Because of the pail,
> the **scraps** were saved,
> Because of the scraps,
> the **pigs** were saved,
> Because of the pigs,
> the **rations** were saved,
> Because of the rations,
> the **ships** were saved,
> Because of the ships,
> the **island** was saved,

> Because of the island,
> the **Empire** was saved,
> And all because of
> **the housewife's pail.**

The importance of bacon to the everyday diet is reflected in the fact that it was included in the first round of rationing in 1940, along with butter and sugar, as the staples most in demand. In response to such a miserable edict, the cartoonist Heath Robinson offered suggestions on 'How to Make the Best of Things'. He proposed a 'neat garden cabinet for growing bacon and mushrooms': his cartoon shows a bald man in a waistcoat offering a bowl of leftovers to a perky pig 'installed in the fireplace of the spare bedroom', with mushrooms sprouting on the mantelpiece and a box below which 'will also lay the foundations of a fine Minestrone' with the simple addition of 'the contents of the carpet sweeper'.

A comic French film, *La Traversée de Paris*, again shows the importance of the pig during the Second World War: it tells the story of two men who defy the city's curfew in 1942 to deliver suitcases stuffed full of pork. In our part of France, the occupying Germans outlawed the keeping of pigs for family use, taking any animals for themselves and forbidding private slaughter, with the intention not only of feeding their soldiers but also, no doubt, of further disheartening hungry households. So the killing of a pig became a secret, dangerous affair, an act of defiance and desperation, a link to life before the war: the men took the pigs out into the far fields at night, under the brilliant winter stars, the women following after with their tools and buckets; the animals were dispatched in silence, quickly butchered under the trees, the meat wrapped and stowed in barns and cupboards before first light. Camille remembers this, even though she was very young. She remembers the cold and the smell of the blood in the night air and the intense, fearful listening. There were gendarmes you could trust, she says, and those you couldn't.

And even then, especially then, when the meat was acquired with such risk, nothing could be wasted, not the blood nor the intestines, the head or the ears. It was not just the pig itself which was treasured, but also the *savoir faire* that meant it could be fully used and enjoyed. Just as it had always been, soldiers or no soldiers, war or no war, in the days after slaughter, each pig was transformed into pâtés and sausages, puddings and terrines, and the nuanced range of cuts and preserves which make up the *charcuterie* (*chair cuite*, cooked meat): *lardons*, *saucissons*, *saucisses sèches*, hams. Affluent Romans had a taste for good ham and the Roman army carried copious supplies of salted, dried and smoked pork; by the Middle Ages, the French had established a medieval *charcuterie* guild to regulate the production of processed meat and ensure its quality, placing the craft on the same basis as farriers or armourers, masons, tanners or bakers – those who made daily life possible. One of the most hated of French taxes, *la gabelle*, was the tax on salt, introduced in the fourteenth century and not finally repealed until the country's liberation in 1945. Its unpopularity was testament to the importance of salt in a cuisine that relished *la charcuterie*. With salt in short supply, or ruinously expensive, and hams to be cured, smuggling became rampant, often organized in a military fashion, and on a national scale, by French troops. The *gardes des gabelles*, the salt-tax guards, were frequently overrun, and in our region, *le pays de petite gabelle*, several wooded routes were established to allow smugglers to avoid main roads between major towns. A local mid-seventeenth-century uprising, which saw 10,000 *croquants* (literally, 'crunchies' or 'crispies' – more accurately, and pejoratively, 'yokels') lay siege to the town of Villefranche-de-Rouergue in 1643, included *la gabelle* among a list of hated taxes to be reformed. Protesting with tambours and trumpets, the insurrection perhaps had more of a party tone than a revolutionary one, and the leaders were duly broken alive on wheels during public executions, their heads later displayed on the town walls.

With such a long history of protecting ancient *charcuterie* traditions at all costs, the inconvenience of foreign occupation during two world wars was unlikely to put a stop to them. During the First World War, a series of wonderful letters from Sister Joachim (a young British woman, Margaret Anne Shippam) at a convent in occupied Ooigem, in western Belgium, shows that even the nuns were willing to defy German orders in the quest for good ham: 'I told you we were having a piggy salted,' she wrote in 1915 to her family back in Chichester:

> Well, his arrival was Accompanied with great solemnity and triumph, at ½ past 7 am Wednesday. Just as we were going to take down our frugal breakfast, piggy arrived in a big cask, carried by three men and a woman. Happily the G's did not get hold of our piggy.

During the occupation in France almost thirty years later, hams were still being made and shared among friends with 'great solemnity and triumph'. Camille remembers a burgeoning black market, but also speaks fondly of the gifting of *charcuterie* between neighbours. There was always a special cut, she says, for *le curé*, the priest, and echoing Sister Joachim, she recalls her parents leaving a ham on the convent steps at dawn so that the village nuns would find it when they woke. 'We were better off here than in the towns,' she says. 'We had pigs still, everywhere, even though they weren't allowed. In Paris they ate guinea pigs.'

Jean-Claude takes us into his storeroom under the house, a dry dark room with onions and garlic hung from the rafters, carrots in straw, jars of pickles arranged on shelves. With some pride, he shows us the box he made many years ago for salting hams. It's plain but well made, with clean dovetail joints in good wood, like a small coffin. 'You just fill it with salt,' he says, 'pop in the leg of meat, seal it up and leave it. Beautiful. You'll never taste better.' We suggest that we might send our hams somewhere to be dry cured. He looks at us and shrugs. For Jean-Claude, the keeping of a pig is a practical way to save money: he can't understand that we might worry enough about the quality of our ham to pay someone else to cure it for us, when we could just as well salt it for free in the garage.

This is a place of self-sufficiency, of proud independence and of making do. Nothing is bought, no product or service, when it can be made or done at home. Camille makes cheese and matures it above the fireplace. She forages for mushrooms, dandelions, sorrel, fruit of all kinds, a variety of nuts: a dealer from the city pays her €2 a kilo for the walnuts she gathers. She has her own eggs, vegetables, rabbits and poultry. She's another of the old women giving this place a sense of stability, doing things as they've always been done, respectfully upholding tradition and country living. But when she talks about her activities it's already with a hint of nostalgia and weariness – she knows such ways are unsustainable both for herself and for the area as a whole. She's winding down. She's fed up, she says, of scratching the fields for walnuts to sell or podding enormous quantities of broad beans for soup. She still goes to market every Thursday, but largely to meet her friends and marvel at the rising cost of living, rather than to barter for staples. She remembers the excitement of going to market as a child, piling into the back of the mule cart and rumbling along the valley in a queue of farm traffic. 'It's just not the same any more,' she says.

We're almost ready to move the pigs. Together, Ed and I have cleared as much as we can around the new fence in the woods and tested it to make sure the current passes right along its length: we've lifted twigs from the wire and listened for the telltale *click*, *click*, *click* that indicates a break in the circuit – a leaf nudging up against the string, wet grass drooping on to it after rain. On the flat patch of meadow at the edge of the trees, we've built a new shelter, roomier than the first, a more solid affair constructed of planks and old wooden pallets, lined with plastic sheeting and roofed with lengths of unwieldy bitumen. We've run the hosepipe round from Jean-Claude's outside tap and set up a drinking trough. We've collected two full buckets of acorns from the tracks, winkling them out of the earth where they've lain since last autumn. We've set aside a supple solid length of ash, a pig stick, something that appears to give the whole process an air of authority and professionalism, the kind of staff that looks like it might have come out of an eighteenth-century woodcut of a proper pig drover. This all seems good.

On Thursday morning, market morning, we go as usual to do our shopping, and our general air of excitement is reinforced by the sudden prosperity of spring stalls. In winter, this town belongs to the bleak heartlands of central France: business at the markets is hurried, frugal, the square hard and bitterly cold, traders braving the ice to set up sparse displays of turnips and spinach. But within a few weeks of spring arriving, the marketplace is suddenly bustling again: stalls are packed with asparagus and *cèpes*, crumbling fresh cheeses, new-season carrots, piles of multicoloured radishes, strawberries, seedlings, flowers, lettuces. Shoppers take their time, pausing, filling their baskets carefully with the delicate produce. The cafe terraces are full and rumble with the burr of patois. This is one of the few ordinary occasions on which you still sometimes hear Occitan spoken (although this is less common now than when we first arrived) and groups of old men in berets gather in the shade of the *halle* to keep an eye on things and chatter in the tangles of their old language. Traders put up their striped awnings, red and green, because the sun can be hot by the middle of the morning; from now until late October this is a place of the south with painfully blue skies, warm stone and deep shadows, relaxed and generous, bountiful.

Firmly planted at the foot of the tall metal crucifix in the square, with a bread stall on one side and packed rows of young tomato plants on the other, a huge white Christ gazing down painfully above, the smallest of the smallholders are gathered: old men with chickens and rabbits in baskets and cages, songbirds, flitting budgerigars; there's a boy with kittens to give away, *chatons à donner*; several women with eggs to sell and bits and pieces they've gathered – dandelion leaves, a few stalks of lilac from the garden, *rapountchou*. It's no longer permitted to sell live pigs in this ad hoc way – they have to be properly auctioned at the livestock market – but it's not that long ago that piglets could be stuffed into baskets and sold to passers-by, not just here but across Europe: an 1890 notice of fees in Sandbach market hall in Cheshire, for example, records that for only 1d you could bring 'any number' of pigs 'in a basket not exceeding 17 inches in length' or pay an extra penny for bringing a hamper 2' 6" long, presumably packed with more, or larger, animals.

There may be no more live pigs at our Thursday market, but the pig is nonetheless much in evidence. In this land of fatted ducks and *Le Veau d'Aveyron*, it's still affordable pork and *charcuterie* products which are most visible around the stalls. This is mostly normal, cheaply produced meat rather than high-end, free-range *Noir de Bigorre*, so there is plenty of it: we can buy confited pigs' hearts;

trotters whole or cooked in jelly; *andouillette* made from daintily named chitterlings which turn out to be robust intestines; ears, lungs and livers; pâtés and terrines of all kinds; a range of *saucissons*. On a plancha grill over a big gas bottle, a man in an Olympique de Marseille football shirt is cooking black pudding to serve with caramelized apples. One of the farmers' wives in the market hall has made a huge sausage pie which she's selling in slices. A young trader has made a big slab of *fritons* with coarse chunks of pork, a marquetry of pig pressed in jelly, and he carves off portions with a large knife. The pig and the market are mutually sustaining: the strawberries may be lusciously red and tempting, but it's the more earthy browns of the pork products that act as the fundamental scaffold for the comings and goings of the season.

We queue for sheep's cheese and yoghurt in the arcaded square which is overshadowed on one side by a heavy bell tower, out of proportion to the church it abuts and evidence of rampant medieval ecclesiastical ambition. The vendor has a spot just under the arch of the tower, coolly shaded in the summer but still chilly now; he stamps his feet and blows on his hands. We talk about moving animals: he's just brought his sheep up into new pasture. 'It's a fragile time of year,' he says. 'Everything's –' he makes a gesture suggesting a brief moment of balance '– *délicat*. You have to be careful with the animals – more than ever. They feel it.' I buy a portion of creamy cheese and wonder if Big Pig and Little Pig feel this fragility he's talking about.

When we've unpacked the shopping back at home, I walk Mo down to the orchard in search of signs of vulnerability: Big Pig is pulling at a thick root, his neck and haunches straining with effort; Little Pig is digging alongside, his head buried deep in the soil, moving rocks with his snout, pawing up clods of clay. They don't seem in the least fragile. But the sheep farmer is wise and experienced, and our conversation reminds me that moving the pigs will be a big deal, for them as well as us, for them especially – a real upheaval.

Perhaps it's just a matter of perception, of anticipation, but it seems that even in the last few days the pigs have outgrown their weaner enclosure. They are pressing up more often against the fence, squealing in indignant surprise if they get a shock. Little Pig is squabbling over space in the shelter. Big Pig snuffles the bare earth disconsolately, in an increasingly fruitless search for shoots and bugs. Around the boundaries and in front of the shelter, the ground is muddy and pitted. The pigs' early inquisitiveness has matured into doughty investigation. Their dependence has grown into demand: they clamour for food, water, company, space. What started a couple of months ago as playful rummaging through the old ivy and at the foot of the plum trees has developed into full-scale, brute-strength excavation which throws out stones, bricks, scraps of metal, which can bulldoze a trench in no time at all and uproot saplings. This small patch of land has, for the moment, been used up; it needs a break from the endless back and forth of snouts and trotters.

And then, as a final prompt, there's an emergency, of sorts. Mo and I walk down early with the morning feed and even before we're halfway along the track, it's clear that something is wrong. The pigs are too noisy. I know them well enough now to recognize this commotion as something new. This isn't the usual low grunt of greeting – this is an anxious chunter, thrown out regardless of anyone's approach, a squeaky garble of distress that can be heard across the fields and down to the lake, flipping back in jittery echoes from the ruined walls of the old farm. This is an unfamiliar sound; untamed.

I go on quickly and Mo stays close; closer than usual. The bucket bumps against my legs, spilling grain. A trail of powdery cereal sits up pale on the mud of the track, marking the point at which the panic kicked in. At the little white door in the wall we both pause, as though to brace ourselves. I say something to Mo, a 'good dog' sort of platitude, and at last the pigs seem to hear us. There's a sudden quiet. They're listening. But it only lasts a second, and then one of them grunts and then they both start squawking again.

And to my surprise, when I push open the door with my bucket, the pigs are there; right there. Upon me: flustered and barging. Usually, there's a gap of several strides between the entrance and the electric fence, a kind of no-man's-land where we can put sacks and pails out of reach and where Mo stands to watch what's going on.

Now this gap is full of pig. Little Pig is at the front, as always, trampling me, shoving against my legs so that I have to step away along the wall. Big Pig is not far behind, closing in from the other side. Both of them have their snouts held high and they're intent on pushing on, pushing forward, anywhere, anyhow. They're taking little account of me. They've noticed me, but only as an obstruction. They don't seem to recognize me, or care that I'm there. For the first time since we've had them, I'm intimidated by this weight of careering animal and by their reckless single-mindedness – by their wildness.

Sensibly, Mo flees through the door. I'm tempted to follow; I back up until my hand finds the latch. But I don't want to be afraid of the pigs. And I've got the bucket, the all-powerful bucket. So I step forward into the scrum of heavy black flanks and I push hard at Little Pig, thrust my knee into his side, kick out at Big Pig, force my way through, ignore the noise. I keep the bucket high and slap it with my palm, so that they'll know it's there, and I call to them: 'Come on, boys! Come on.' My voice is high and strained.

I make my way clear and can drop the bucket to my side. I begin to see what has happened. The fence is down. It's not just the wire loosened or one of the posts pushed over: the whole fence, posts and wire and everything, is trampled into the ground along a length of perhaps five metres. Inside what was the enclosure, the shelter is more or less demolished. There's a tangle of plastic table leg and corrugated metal and straw, but little else. The feeding trough has been kicked away into the mud; I right it and scrape off the worst of the dirt with the toe of my boot before refilling it. As I do this, the pigs slow and quieten. They watch me, properly, with interest. Their eyes are soft where they had been hard; their heads drop as the tension subsides. They know who I am. I'm the person who brings food. I'm a good thing. And abruptly, as though a switch has been flicked, they are domesticated again, recognizable, shuffling back and forth along the length of the trough in the endless search for the best mouthful of grain, their noses floured with cereal dust, their ears lolling, their tails flicking contentedly.

But I'm unnerved by what I've seen. Unnerved for two reasons. Firstly, I've seen, for the first time, Little Pig and Big Pig as grown animals, heavy, unpredictable, capable of crushing limbs without compunction. The weaner days are well and truly gone. These are mature beasts, wilful, independent, a bit anarchic; not pets or playthings. I knew this, in my head, but now I've seen it and felt it, and been afraid of it, and I actually, properly realize what it means – a day or two before we attempt to take these animals out of their safe place, walk them through the neighbourhood and set them loose on a much bigger, wilder area of land with only a few lines of electric fence to keep them from people's homes and gardens, the village at the foot of the woods, absolute freedom beyond. This is the first thing that unnerves me.

The second is this: when I look at the flattened fence I realize that it's been trampled from the outside in. The damage is not the pigs' doing. This is not an attempt to escape. Probably they had the shelter down in their panic; probably they upended the trough; probably they made the wreckage worse – but this was because they were frightened. The danger has come from outside; the fence has been pushed to the ground by something, or someone, forcing a path to the pigs. That's what all the noise was about. The dismay. The confusion.

There's been an intruder. A threat. An attack.

An attack, a ruffian, an intruder. History repeating. Bisset's black pig, living such a different life to Big Pig and Little Pig, nonetheless has his own assailant, an assault out of the blue. His tale takes a darker turn. I read this latest episode in the eighteenth-century story on the evening after I've cleared up the scattered fence at the Mas de Maury and I'm struck by how vulnerable Bisset's pig is as it adapts itself to stardom in a new environment. No matter how learned he might be, he's a pig out of place, an eccentricity. I recall the fear so clearly evident in Big Pig and Little Pig earlier that day, even in the quiet safety of their own enclosure, and I feel sorry for Bisset's pig, dragged from the known and the habitual into the uncertainty of spectacle.

It's the middle of a performance: the Dublin crowd is enthralled. This night is going just as well as the previous two nights, perhaps better. The spectators are clapping, cheering, laughing. There's banter, of course, prattle and joking. People are excited, fascinated. They like what they're seeing. They love the pig. Who doesn't love the pig, so sage and solid?

And the pig, deliberate and equable in the fuss and heat of the room, has already accomplished several admirable acts of mathematics and is poised to spell the name of a young lady in the second row, the lady in the flouncy hat with pinkish ribbons and pinkish cheeks. On the floor, there's an alphabet of cards laid in a circle, a circus of bold red letters. The pig is in its place in the circle; its eyes are bright. Bisset has his hand on his pig's neck, his palm flat just above the point where the red of the pig's waistcoat gives way to thickening black hair below the ears, and he is leaning towards the woman, smiling broadly, tantalizing her, holding them all entranced in this moment of anticipation. He's the showman, the performer, the tease. Will the black pig do it? Will it spell? Again? As it did last night? What's the woman's name? How can the pig know it? How does the animal do it?

'Poor Bisset', say the papers the next day. 'Poor injured Bisset', laments *The Sporting Magazine*. There will be no spelling tonight, no magic, no romance. Instead, from out of nowhere, there's a gate-crasher. A man with no ticket and no smile, who bursts into the room and pushes rudely through the crowd. And he's quickly on to the stage, scattering the spelling cards, breaking the props, stamping on everything he can find, throwing letters and balls and books against the walls. Perhaps, for a moment, one or two of the spectators imagine all this is part of the act, but they soon see this can't be true: there can be no mistaking the intruder's steady anger or his will for destruction, and now he's pummelling Bisset, too, punching him in the face and stomach, kicking him when he falls. This is no panto-mime beating.

The intruder takes no notice of the howls of protest; he's glaring around him, cursing those who've encouraged such a foolish spec-tacle. He wants to put a stop to it, immediately and at any cost. And he's a policeman, of sorts, with the power to make them obey him, and so the woman in the second row gives up hoping the pig will spell her name and backs away, and several other women cluster together in the far corner of the room where things are quieter, and though the men shout and complain and one or two throw their fists in the air, the intruder ignores them. Instead he draws his sword. He wants to kill the pig.

Poor Bisset, breathing hard, dizzy with pain, pleads his case. He explains that he has all the correct permissions, all in order, everything as it should be and agreed by the Chief Magistrate. He pleads for the life of his pig, his special pig. He is as bold as he has ever been, as sincere as he can be, and he forces himself to stand up straight and place himself between the pig and the sword.

The policeman of sorts pauses, stays his hand, but his sword remains drawn between them and the pig is trapped now against the wall, quiet enough but uneasy, its tail swishing. This is not part of the show. The pig has not been taught how to behave on such an occasion. And the policeman of sorts gives no ground. He hears Bisset's defence but he doesn't want to believe what he hears. He scowls at the big black dirty animal; he shakes his head, grimaces, thrusts forward with his sword so there can be no mistake and makes a threat: if the show is not halted at once then Bisset will be dragged away to prison and the pig slaughtered. He's flushed, pleased. He addresses the crowd with a flourish and sends them home. The entertainment is over.

Poor Bisset. On the brink of another great success. The intruder, the policeman of sorts, struts from the room, leaving a trail of indignant quiet behind him. The crowd ebbs away. One or two of the spectators offer Bisset a sympathetic word, a kindly glance, but he hardly knows where he is and he does not respond.

All the accounts I come across agree that Bisset is blameless. He has the right permissions and he's doing nothing wrong. It appears to be an unprovoked, unreasonable attack by a jobsworth law enforcer – one of the reports concludes that the pig 'in the practice of good manners, was at least the superior of the assailant'. But still Bisset has to go. The policeman of sorts may return, may be as good as his word and haul Bisset to the stinking Dublin gaol. So he gathers himself, tries to collect his thoughts and rally his spirits. He has the pig, after all. Worse could have happened. He aches badly from the beating;

there's a wound from the blade of the sword; his agitation makes him woozy, but he's proved himself here on Dame Street; he's been the talk of Dublin; he has fat bundles of banknotes in his pocket. He can go on to better things, to London. The pig is already a star; there'll be crowds every night, genteel crowds, the wealthy, no ruffians with swords. Bisset takes a breath, pats the pig.

Early next morning Bisset pays half a guinea and takes the boat from Dublin harbour to Holyhead; the pig travels with him, for another half-guinea. It does not mix with the farm animals below deck but has special passage as a pig in a waistcoat (and perhaps boots), and they stand together by the rails as the Irish Sea swells below them. Bisset is feeling the effects of the attack; his usual energy is drained, his head aches, his vision wobbles. He wishes he did not feel so sick. He wishes they were already safely in London. The pig, on the other hand, seems unaffected by the traumatic events of the previous night or the roll of the boat on the waves. A stoic pig.

The boat docks; the passengers disembark. One or two people stop Bisset to ask about the pig, but he doesn't want to bother with them. He's quite rude. He wants to get on. But a day or two later the travellers are still only at Chester. They should have been well on their way to London by now but they've been forced to a halt. Bisset has had to take lodgings. He's not well. His thoughts are scatty, lathered; he can't remember where he is, or why. He's anxious all the time and afraid; he sees intruders in the shadows and calls out; his agitation stifles him; he does not eat. He's in his bed. He's cold. Done in.

Done for.

In August 1783 Samuel Bisset died in a room in Chester from the effects of a beating in Ireland, and for the sake of a pig. He was not known in the city, and his death was ignored. There were no notices in the newspapers; the town crier had nothing to say about the matter. No one bothered much about his family. The pot of money he'd brought with him from Dublin – the fruits of three splendid performances – was never seen again: lost, or stolen; perhaps taken by the landlord to settle the account. The burial had to be paid for, after all. But the money wasn't everything, of course, and as I reach the end of this part of the story, I'm left wondering about the pig. In these last few days of Bisset's life, when he was shivering on his deathbed in some dingy Chester backstreet, where was the pig? Nothing is said in any of the accounts about who might have stepped in to take care of it, if anyone, or about what was decided for its future without the man who had been so long its companion. The death notice appearing almost six months later in the *Westmeath Journal* even gets Bisset's name wrong, calling him John. In all this confusion and uncertainty, the tale appears to grind to a halt leaving the most important question unanswered: what on earth happened to Bisset's pig?

We clear up in the enclosure. We push the fence posts into new ground and trail the wire from one to the other. We rebuild the shelter, again. Since the entire place will be emptied in a day or two when the pigs are moved, it feels like a chore; but we're careful, nonetheless, because it's not clear what happened during the night, nor what came here to the old orchard. We turn up the current on the electric fence. We check for gaps in the wall.

I think about poor old Samuel Bisset dying in defence of his pig. I wonder about jealousies and grudges. Would anyone want to do harm to our pigs? Would anyone care enough, harbour enough spite? It seems a ridiculous idea. We're still strangers here – we're still English interlopers, it's true – but everyone we've spoken to about Big Pig and Little Pig has been kind; amused and curious but kind. Like Bisset, we've broken no rules. Besides, who would go to the trouble of breaking down the electric fence, charging into the enclosure and chasing the pigs from their shelter when you could just stand at the entrance and shoot them with a shotgun? Was it all for fun? For a laugh? It doesn't make sense.

Perhaps this was some kind of 'nature' thing; perhaps we should blame wild boar. The door was closed when Mo and I arrived, so they couldn't have sneaked in from the track, but perhaps they somehow found a way over or around the orchard walls to attack their pampered cousins. They could have been drawn by scent and then found themselves trapped, trampled the fence . . . But this is ridiculous, too, isn't it? What are the chances of cavorting herds of boar plunging out of the woods, rampaging through the enclosure and then vanishing without trace?

Dogs, then? Foxes? Cattle? Not long after we arrived in France I was walking down the lane to the village at night. It wasn't late – perhaps eight or nine o'clock – but it was softly, impenetrably dark: no street lights or house lights, no moon, a tangle of stars. I hadn't brought a torch. I tried to pick out the paler surface of the road against the thicker blacks of the hedges and fields, but this turned out to be more difficult than you might think, and familiar ground was proving treacherous. I was disorientated, already jumpy, wary, the absolute dark new to me. As I made my way up the slope to the point where the lane turned along a line of pine trees, I began to hear an odd sound, an intermittent, hollow *clunk*, a kind of bodiless sound, clear and sharp but not quite physical. I'd heard nothing like it before, I was sure. It came at me from ahead and then from behind, from one side and then from the other. It seemed close, but I couldn't judge because it echoed, too, as though ringing on stone.

I was terrified. I turned tail. It took me perhaps fifteen minutes to get home and then I retraced my route by car, still trembling. The headlights, of course, showed everything in its familiar form: Solange's farm next door, the hay barn, the tracks off on either side, the tall oak, the pines . . . the donkeys. Donkeys! Five or six donkeys broken loose from somewhere, grazing quite happily in the dark, nudging each other across the lane, languid, unconcerned. *Clip-clop.* Hooves on tarmac. The ordinary recomposed. A lesson in the power of night.

Probably something humdrum happened at the enclosure. Even in the wild, adult pigs have few natural predators: there are no bears here at Mas de Maury, or leopards; to my knowledge there are no alligators in the lake. And with the added protection afforded domesticated animals, attacks on free-range farm pigs are extremely rare. Certainly something spooked them and brought down the fence, probably in the shuffling, unsettled hour or so around dawn, not long before Mo and I arrived, but we'll never know if it was an intentional assault by man or beast, or just confusion of some kind: a family of deer, perhaps, unexpectedly finding itself confronted, alarmed and skittery. We're just grateful that Big Pig and Little Pig are both unscathed. No tragic ending here, unlike Bisset's sorry tale. And we take comfort that the new piece of land at La Graudie is better protected: the pigs will be out of view of conniving humans, further from a track and sheltered by the sloping woods; the houses and barns, geese and dogs will put off animal marauders; the huge enclosure will allow room for evasion and escape.

There's no doubt now: it's time to move.

It's midweek, mid-morning, a time of stillness. A bright day with birds circling high, the hay growing thickly and scenting the dew, the light already hardening towards summer. The verges are speckled with campion, poppies, mallow, bindweed, daisies, scabious, thyme, feverfew, saxifrage, stitchwort – and all the jewelled bugs, beetles and hoppers that skitter among them. It feels like a cheerful day for moving pigs and we set off to the orchard in high spirits, each with a bucket full of acorns. Only Mo, left at home, is glum.

We leave the buckets outside the little white door and go into the enclosure. Big Pig is truffling at the far end under the plum saplings, his nose deep in soil. Little Pig is lying on the straw in the sun, lazy, but he's the first to see us and he squirms to his feet with a grunt and rushes over for food. Big Pig raises his head, shakes the earth from his skin and trots over to join us. I scratch him on the neck, behind the ear. It's difficult to know whether he feels my touch through the thick dark skin, but there must be some pleasure in it because Little Pig nudges, demanding attention, too.

Ed turns off the battery that runs the electric fence. We remove the three posts nearest the door and drop the wire, pulling it out to create a wide passage. The pigs watch. We step back towards the door and encourage them through the gap. 'Come on, then! Come on.' Two mornings ago they were here, charging at me, a heap of pig beyond the enclosure, but now they stand resolutely still, exactly at the line where the fence had been, exactly where they usually do. We fetch the buckets and rattle the acorns. They know the sound; they want the treat. But they daren't cross the line they've learned. They're frightened of a shock, of pain. So they gaze at the bucket and grumble and shove sideways against each other; they make a tiny movement forward, nothing more than a flinch.

I run my hand in front of their noses. See? No wire. I step back and forth to prove that things have changed. The pigs eye me suspiciously. Ed rattles the acorns and moves away with the bucket towards the door. 'Come on. Last chance!'

They're desperate now. They want the acorns more than anything. They want to burst forward and follow Ed. And they suspect that it might be all right. They've begun to understand that the rules are being rewritten and they hold themselves tight and unusually still, suspended between learned fear and new desire. 'It's OK. You'll be OK. Come on.' But they can't bring themselves to risk it. They discovered the sting of the fence as tiny weaners, and ever since they've respected its authority. Quite sensibly, they don't want to get hurt. Even for a big bucket of acorns. And it occurs to me that much of their misery after the 'break-in' at the enclosure might simply have been because they'd been forced across the line that night, driven over, compelled to defy safe habits.

So it's an impasse, a stalemate. We can't drag or push them out; they're simply too heavy and determined. They'll have to do this for themselves. But what if they won't? What if they refuse to step over the now non-existent boundary? We'd envisaged all sorts of problems walking the pigs along the lane but not this; we'd never considered that we wouldn't even get started. I step behind Little Pig and try to edge him forward, prodding his round bottom gently with my knees, talking to him. But the sense of a limit is too ingrained. Even this slight encouragement to cross it causes anguish: Little Pig protests and backs heavily into me, shying away; Big Pig, too, pulls noisily, anxiously aside. They're edgy for a moment, the acorns forgotten.

We fetch both buckets and put them on the ground a few feet from the door. I kneel by one of the buckets and rummage inside it, presumably throwing up a delightful aroma of oak mast. We take a handful or two of acorns and scatter them in a trail from the enclosure. The pigs can now see the potential feast, as well as hear and smell it. On the whole, pigs use their noses and ears much more than their eyes, but anything's worth a try. We sit with our backs to the wall, the stone crumbling over our overalls, and we wait. The pigs fret and fidget, tormented by the thought of acorns out of reach.

Finally, warily, it's Big Pig that makes the move. Little Pig may be greedy, but Big Pig is brave. More thoughtful, too, if that's possible. He fixes his attention on the buckets, steadies himself, and takes a single, slow step over the imaginary line. He seems still to expect to be zapped; when nothing happens, he collects himself and gingerly takes another step. 'Well done. Good pig.' We get up slowly, so as not to cause alarm, and move across to rattle the buckets. He's extremely cautious, but he's approaching the acorns. Little Pig, apparently terrified and furious in equal measure, stands stiffly behind the non-fence and glares.

We can't separate the pigs. We can't leave one untended while we take the other. We have to move them together. Two pigs, two people: a proper drove. But Big Pig is growing in confidence. He's worked his way along the trail of acorns and it's obvious that he's enjoying himself. His tail swishes happily from side to side, his snout is lively, twitching; he's trotting towards the buckets. We pick them up and step away and, just as planned, he follows. If we don't keep moving so that we're just ahead of him, he'll press his head low into the bucket, then his strong neck, eventually his trotter, and he'll force us to stop or spill the entire hoard of acorns, or both. But Little Pig is still hesitating. He wants to come, he's desperate to come, but he can't yet bring himself to take the plunge. It's like watching someone tackle their first bungee jump: will they? won't they?

And we wheedle and encourage, and I wrap my arm gently around Little Pig's neck and tug very slightly, and Big Pig is flaunting his feasting and his freedom, and in the end, inevitably, Little Pig comes, too. In a bustle of unease, he crosses the line, still afraid of a shock but much more afraid, finally, of losing out or being left behind.

So: we have two pigs, at last. We can begin. At a merry amble and with the constant brisk jiggle of acorns, we set off together through the little white door and into a new world.

★

The care of the family pig has never been a particularly gendered activity. Women kept poultry. Men tended cattle. Goats and sheep: that was women's work, mostly, or children's. Mules, horses, miscellaneous meat stock: men took charge of that. But the pig was different. Keeping the pig was a shared task. Men often foraged handfuls of greens to supplement kitchen scraps: 'During the Spring and Summer months, every labourer, who has industry, frugality, and conveniency sufficient, to keep a pig, is seen carrying home in the evening, as he returns from his labour, a bundle of Hog Weed,' noted the agricultural writer William Marshall in 1798. A boy in nineteenth-century Northamptonshire noted that his chores included sorting 'all the small potatoes and any diseased, with some swedes [. . .] washed and boiled in the copper' for pig food. 'When it was cooked, put in a tub and mash it.' Because the pig was kept alongside – or even inside – the house, women and girls, too, were inevitably involved in raising the animal on a day-to-day basis, and when pigs were let loose to forage in orchards or woodlands, it was usually the housewife who took her knitting or sewing along and sat with them. In *Lark Rise to Candleford*, a rural memoir of late nineteenth-century life, Flora Thompson remembers that the pig became 'an important member of the family' and everyone, from the oldest to the youngest, took an interest in its well-being:

> its health and condition were regularly reported in letters to children away from home, together with news of their brothers and sisters. Men callers on Sunday afternoons came, not to see the family, but the pig, and would lounge with its owner against the pigsty door for an hour, scratching piggy's back.

Similarly, the French belle époque of the late nineteenth and early twentieth centuries revelled in the idea of the family pig: series of popular photographic postcards proudly displayed mother, father and children all posing with their animal; some of the captions showed the women declaring a preference for piglets over their men, while others had the man of the household with an armful of pigs in his embrace. Comfortable, affectionate family life without a pig was unthinkable. Apparently, even into the early twentieth

century, newly-weds were as excited about the prospect of owning
their own pig as having a private space for those first few nights
together: 'To have a sty in the garden, or, as often, abutting the
cottage, was held to be as essential to the happiness of a newly married couple as a living room or bedroom,' suggested Walter Rose, a
rural carpenter.

Walking the pigs with Ed is an act of shared domesticity. I'm at the
front of the procession with a bucket in each hand, going on slowly.
I have one pig to each side of me, slightly behind me, ambling. Ed is
a pace or two further back, wielding the drover's staff. We've made it
on to the Mas de Maury track that leads up to the stone cross marking
the junction. To our right is a high hedge of hawthorn and blackthorn and brambles, twittering with small birds. To the left, with the
sun slanting across it, is a row of very old and large oaks which mark
the perimeter of a field. The field is sprouting something green; a
flock of starlings shimmies across. There's no sign of anyone else.
We don't talk much – we're concentrating on the pigs – but still it
feels special, this moment together, intimate, slightly festive. It's perhaps the strangest thing we've done since we've been married, and
perhaps the most beautiful.

From time to time, one or other of the pigs will pause to snuffle at
something. Little Pig: nose in the hedge. Big Pig: deep in the debris
at the foot of an oak. There are acorns, of course, buried and delicious. There are new leaves, insects, general bits of tasty this and that.
But on the whole they're as interested in the journey as in what they
can scavenge, and one rattle of the bucket has their attention. They
look up, they remember: ah, yes, that's right, we're on the move.
They sense more discoveries, or hope for them. And they're off again,
the pace quickening.

As we make our way to the end of the track I turn and look back,
just once, and I see a scene I'm not quite in and which doesn't seem
quite real: a bucolic, ancient frieze of two fine, rounded black pigs
sauntering through the light and shade of spring; the drover a few
paces behind, unconcerned; the frame of trees and hedges indeterminate, unchanging. For the briefest, most exhilarating of seconds,
I slip through time.

We reach the cross. It's a plain blunt cross on a corner of drystone wall that abuts the hedge: three large pieces of pale weathered stone stacked unevenly, one upon the other. The walnut tree, above and behind, is not yet in full leaf. It dangles reddish catkins into the shadows. Here, the dirt and gravel of the track give way to the metalled lane; from here, for a distance of about twenty yards, we'll be on the road.

It's only a country lane, no more than the width of a small car, but the pigs have never experienced a hard surface underfoot. Ed comes alongside and takes a bucket. We pause and the pigs have a handful of acorns each as reward for such good behaviour so far. There's no sign of any traffic: you can usually hear a car coming from at least half a mile away, and just now it's quiet. We've chosen a good time, after the children have been taken to school and before people start coming home for lunch, but it's still a relief to find the road deserted. I'm not sure how the pigs would react to a vehicle coming alongside them; I'm not sure I want anyone to see us clip-clopping comically along the highway; I'm not sure the appearance of a 4x4 wouldn't shatter the spell.

We manage the road. The pigs are unimpressed by the discovery of tarmac. But they love the narrow, grassy path that comes next. It's damp here and shady, soaked with smells, littered with the fruit and nuts of past summers. Big Pig trots past me with confidence on the trail of some particular scent. Little Pig buries his head in a tangle of undergrowth. We come to a standstill. The rattle of the acorn bucket has no effect. There are better things here, just now, than last year's dried-out acorns. And we've been walking already for fifteen minutes or more: the pigs seem to want a rest.

I expected the pig walk to be anxious and stressful, a chore, and instead it's turned out to be a thing of great pleasure and romance. I'd like the experience to last. I'd like to remain here on this path with the pigs and Ed, cradled in green shadows, admitted to this non-place, seduced by this non-time. But we have to get to the new enclosure. We have to get the pigs settled and secure. I hurry to catch up with Big Pig; grab hold of a fistful of hairy black hide, enough to slow him. I jink the bucket above his head. He remembers the sound of acorns, thinks about it; looks at me. It's some kind of negotiation. He knows I can't bully him. He knows he could run away, if he wanted, crash through the hedges, turn on me and bite and kick. He knows the bucket's a ploy: a good one, a tasty one, but only a ploy.

Big Pig's deciding something enormous. If he chooses to walk on now and follow my direction then it's because he trusts me; it's simply because he likes me enough to come with me. The alternative is life as a pig, purely – a life without humans – setting off into this wide land and fending for himself, abandoning what he's known for the lure of space and liberty, fields and woodlands without boundaries. He's deciding how much he wants to be part of this 'family'. And how much he wants to break free and run wild.

Can a domesticated animal ever decide such a thing? Is there ever a choice? Big Pig looks at me again; I nudge him with my knee. I step past him, begin to walk, rattle the bucket. Big Pig follows, of course he does, and Little Pig trots on quickly, grunting loudly at the thought of being left behind. And very quickly we're at the end of the path, crossing the road to La Graudie, finding our way on the verge beside the hedge to the open gateway that leads to the scruffy field that leads to the meadow and woods of the new enclosure. In no time at all, we've taken the pigs through the gap under the ash tree and emptied the acorns on to the ground to delay them while we loop the wire of the fence across behind us; we've connected the battery and thrown the switch for the electric current. The little green light flashes: the pigs are in.

The walk is over. But in the time it's taken to make our way with a rattle and a snuffle from one enclosure to another, my relationship with the pigs has changed. I knew they had different characters: in the orchard pen at the Mas de Maury, I could see that they had grown to be unique animals. Big Pig was a bit calmer, I thought; Little Pig more friendly. But this didn't mean much. It was a curiosity. It was setting out on to the tracks and lanes which tested the pigs, gave them the opportunity to be themselves, provoked them, teased them, and confirmed them completely, absolutely, as two distinct animals. Yes, Big Pig is the level-headed one, but he's bold, too, and loyal. Little

Pig's curiosity makes him flighty; his exuberance and joy in life mean he's quicker to act and react, more easily distracted. He seems to care about us less. And now this realization involves me, too, because as I've come to know both of the pigs, I've come to treat them differently. I trust Big Pig; I like him. I appreciate his solidity. I find I think of him as wise. Whereas my relationship with Little Pig is more fidgety, slightly wary: I'm fond of his openness but suspicious of his antics. I think of him as selfish, perhaps even spiteful. I keep a closer eye on him, allow him fewer freedoms.

How fair are these judgements? How sound? I've no way of knowing. Ed has come to similar conclusions, but we could both be mistaken. These are our first pigs. How can we hope to really understand them? Can we ever understand a pig, or are we just indulging in careless anthropomorphism? Maybe it doesn't matter. Except that because I've come to know so much about Big Pig and Little Pig, I've begun to treat each of them as individuals, as characters. I've formed a bond; well, two bonds. And isn't this like an executioner falling for someone on death row? These are pigs for meat: Big Pig and Little Pig, not pets, not companions. We haven't even hinted at any change of plan – neither Ed nor I have so much as raised a doubt. We're thoroughly enjoying the pigs, but when the time comes, as it must, we'll kill them, ourselves, at home. That's the intention, still, unaltered.

But when I go back to my reading, I'm struck again by the brutality and trauma of the slaughter. Take this account by Flora Thompson, for example, like a review of a horror film, with the emphasis on blood and shadow: 'the killing was a noisy bloody business [. . .] the whole scene, with its mud and blood, flaring lights and dark shadows was as savage as anything to be seen.' Or this, from an Essex cottager recalling the terrible noise of a frantic pig: '[I] lifted the pig to the slaughter [. . .] kicking, squealing, anticipating its end, and struggling to get free [. . .] there was a louder scream and blood spurted.' Time and again when I come across historical reports of pig-keeping, I'm confronted by pain, fear, panic, and I wonder how I'll feel when it's me in the midst of all the din and gore. I have no experience of anything like this: I save bees and butterflies that find their way into the house; I rescue injured birds. Am I really the sort of person who will kill a pig: Big Pig or Little Pig? In the accounts I read, the task is often regarded as too violent and stressful for children to watch, even in farming families who might be considered to take a robust attitude to livestock: in Scotland at the end of the nineteenth century, one woman recalled that 'we were sent away from home the day the pigs were killed, we went to Grandma's house because the pigs were – you know, pets [. . .]' Pets. Animals you've grown to know and love, kept for pleasure, companionship.

But the reading makes no difference. The end is still fixed. That's what I tell myself. Big Pig and Little Pig will be killed, by us, quite soon. I can't see an alternative; it's surely not worth thinking about changing our plans. What on earth would we do with two hungry, fully grown, unruly pigs if we don't kill them? The children of nineteenth-century Scottish farmers clearly didn't want their pet pigs to die but their attachment made no difference in the end, because practical necessities demanded the slaughter go ahead. For us it will surely have to be the same: we'll just have to face up to our squeamishness and press on, won't we? And so I watch them nudge each other forward into their new enclosure, brushing through the meadow, heading towards the bank of celandines, a sprightly yellow at the edge of the woods, and in the new promise of spring I think about death, their deaths.

Two pigs to be raised and killed at home. How difficult can it be?

3

I'm resigned to the dissatisfying disappearance of Bisset's pig. That's it, then. A doleful end to a brief career. But I can't help rummaging, reading on, and I quickly find more accounts of a performing pig. They're confused in places, a bit uncertain, but it's a black pig, they're agreed about that, and they date from the summer of 1783, just after Bisset's sorry death. Suddenly the story begins again, refreshed, reconfigured; the same but not quite the same, fattening like a sow in acorns. And there's a new hero. For a long time, I know him only as Mr Nicholson. He has a fine troupe of performing animals. He has a hare that plays the drums and a tortoise that can fetch and carry like a dog, only more slowly. He has six sprightly turkey cocks that toddle through a country dance to much acclaim. Eventually, a chance piece of research throws up his first name – John – and confirms what the newspapers were suggesting: he is now the owner of Samuel Bisset's prize pig.

John Nicholson is a professional, that much is clear, a seasoned impresario, already sixty years old, short, bald, rotund. Perhaps he was in Dublin to see Bisset perform. Perhaps he's been tracking his rival's career through the newspaper reports. Perhaps it was chance that found him in Chester in August 1783 when there was a bereaved black pig for sale, although I wonder how, in that case, he discovered the animal's talent for spelling and telling the time and reading minds. However it happened, Nicholson sees an opportunity and steps in, takes over. He sniffs out a fortune. And the pig finds itself with a new home, a new master, and a resurrected career.

A year passes while Nicholson imposes his own training regime and tweaks the spectacle to his own tastes. The pig, as ever, practises, learns, performs. It's a good pig. Does it miss the old days in Ireland, slouched on the floor of the pub under Bisset's bar? Does it miss

Bisset? There's no way of knowing, of course, and Nicholson has no time for such questions. He's off with his new menagerie. They try the spa town at Scarborough where the wealthy take the waters and bathe. This is a genteel resort, a far cry from the rough-and-tumble of Dublin's theatreland; a long way heading east from Bisset's last stop at Chester. The show goes well; it's a promising start. Nicholson, like Bisset before him, begins to realize just how much people like the pig. The stylish Scarborough citizens want novelty; they have a taste for absurdity and excess, but they like to seem learned, too, and abreast of the very latest progress. The pig panders to their vanity and their curiosity; he cannot fail.

Nicholson takes the troupe inland to York. Avoiding the butchers' shops on The Shambles, they set up with the strolling players and run through the routine: ladies and gentlemen, the unique, the astounding, the marvellous Black Pig. A few nights; a good crowd; a decent profit. And they're on the move again. It's the season of country fairs, when farmers and labourers, parsons and merchants, townsfolk and countryfolk converge in the hope of finding work or love or trade or entertainment, and Nicholson and the pig roam from one fair to the next, working their way south from York through rich green pastures and towns gossiping of Industrial Revolution in the offing.

At Michaelmas 1784, Nicholson and the pig arrive in Nottingham. Their act is beginning to find its way into the popular press; they're attracting attention. And the Nottingham Goose Fair offers a big opportunity to become even better known. Here, they have the chance to reach an audience of all types and professions and classes. There is wrestling, dancing, a marching band; booths, tents and stalls for eating and drinking; gambling, peep shows and puppet shows. There are pigs for show, pigs for sale, greased pigs for sport, and among all those pigs one that stands out: Nicholson's pig, Bisset's pig, our pig. And in the flurry of the fair, it's not just the raucous pleasure seekers who flock to Nicholson's show, to lap up the unusual and the absurd, but the cultural elite whose approval could give the act respectability, even prestige, and who might just secure the black pig a place in the history books. One of those who see the show, for example, is Anna Seward who lives with her family in the Bishop's

Palace at Lichfield where her father is the cathedral canon. Anna is a poet. She's part of a literary circle that includes Sir Walter Scott and Erasmus Darwin, and she corresponds with Josiah Wedgwood and the politician and inventor Richard Lovell Edgeworth. After her visit to the Nottingham fair, she sits down at dinner with Samuel Johnson and regales him with an account of the 'wonderful learned pig' she witnessed in action that afternoon. She is enthusiastic about what she's seen and clearly intrigued by the pig's apparent abilities. And Johnson, eager to hear all about it, is suitably impressed by her story of a black pig displaying such intelligence and style: 'Pigs,' he concludes on hearing her report, 'are a race unjustly calumniated.'

As the pig's achievements come to be discussed in the highest of circles and at the best of tables, it becomes clear that one of the reasons for its success lies in the puzzle of a paradox: here is an animal known for its stubbornness, filth and perversity showing itself to be wonderfully docile and intelligent. One of nature's most obstinate creatures has not only been tamed but is proving cleverer than those who pay to watch it, performing card tricks and reading minds in feats that even seasoned performers would struggle to pull off. Here is a stupid hog that can read letters well enough to spell – at a time when many claim it's the act of reading which separates humans from animals and demonstrates humans' innate superiority. Such achievements raise potentially difficult questions, so that for every pleasure seeker who takes the pig's antics at face value there are many more who believe Nicholson's act challenges the fundamental philosophies of the age. What does such a special pig mean, in an Age of Enlightenment, for our view of animal capabilities? What does it suggest about natural hierarchies and the human place in God's world?

I'm impressed, and rather surprised, by the public's faith in the pig's apparent intelligence and its slick, seductive routine. I don't come across many derogatory accounts of the sapient pig's antics; remarkably few spectators dismiss Nicholson as a cheat or a swindler. There's a little gentle mockery of over-eager audiences from time to time, but mostly this is offset by what appears to be genuine excitement at the pig's achievements. What I do find, however, is that the pig's demonstrable abilities are so unexpected and such an inversion of the accepted order of things, that some spectators are terrified by what they see and hear. They baulk at the unnatural talent on display and suspect black arts and witchcraft. Several commentators call 'for the Pig to be burnt, and the Man banished', since both are clearly in correspondence with the Devil. It's perhaps no coincidence that Scottish folklore often put the Devil in the shape of a pig, referring to him as 'The Big Black Pig' who was in the habit of 'visiting young people who played cards'; superstitious sailors, too, traditionally refused to carry pigs on board because their cloven hooves were too devilish for comfort. Since the middle of the seventeenth century, stories of pig-faced women had surfaced across Europe, telling of beautiful women whose faces were transformed by witchcraft – the spell could only be broken by the love of a man undaunted by the prospect of marrying a bride with the features of a hog, a woman who grunted and ate from a trough. By the 1670s, the folklore had been memorialized in a song, 'The Long-Nos'd Lass', which proved popular with 'lovers of the monstrous'. The lyrics gave all the gory details of the poor bewitched heiress whose 'visage was perfectly just like a sow'.

The connection between the pig and the Devil may have harked back to a verse in one of the New Testament gospels in which devils are heard to plead with Jesus: 'If you are going to cast us out, send us into the herd of swine' (Matthew 8: 31). However the association came about, it was unfortunate but by no means calamitous for Nicholson. If there was a frisson of menace or magic about the act, a hint of the dark and mysterious, then so much the better. It certainly didn't deter the crowds. As the summer fairs drew to a close, Nicholson had cause for celebration: he had never been so wealthy, or so well known. The pig had performed impeccably. People had marvelled and chattered; word had spread. With his eye on the big-gest audience of all, among the theatres and playhouses of London, he decided to take time to polish the act and withdrew his animal performers from the public eye for the winter. The pig was rested and, like any old pig, passed the short days in a cold sty. At one moment, reading his letters and adding up his sums, the pig was almost person. At another, quite simply pig.

★

I wonder which of my pigs would be the performer. Little Pig has a certain star quality: he shows off, flounces and pouts. But Big Pig is the one you might consider training, if you had to. He's the one you'd stake your house on if it came to selecting the right cards to spell out a tricky name from the crowd. He's the one that would listen to you and pick up on those tiny signals you'd spent months together perfecting.

I wonder about Nicholson's act as I watch the pigs explore their new surroundings at La Graudie. They're examining the shelter, flicking their noses against the plastic sheeting: they've never encountered this sort of plastic before, and they're enjoying the new sensation, the new game. They rummage through the straw, as always, rearranging it deftly to their liking. They move around the back of the structure, nudge at the corners, scrutinize the planks, test it all. Then they move away. The field has not been worked for years. It's so scruffy and overgrown that it's difficult to determine the boundaries in places and impossible to be sure of the contours: the land inclines suddenly, throwing you off balance, or pushes up a hidden ridge, perhaps a lost wall or a piece of buried machinery. We hacked through brambles to set up the fence but there are plenty more, thick at the edges and in one corner; there's a rampant hedge of blackthorn, spindle and elder; there are dense patches of weeds. None of this disturbs them. Little Pig ambles off, pulling his way through the brambles, eating, nosing, eating; Big Pig follows and they go on together, slowly, side by side, so close that they bump together at each step. They shove, grumble, explore. My pigs are definitely more 'person' since the move – or I think of them more in that way since our walk together – and I find myself watching them as Nicholson's spectators must have watched his pig: look at that! How skilful! How clever!

If I'm giving them human attributes and human emotions then the pigs' response to the sweep of woodland that shelves away at one side of the field can only be described as pure delight. I can imagine them – see them? – smiling. They certainly gambol. It takes them a while to discover they've got such a place. The trees are dense where they edge the meadow, stuffed with undergrowth; the slope begins sharply. For most of the day they ignore this margin and content themselves with foraging on the flat ground around the shelter. This would entertain them for weeks, I know; it's larger than the enclosure they've just left and must conceal an enormous amount of good stuff. But I can't resist showing them the woods, because I know they'll like them and because their pleasure would give me pleasure. So I go to the edge and call them. And as they come towards me, I take a pace or two down, into the trees.

They stop at the brink. Together. Their experience of the world to date is flat. Here is something disconcerting: land that shelves, abruptly, steeply. Gives way underfoot. They're not at all sure. But crossing the boundary of the electric fence earlier in the day seems to have given them a certain courage, or at least a grasp of the unexpected, and it's only a minute or two before Big Pig plunges, Little Pig quickly following, both of them slipping on the dry precipitous ground, floundering on the stones; both of them knocking into me so hard that I stumble, too, and we helter-skelter through the trees in a bundle of surprise until I grab a trunk to steady myself. The pigs slide on some more before finally finding a way to get their footing on this unpredictable terrain.

And now they're here, they're delighted. Really, truly delighted. It's the scale of the place, I'm sure, that thrills them, the sense of land stretching away and freedom; it's an instinctive fondness for ancient woodland and everything it offers; it's the novelty and the promise – but just as much as any esoteric reaction, it's the acorns. There are some chestnut trees here, some rowan, one or two ash, but mostly it's oak: tall, old oak. Just like the field, these woods have been unused for years, which means each autumn the acorns have fallen and lain unused, composting over time into a thick, rich mulch. The acorns from the last year or two sit on top, dry but intact, spiked with insects: a crunchy, tasty carpet. 'My brothers and I had to collect acorns [. . .] we used to go for miles with a little cart for acorns for the pigs,' recalled one East Anglian shepherd at the beginning of the twentieth century. In the Domesday Book, woods tended to be classified according to their capacity to hold pigs, with oak and beech woods at the top of the list. In the Middle Ages, villagers beat oak trees in the autumn so that the acorns would fall for the pigs: a page from the fourteenth-century manuscript known as The Queen Mary Psalter (in the British Library) shows two energetic men wielding long clubs, and the fruit falling to a herd of brown spiky hogs below, some of them reaching skywards to catch the windfall and some of them quite obviously grinning at such a treat. *Jamón Ibérico de Bellota*, often considered the finest ham in the world, is made from black pigs that roam Spanish oak groves getting fat on acorns. Pigs and acorns: the affinity has been recognized throughout the world for centuries, and hardy breeds, like the *Noir de Bigorre*, were specifically developed to make the most of it, so that animals could be driven into woods in autumn and winter and left to forage. And here are Big Pig and Little Pig, installed in an ancient oak wood. A 'pig in clover'? No, pigs in acorns. So much better.

Spring careers into early summer. On the ridges of high stony land the orchids are in full bloom, speckled pinks, whites and purples; there's a cluster of *trompe l'oeil* bee orchids in the pigs' meadow for a while, until it's trampled. I hear golden orioles fluting in the woods in the mornings when I go to do the early feed; wrens and great tits nest in the walls around the enclosure, flitting backwards and forwards, fidgeting.

For a few intense, blustery days, there's a howling low-level wind, *le Vent d'Autan*, a southerly wind, fickle and ferocious. Up high the skies are still, the clouds hardly moving, but down below trees are buffeted, sometimes cracking, the hay fields swell like stormy seas, tiles and plant pots smash; Mo, the hens and the pigs all head for shelter. Sweeping up from the Mediterranean, trapped between the high land of the Pyrenees and the Massif Central, *le Vent d'Autan* is gusty and warm and said to send you mad. Milk turns sour: when this wind's blowing, my neighbours say, never carry any fertilized hen's eggs or they, too, will turn bad; don't open a wine barrel or bottle or the wine will surely go rancid. Above all, *surtout*, don't kill your pig.

Le Vent d'Autan dries the soil quickly and we finish digging the garden and putting in the young plants. Peas and broad beans, sowed from seed, are already sending up tall tendrils, and waiting to be staked. Now we add tomatoes and courgettes, squash, cucumbers, aubergines, chillies and peppers, chard. There's a special Sunday market at a village not far away, a once-a-year extravaganza of herbs and flowers and plants. We join the other shoppers with their boxes and baskets, making our way to the hidden square, set back from the river and the road, where the stalls are set up higgledy-piggledy, the castle ruins stately above and swifts screeching between the eaves. For this one day, the austere, rather shabby village becomes a place of scent and colour, bustle and anticipation: geraniums and petunias and bougainvillea spilling pinks and reds on to the street; mint and sage and lavender brushing against bags and legs and dogs; rows and rows of tomato plants promising summer salads. It's a place where you hear a lot of English spoken – British expats are not easily separated from their flowery borders – but every French family in the neighbourhood has a vegetable garden, a *potager*, even if it's small, and it's these families who buy with the most determination and energy and knowledge, discussing cabbage varieties at length, comparing prices, selecting plain, robust plants that will ensure good harvests.

In the exuberant, flowery excitement of it all, Ed and I throw ourselves into this market that is so much about good things yet to come – plants that will grow tall, vegetables that will flourish, a rich harvest. We don't quite know what will happen at the end of the summer but we do know we might have to face up to the terrible prospect of leaving Big Pig and Little Pig too soon. Or, worse still, killing them early. If we can't find a way to make ends meet, we'll be forced to go back to the UK, where we can more easily find work. And, of course, we can't take the pigs with us – nor even the meat. This would seem such a sad conclusion to such a joyful experience that we hardly talk about it , but it's in the back of our minds, nonetheless, a bothersome thought with a nasty sting, like a biting fly on a soft pig underbelly.

We're still making calls to hotels, as many calls as we can. In fact, we're beginning to get to know some of the staff quite well. But the income isn't enough to live on – or to pay for pig grain. In Micawber fashion, we keep thinking something might turn up, a happy solution to all our troubles, but we're also well aware that poor Mr Micawber ended up stuck in debtors' prison. Something will have to be done. Sooner or later, we'll have to make a decision: to stay or to leave; to keep faith with the pigs or to give up on them.

This market, though, is a joyful, hopeful occasion. We don't think too much about the future; for this morning, we don't worry about our time with Little Pig and Big Pig being cut short. In the spirit of optimism we buy more than we can comfortably carry. We sit in the sun outside the cafe, surrounded by our food larder in miniature – *One more chilli plant, do you think? Just one more of those lovely orange tomatoes?* – and our minds drift to the glutted days of summer, of ripening fruit and fattening pigs.

The market is well timed. *Le Vent d'Autan* stops as suddenly as it began and in an explosive, choreographed burst of life everything becomes full and vigorous and noisy: the lawn is shin-high, the terraces are pocked with weeds, the hedges fill out. In the pond, the irises flash yellow and frogs blob on the surface of the water, croaking lazily. Crickets sing; the hoopoes arrive with their cartoon strut and infuriating *hoo-hoo-hoo* repetitions. The hens set to laying with gusto. Nature is flourishing.

But Little Pig is sick. At this time of year, when it's fully light by six, the pigs have already been rummaging for hours when we come to do the morning checks: water, food, fence, shelter. Usually they're deep in the woods when we arrive; we go to the top of the slope and call them and are treated to the sight of two hulky puffing animals slipping and sliding their way up the bank. Little Pig is last, always. He's fatter, his legs are shorter, he doesn't like the climb. But today when Ed goes to the enclosure as usual, Little Pig is still tucked down in the straw and Big Pig is loitering a yard or two from the shelter, uneasy. I'm in the garden, picking rhubarb; I've been watching buzzards wheeling on the warm currents above the field opposite, five or six of them, rolling and diving, mewling; out of the corner of my eye I see Mo, galloping along the lane, a flash of white, and just as I go to call him I see Ed following some way behind, his head down. I'm surprised to see them so soon and I go to meet them at the fence: 'It might be fine,' Ed says, breathless, 'by the time we get back there, he'll probably be on his feet. I just want you to come and look and give a second opinion.'

But there's no mistake. Little Pig is lazy; he likes his comforts, but this morning he won't get up for anything, not for food or attention, not even when Big Pig has a trough of grain to himself. There's nothing obviously wrong with him: he's not injured, as far as we can see; there's no wound or bleeding or diarrhoea or vomiting; he's not coughing. But there's a dullness about him – a lethargy – that rings alarm bells, and he seems to be breathing hard. Our considered medical assessment is that he's 'not right'.

We wait. We perch on the wall between the field and Jean-Claude's garden and we watch. There's no real need to worry, surely, and Big Pig, at least, seems happier now we've taken over the vigil. He potters off into the shade of the woods before the day gets hot. But Little Pig doesn't move. Now and again, too frequently, we go back to the shelter: I kneel in the straw and run my hand over his floppy stomach, up his flank, through the long hair on his shoulders and neck; I rub his nose. 'Come on, then. Shall we get up? Come on, h'up.' He grunts quietly in reply, sometimes, but is too still; he hardly lifts his head. The evening before, both pigs had been fine. We'd taken them a tub of leftovers from the kitchen – carrot peelings, a lettuce stalk – and they'd grubbed through it with glee, but now . . . What on earth could have brought on such a change so quickly? Is it a touch of stomach ache from something he's eaten? Something congenital and fatal? *Le Vent d'Autan*?

We think of pig breeds as recognizable and distinct. One breed has to look like this; another breed is like that. Tamworths: long of body and snout, ginger. The American Landrace: the palest of pinks, sleek, nondescript, a 'factory' pig. The Middle White: rotund, snub-nosed, pert-eared. But it wasn't until quite recently that these characteristic features became set in place: in the eighteenth and nineteenth centuries, cottagers and farmers bred their sows with whatever type of boar a neighbour or friend happened to have, and the name – Berkshire, for example – tended to refer more to the locality in which the animals were kept than to any agreed characteristics. Paintings and lithographs show a range of colours, shapes and sizes: 'no two pigs are the same,' marvelled a traveller to Kent in 1793; a few years later a Derbyshire farmer noted that the local animals were 'a complete mixture of colour and types in this county as elsewhere'. Even when we went to see the litters of weaners at the farm where Big Pig and Little Pig were bred, there was the occasional odd one out among the herds of black pigs: one or two with pale spots; one with a white belt; one almost entirely, classically pig-pink.

By the middle of the nineteenth century what mattered most was size. By 1843, pigs at the Royal Show were being divided simply into two types: small and large. And it was the large ones that got all the attention. In a print of 1809 you can see a proud gentleman farmer, in top hat and a tailcoat, dwarfed by a black-and-white monster of a pig, apparently weighing in at 12cwt (609kg); the contest at the Royal Show in Chester in 1858 was won by a boar of 1,148lb (521kg). Huge old pigs, however, were good for nothing other than freakish display. You could not breed with them, nor was the meat decent, and by the end of the century the influence of the gigantic show pig was waning: 'it is painful to see prostrate masses of fat grunting and sweating under a weary life in the heat,' complained a judge at the Derby fair of 1881, 'the time has come to put a check on the unlimited exhibition of animals that plainly cannot be in a fit state for breeding.'

Big Pig and Little Pig will be about a year old when we kill them. According to our graph, they're already around half their finished weight and should reach close to 180kg by the end of the year, which is about as big as any modern meat pig tends to get. Abattoirs don't like dealing with huge carcasses, and after a certain point it's fat, rather than flesh, that's being 'grown'. In the twentieth century, it was this distinction between lard and meat which became the battleground for pig breeders, and which finally led to genetic narrowing as older breeds died out in the face of competition from new hybrids. In an influential series of essays in 1821, published under the title *Cottage Economy*, the farmer and campaigner William Cobbett suggested that 'lean bacon is the most wasteful thing a family can use. In short it is uneatable, except by drunkards, who want something to stimulate their sickly appetite.' He urged his readers to let their pigs run to lard: 'make him *quite fat* by all means. If he can walk two hundred yards at a time, he is not well fatted.' But tastes changed. People began to prefer lean meat, and British breeders raced to catch up with European farmers who had not succumbed to the English obsession with lard: by 1924, Britain was importing 8 million cwt of bacon each year, half of which came from Denmark. The new emphasis was on breeding sleek pigs that matured quickly and had a good proportion of muscle to fat. This ideal drives the market so thoroughly these days that commercial pig farms rely on only one or two breeds, and work continually to raise the percentage of meat in their pigs. The US pig industry, for example, produces well over 20 billion pounds of pork a year. Carcasses are graded and priced from US1 (the best) to US4 (the poorest), depending on the expected amount of four lean cuts – ham, loin, shoulder and arm – each one produces. The system was introduced in the 1930s, but since then breeders have reduced the breeding herd by half to refine the gene pool and increase the amount of lean meat, aiming for a pale, uniform, easily packaged product. They've been so successful, so rapidly that the scale has had to be completely recalibrated twice: in 1968, and again in 1985.

My pigs will put on a good solid layer of fat. The meat will be properly red, dark, almost as dark as a young beef. French butchery cuts vary from traditional British ones – some of the tastiest, such as *levure* and *araignée*, don't make their way into British shops at all – but it's easy enough to see that Big Pig and Little Pig will give us a range of tasty options, whichever national practice we follow: already it's clear that Little Pig has a floppy, fatty belly; Big Pig has muscly, dense shoulders. Old breeds, now rare breeds, are like this – each animal is likely to have a particular strength. It's one of the reasons we value them. But there are others, too: often old breeds are healthier, because they've not been subjected to such intensive breeding and selection programmes. Outdoor, free-range pigs are also healthier, on the whole: in packed barns animals easily transmit coughs and diarrhoea, they bite and scratch each other in fights, or chew off each other's tails, because they're bored. But Little Pig is proving the rule by exception. I'd like to think a few hours in the sunshine and a bit of coaxing will get him well again; I'd like to believe that this stout, hardy pig will be strong enough to recover naturally from whatever it is that's ailing him. But as the day goes on, such an outcome seems less and less likely. We're going to have to do something. We're going to have to intervene.

For pigs raised in intensive conditions, antibiotics are routinely mixed with food and drinking water so that whole herds can be treated. This blanket approach notoriously increases the risk of resistant infections: experts estimate that twice as many drugs are prescribed to healthy animals than to sick humans. It was only in 2006 that the EU outlawed the use of antibiotics simply as a means of enhancing growth; in the USA, South America and Asia, pigs are still treated with antimicrobial drugs to help them fatten more quickly, and worldwide over 63,000 tonnes of antibiotics are annually fed to cows, chickens and pigs. Treating one pig, one sick pig, is unlikely to add anything to these kinds of figures, but still we're wary. What if we're overreacting? What if unnecessary treatment taints the meat? What on earth might pig medicine cost?

Transporting Little Pig to a vet is beyond our logistical capabilities. Our small, old domestic car is already thoroughly trashed from carrying sacks of grain which, without fail, spill over the back seats and into footwells, from ferrying dirty tools and buckets and from driving in pig-poo wellies. Nonetheless, trying to find a way to squeeze an adult pig into the boot is a step too far. So we look up a few useful words of French and head off to the surgery in town with nothing more than a faltering description of what might be wrong: what's the French for 'he's just not right'?

We know the vet from taking Mo along on occasion. He's patient and thorough and familiar with many of the local farms. He listens to our garbled and amateur explanation of Little Pig's state and then, predictably, proposes antibiotics. 'Two doses,' he says. 'One now and one in twenty-four hours. You'll have to inject them.' It's not as expensive as we'd feared, and he takes us calmly through the procedure, explaining how and where to inject. This is an intramuscular injection: we don't have to find a vein or be too exact. It doesn't sound difficult.

But what seemed simple in the vet's clean blue room becomes immediately fraught and problematic outside, in a ragged dusty shelter, in the face of a burly, squirmy lump of pig. Put it just behind the base of the ear, the vet said, where the flesh starts to thicken; keep the needle at an angle of 45° and let the liquid come through steadily, without rushing. *Facile*, easy. Except Little Pig knows something's up; he knows that it's unusual for the two of us to be crawling through the straw alongside him; he's distrustful, curious. He flops on to his side, away from us. Under the low roof of the shelter, it's awkward stretching across his prone body to reach the correct spot above his shoulder for the injection, and as Ed pulls back the black hair to try to reveal bare skin in the right place, Little Pig pulls away. We start again. There's a moment when Little Pig is still, just after Ed clears the patch of skin, and I need to be ready, rapid and sure with the needle. Here we go: reach across, bare skin . . . But the needle is long and quite fragile; Little Pig's hide is tough. I'm anxious to inject at the angle the vet advised, but I'm aware that I also have to be quick; I hesitate, then hurry. I've only managed to get the very tip of the needle in place, not enough, and Little Pig is on the move again, turning, floundering. The needle breaks.

It could be some kind of parlour game, like pinning the tail on the donkey. It could be fun, laughable. Uproarious, even. But it just feels distressing. I rock back on my haunches. We have to start again.

Other people must also struggle to inject their animals, because the needles come in packs of two. We fit up the injection carefully again and creep back through the straw. Ed does the thing with the hair; the needle goes in. Not quite a perfect 45° perhaps, but no one has a protractor to check. I press the plunger. Ed rubs Little Pig's ear. In just a few seconds, the dose is delivered. Little Pig shuffles, but gives no indication of having noticed that a medical procedure has been carried out. You see, just like the vet said: easy.

Now we have to wait. The vet didn't have much idea of what might be wrong. It could be many things: it could be a lung infection, intestinal torsion, heart disease. Any of these could be fatal. Or it could be a virus, a cold. Nothing to worry about. The antibiotics might do some good; they might not.

We plunge into morbid Internet pages: pigs dying, everywhere, from all manner of unaccountable maladies and horrible twists of fate. Farm pigs choking, pet pigs constipated to death, free-range pigs slipping away from calcium deficiency. Who'd have thought there were so many ways for a pig to die? We stop googling. We have to accept there's nothing we can actually *do*. We have to just wait while Little Pig rests, and the antibiotics take effect. We'll go back later and just see what's happened.

While we wait we dig and then repot some late tomato seedlings. The rabbits have attacked the first lot of plants we dug in so carefully. During the day, they sit on the lawn, cute and fluffy, grazing quietly among the chickens; as soon as dusk falls, they scamper over to discover what tasty treats have been grown for them in the vegetable patch and they lay waste to our efforts. So we're in need of reinforcements, and by the middle of the afternoon there's a satisfying row of little pots on the table-tennis table: round and square; green, white, purple, blue, yellow – a complicated, unreliable system of colour coding that we'll have forgotten by the time we come to plant out. While we work, we talk, of course, about Little Pig. We reminisce: remember when he . . .? Remember how he . . .? I realize how sad I'd be if he died.

But when winter comes round again, I'm going to kill him. Aren't I?

I wonder about what constitutes a good death. One way or another, Little Pig is going to die. So should it be on my terms, when and how I want it, so that he can contribute, as intended, to the family economy? Does this kind of death have a purpose, an animal-killed-for-meat purpose, which therefore implies it is a good end to things, or at the very least, orderly? Or does Little Pig have a right to a different fate, unplanned? Once again, a pig and a paradox. A conundrum. Would I rather my pig passed away in his straw bed that evening, naturally – or would I prefer him grazing through a few more months, so that I can then dispatch him with a large knife?

There's a moment in Thomas Hardy's *Jude the Obscure* (in chapter 10) when Jude and his wife, Arabella, are forced to kill their pig – the usual slaughterman has been held up by a sudden snowfall. It doesn't start well:

> Jude, rope in hand, got into the sty, and noosed the affrighted animal, who, beginning with a squeak of surprise, rose to repeated cries of rage [. . .] while Jude held him Arabella bound him down, looping the cord over his legs to keep him from struggling. The animal's note changed its quality. It was not now rage, but the cry of despair; long-drawn, slow and hopeless.

Jude loses courage, unwilling to kill 'a creature I have fed with my own hands', but Arabella is made of sterner country genes and, more-over, has clear ideas about how the process should be accomplished:

> The meat must be well bled, and to do that he must die slow. We shall lose a shilling a score if the meat is red and bloody! Just touch a vein, that's all. I was brought up to it, and I know. Every good butcher keeps un bleeding long. He ought to be eight or ten minutes dying, at least.

Thankfully, for the reader as well as the pig, Jude ignores his wife's instructions and the killing is 'mercifully done'. Nonetheless, Hardy makes much of the continuing drama. First there is the death itself, in which human emotions such as blame, betrayal and friendship are assigned to the poor pig:

> The dying animal's cry assumed its third and final tone, the shriek of agony; his glazing eyes riveting themselves on Arabella with elo-quently keen reproach of a creature recognizing at last the treachery of those who had seemed his only friends.

Finally, after much mess and confusion – 'forming a dismal, sordid, ugly spectacle' – we become aware of the impact of the event on Jude: the pig-killing provokes much soul-searching and self-doubt. Perhaps more significantly, the whole experience, Hardy suggests, is not just a matter of private discomfort but an act with more

far-reaching implications about what it is to be human and about the
nature of our relationship with the natural world:

> Jude felt dissatisfied with himself as a man at what he had done [. . .]
> The white snow, stained with the blood of his fellow-mortal, wore
> an illogical look to him as a lover of justice, not to say a Christian; but
> he could not see how the matter was to be mended. No doubt he was,
> as his wife had called him, a tender-hearted fool.

I think about Little Pig lying in the straw and Jude's distress at dis-
patching an animal he's fed with his own hands. I wonder how much
stronger such an attachment would be if it arises not only from feeding a pig, but from nursing it through sickness, how much more
'illogical' the justice of slaughter might seem. Am I, like Jude, a
tender-hearted fool? If we coax Little Pig back to health, will I really
be able to kill him afterwards? I don't have an answer to such questions, and the asking of them disturbs me.

Spring 1785. Nicholson has brought his menagerie out of winter
retirement to London but his pig, like ours, is causing concern. It's
thin; too thin for a pig. Eighteenth-century pigs are rotund and lardy
but Nicholson's sagacious black pig is skinny like an old dog. In the
reports I unearth of the new season's entertainment, it becomes clear
that some of those watching are concerned about its well-being:
'what with the weather, and the concourse of visitors, the poor animal is so *roasted* that its skin is almost *crackling*,' writes one sympathetic
observer. This is the age of the cottage pig; more and more people
have one or two pigs of their own, in the garden, on the street, in a
sty or in the house. My house was built around this time and follows
a pattern for many of the local cottage-farms: living accommodation
on the first floor and, beneath it, a small dark room – a den rather
than a room, really – where the pigs and cattle were kept, warming
the residents above. There's still a stone manger built into the wall.

More people keeping pigs means more people knowing what a
healthy animal should look like; more people growing fond of their
family pig means more people complaining about unhappy practices.
Nicholson is known to be a disciplinarian, coaching his performing

troupe with fervour. Some of those watching begin to suspect he's being unkind to his pig: 'great torture must have been employed ere the indocility of the animal could have been subdued,' complains Henry White, a young clergyman.

When the whispers of ill-treatment reach Nicholson, he defends his methods, and his slim pig, but without giving away his secrets: 'a plenitude in the belly,' he explains to *London Unmask'd*, a popular journal, 'would diminish his pupil's adherence to discipline.' A fat pig cannot be a wise pig, he suggests; a well-fed pig will have little incentive to learn. All those engaged with training a pig know that what works is patience and companionship, not brutality: 'You are not to beat him into the knowledge of your design, but coax him to it, if possible.' The pig will want to please, and will try to understand you. He'll make an effort. If you begin with a secret language of 'snuffling', talking to the pig through your nose, in time you won't even need that: 'the animal is so sagacious that he will appear to read your thoughts.'

There's a lesson to be learned here about the best way to go about things, and the right way to treat an animal, and in an age of moral certainty, publishers pick up on Nicholson and his black pig as a good model for children. Alongside the robins Pecksy, Flapsy, Robin and Dick in Sarah Trimmer's popular book *Fabulous Histories Designed for the Instruction of Children, Respecting Their Treatment of Animals* (1786), for example, appears a learned pig very much like Nicholson's:

The creature was shewn for a sight in a room provided for the purpose, where a number of people assembled to view his performances. Two alphabets of large letters on card paper were placed on the floor; one of the company was then desired to propose a word which he wished the Pig to spell. This his keeper repeated to him, and the Pig picked out every letter successively with his snout, and collected them together till the word was compleated. He was then desired to tell the hour of the day, and one of the company held a watch to him, which he seemed with his cunning little eyes to examine very attentively; and having done so, picked out figures for the hours and minutes of the day [. . .] And do you think, mama, said Harriet, that the Pig knows the letters, and can really spell words?

A few years later, *A Present for a Little Boy*, which features remarkable animals of all kinds, was to urge its young readers to consider their own conduct in comparison with such a well-behaved pig: 'some pigs have evinced so teachable a disposition, that children might take a useful lesson from their conduct,' the author suggested. The anti-cruelty message is clear and personal: 'for little boys have obstinate tempers, some have been beaten, others have had their hair pulled, or ears pinched, to make them mind their spelling: how difficult then must it be to teach a pig to converse with men?'

Mr Nicholson is fat; his pig is thin. Neither fact seems to deter spectators. Nicholson installs himself and his menagerie in suitable lodgings at 55 Charing Cross, a stone's throw from the Admiralty building. He puts together an ambitious programme, and works his troupe hard, advertising four shows a day, seven days a week. They all sell out. And it's not the singing ducks or dancing dogs or per-forming rabbits which sell tickets – all of these have been seen before, so many times – it's the one and only, not to be missed, never to be forgotten Learned Pig.

Despite the stir they've caused in country fairs, it appears that Nicholson is rather taken by surprise when the metropolitan crowd warms so quickly and so fervently to his pig. According to the enter-tainment schedules for the summer, it seems as though the plan had been to run the show for a few weeks in London and then move on to Oxford and Bath. But clearly Nicholson can't bring himself to turn his back on such enthusiastic and affluent audiences. He makes the decision to remain in the capital, and instead of taking his learned pig to the learned streets of Oxford, he goes off in search of larger, more fashionable premises.

Poor Samuel Bisset. Lucky Mr Nicholson. The black pig appar-ently cannot fail. It makes people marvel. It makes them laugh. It makes a fortune. At a time when science (and pseudo-science) is cap-turing the popular imagination, a performing pig fits nicely into an atmosphere of experimentation and theory, mystery and invention. It's a genuine curiosity, a scientific feat of training, if you will, which raises intriguing questions about the nature of beasts and about civil-ized society. It prompts discussion and disrupts convention: here, after all, is a creature of the working classes performing to everyone, regardless of income or rank, most certainly including the wealthy and the influential among its greatest admirers. With a quiet nod to revolution, here's the mundane hog of impecunious families laying on a show for the gentry. Like the best of performers, the Learned Pig captures something of the spirit of the times; the act is modern and risky and tucked below the glamour there's something just a little dangerous. John Nicholson and his pig probably don't know any of this, or pause to consider the wider implications of a black pig that can spell, but they ride their wave of luck and good-timing with flair, and through the baking summer of 1785 they line their purses with gold.

It's not a surprise that Nicholson's pig struggled with the heat during packed performances at Charing Cross, 'its skin [. . .] almost crackling'. Pigs don't have sweat glands and don't pant like dogs, so they can languish in warm conditions. When the opportunity arises, they love nothing better than to wallow in thick, wet mud. This is not just sloth. Mud acts as an efficient coolant, and when it dries on their skin and in their bristles, it provides a valuable protective layer against the sun.

In central London, the chances of Nicholson's pig finding a refreshing wallow were slight, but our field is set up with just such a thing in mind. There's a natural dip in the land close to a hedge, about the size of a family bath, shaded, hemmed in by exposed tree roots. The hose snakes to it, over the wall and through the brambles from Jean-Claude's tap, and the soil there is naturally heavy with clay. We've tried soaking the depression with water: it quickly becomes squelchy and remains damp for hours. When the weather turns hot, the pigs can loll here in the shadow of the oaks; as they wear away the grass and weeds it will rapidly become a doughy mud-tub.

At the end of the afternoon, when we walk round to the enclosure to check on Little Pig, it's not hot. But the day has been warm and close, and the sun has come through now with sudden brutality, wilting the daisies against the barn wall. Since we left Little Pig so mopey and sick, we're naturally concerned about what we might find, and we approach the field quietly, in the hope of seeing the state of the pigs before they know we're there. We swish through the lengthening meadow grass as we cut across from the lane and creep under the ash; from here we can peer round and see the mouth of the shelter and most of the field.

Little Pig has gone. There's a large dent in the straw and more straw scattered on the ground all around the shelter, but there's no pig. The field, too, appears empty. Is he well enough already to tackle the slope into the woods?

We straddle the fence, inelegantly. Ed goes quickly to the woodland boundary and crouches, peering into the trees, trying to catch sight of a black pig in black shadows. At the same time, I take a few steps along the perimeter, down the shallow slope behind the shelter, in front of the nettle bed. I see Little Pig a few yards away; his snout, the top of his ears, his thick round buttocks, all poke up above the grass and dock and clover, the rest of him is out of sight in the wallow. I call Ed. Little Pig doesn't move. Ed and I approach together. The pig's ears twitch. He snorts quietly, nothing more than a strangled breath. But still he doesn't move. Then, just as we reach him, he realizes we're there. Slouched deep in the cradle of damp, cool soil he hasn't heard us approach and now he starts violently, squeals, yanks himself from the wallow and scatters towards the nettle bed.

A startled pig, not a sick pig.

The commotion has brought Big Pig from the edge of the woods where he must have been foraging not far away. He's pleased to see us and trots over happily. Little Pig, reassured that we're not murderous intruders, nods and puffs and barges me in the leg. We watch them for a while, astounded. Can Little Pig really be this well, already? It's been little more than half a day since we found him slumped in the straw, panting and miserable. Now, there seems to be nothing wrong with him. When we put food down, he tucks in with gusto, nipping Big Pig on the shoulder with his teeth when he feels he's missing out. He's moving fluidly; his eyes are bright and clear; his breathing seems to have gone back to normal. He's noisy and active. And as soon as he's full up with grain and tired of our company, he takes himself back to the wallow. Perhaps he just needed some spa treatment.

All of this is excellent news, of course, and we're delighted. We walk home in the dusk with the nightingales casting circles of song along the lane, basking in the satisfaction of having averted disaster. But the following morning, we realize that we have to administer the follow-up injection to a healthy, spirited, capricious Little Pig. If injecting a poorly pig is difficult, how much more testing is it going to be now? We consider scrapping the dose, but we don't want to do irresponsible things with antibiotics, and we're concerned that without the full treatment there may be some kind of relapse. So we head off to the enclosure with the bottle and the needle; the last needle.

It's Ed's turn to be vet. We lure the pigs to the trough with a sludge of peelings and Ed hovers, poised, waiting for a rare moment of stillness. He makes a jab; misses. Little Pig has his snout in the food; the recommended injection site, between the base of the ear and the shoulder, is at the action end of things as he rummages and snuffles. He flips aside carrot peelings in favour of apple cores with a quick, strong movement which forces us backwards; Big Pig, an added complication, thrusts his head under Little Pig's and they jostle for a while, their necks entwined. It takes them a long while to settle the dispute. Eventually, Big Pig moves to the other side of the trough and there's a lull in the bickering. But now the food is nearly gone, and when it's finished the pigs will be gone, too, off into the

woods where we'll have no chance of keeping up with them, let
alone catching them.

I put a hand to Little Pig's head, slide it down the neck. Here . . .
the hair is parted. Ed is quick. The needle goes in. In the second
or two before Little Pig shrugs us off and prods his foot into the
trough to upend it, scattering the last scraps so that the pigs scatter in
response, the dose is delivered. Well, most of the dose. The rest drib-
bles into his bristles; the final drops drip from the end of the needle
into the grass below. The pigs loiter briefly and then set off for the
woods, one behind the other, their haunches sashaying, their tails
twirling like the ends of skipping ropes.

And so it's June; summer. Full-blown, balmy-night, heat-like-fist-
fights summer. The cockerel is crowing the advance of dawn in the
early hours, the frogs are languid, the gloss of spring is tarnished. In
the fields all around the house, the hay is being cut and turned.
Ancient red tractors growl up and down clearing wakes, swallows
ducking and diving above them to catch the flies. The air is thick
with dust, seeds, pollen, the light only dribbling through. The hens
scrabble delightedly in the piles of drying grass. We sneeze. Both pigs
are rumbustiously healthy.

When I see Big Pig rummaging through the summer hedges or
Little Pig lazily nosing grubs from the dry stones of the wall, it gives
me pleasure. They are living well. But sometimes I'm troubled, too,
because I know that very few pigs have the kind of genuine free-
range existence that ours do; very few are able to indulge their
insatiable instinct to labour and forage and explore. Some are kept
outdoors, with a roomy pen, natural light and freedom to wallow
and graze. Many, many more are confined inside sheds and barns,
their noses ringed to prevent digging, their movements restrained;
others spend at least part of their time packed into crates. Most pigs
raised for meat endure short lives in a restricted, unnatural environment. If we buy cheap, mass-produced pork, this is the system we're
buying into. We know that. But the more I get to see of Big Pig and
Little Pig, the more this thought of wholesale intensive farming dis-
quiets me. And there's something else, too. Because I begin to realize

that at the other end of the scale, when we give our pigs the 'deluxe' version of life, with oak woods and meadows, entirely natural habitats and rhythms, it perhaps becomes more, rather than less, difficult to justify their deaths. There can be no argument, after all, that we'll be putting them out of any kind of misery, only that we'll be denying them further months and years of contentment. Surely if we care this much for our pigs, we won't kill them?

We've struck some kind of implicit deal with Big Pig and Little Pig: we allow them to range and eat as they like and in return they do the work converting all that exercise and nutrition into excellent pork. Their lives are given over to a purpose. This, for us, is an acceptable transaction but, of course, it's a one-sided agreement. The pigs have no say in it. And while on a day-to-day basis this smallholding bliss is infinitely better for them than a battery existence in a huge commercial farm, the outcome is ultimately exactly the same. It's a riddle which taxes me. I'm determined to give my pigs good lives, the best I can. I'm committed to raising them responsibly, with their welfare constantly in mind. But the agricultural animal is a unique and curious beast, neither companion nor wild animal, an in-between creature which, in the end, is reduced to its role as a food source. The smallholder's animal, or the cottage pig, inhabits an even more ambiguous place, close to the family that's raising it but destined to be stewed in their pots. I'm not quite sure what it will take to extricate myself from this ambiguity. I'm not sure that I'll be able to see Big Pig and Little Pig clearly, when the time comes, as nothing more than meat.

The pigs, happily unaware of any life-and-death debate, throw themselves into summer with enthusiasm. As a result of their constant industry, their meadow is already more shorn than any of those being harvested by the farmers – the grass and weeds are trampled or eaten; soil is bare by the shelter and along the line of the fence, trodden and hard, turning dusty; the nettle bed has been conscientiously devoured – and in the woods they've begun to construct an impressive system of terracing as they work sideways along the slope, digging out things they want to eat and nipping off all the fresh greens. This is their place now, every stone and log explored, every

fallen tree hollowed, every damp nook gouged. Sometimes we follow
the electric wire as it winds through the woods to check it's not been
obstructed or broken, sliding down the hill from tree to tree to the
flat land at the bottom where there's younger, lighter growth and
glimpses of the meadows that skirt the village, the church steeple visible beyond. It's clear, then, how much work the pigs have done and
how thoroughly they've inhabited the whole plot. What had once
been marked only by our arbitrary fence-building is now different
entirely from the woods on either side: balder, airier, neater.
Traditionally, pigs have been used to manage woodland, to clear and
regenerate it so that new growth can force its way through; here
they've already made an enormous impact. Even though there are
only two pigs in such a large stretch of woods their constant excava-
tions have thoroughly tilled the soil to a depth of several centimetres,
much more in places, and they've sorted weak from strong growth,
opening up glades and unclogging the bases of the stately old trees.

They've done a good job of the field, too. The nettle patch has
gone; the stone wall behind is visible for the first time. Little Pig, in
particular, has a taste for bramble flowers – preferring the pink ones
to the white – and they both love blackthorn berries (sloes) so the
hedges have been well trimmed back. They've dug away around
fallen stones, revealing buried bits of this and that: a broken spade, a
bottle of thick green glass, some kind of small iron farm contraption
that looks disturbingly like a scold's bridle. When they hear us coming now, they hurtle across the enclosure or up from the woods,
unconstrained by thickets or weeds.

And they plunge at us in expectation of something more interesting than grain. At home, the garden is nothing like as clear and tidy
as the pig enclosure: it's knee-high with docks and gripped by bindweed; brambles claw at us from all sides and torn netting trails from
the blackcurrants. But this is a climate where even untidy gardeners
can thrive, and we stumble up to the house every morning and evening with armfuls, bucketfuls, barrowfuls of produce. When we've
sorted and stored, pickled and frozen, Little Pig and Big Pig get their
turn, have their fill. But despite a pig's reputation for guzzling anything in sight, they can be surprisingly picky. Empty pea pods they

love; broad bean pods they hate. Tomatoes, melons, fruit of all kinds and pumpkins they squabble over with spite. Lettuce stumps they'll tolerate, if there's nothing much else; cabbage leaves they tend to pick at, disgruntled at being forced to tackle such fare; cucumbers they can take or leave. And they won't touch courgettes. This is something of a disaster because, of course, we have far, far too many courgettes. We try cutting them up to reveal the seeds, dicing them, peeling them, hiding them at the bottom of the trough. But nothing works. At the end of every feeding time, the courgettes remain untouched, neatly shunted to the side of the trough so that they're not in the way of proper food. But we're desperate to get rid of some of the glut, so we resort to boiling them down in big vats until they're a pale green sticky mush and we mix this with the grain. We dole the slop out like Dickensian schoolteachers, and the pigs tuck in. Suddenly it's a favourite. Stewed courgettes – mmm, that's different altogether; that's sweet and tasty. And so we have a reliable outlet for the mountain of courgettes, which is a good thing, but now, in addition to all the other chores we do for the pigs, we have to cook for them.

It's hot now, really hot, a dry, inland heat that seeps silently up from the Mediterranean and hangs here, still and stately. Within days the verges are brown and hard. The hens stop laying and hide away instead, flopped under the conifers at the end of the garden; Mo staggers from sun to shade, sun to shade. In the house we siesta on the tiled floors, until they, too, get warm. As the enclosure field dries out and the vegetation becomes scant, and even supplies in the hedges and woods die back, the daily delivery of choice, organic garden produce seems to keep the pigs content. But food is not really the problem: it's lack of water that could quickly cause harm. The local farmers trundle back and forth with metal water vats attached to the back of tractors. There's a queue at the *fontaine* in the village. Water collected from roofs and drainpipes through the spring is channelled into barns and stables. We go to the enclosure three or four times a day to fill the drinking trough, and especially the wallow.

The pigs have worn the wallow wider, longer, deeper. It now fits two pigs perfectly. The clay ground has been pressed smooth and hard, and so water gathers, creating a claggy layer on top, thick and cool. The tree roots at the side act as a kind of backrest. It's all very comfortable. They spend a lot of time here, remarkably harmoniously, and as a result they've become brown pigs, a thick coffee colour on the rump and stomach, snout and ears, a more dappled black-and-tan above. When you pat them, or when they barge into you, a gritty dust puffs out of their bristles. In the heat they're moulting, too, shedding the excesses of black hair, and so they seem sleeker all of a sudden. Brown and sleek: summer pigs.

A couple of times a day, we hose them down. We stand just inside the fence, turn the water pressure high, fit our thumb over the end of the pipe and spew a shower into the air a foot or so above the pigs so that it patters down steadily all over them, heads and backs, turning the dust on their skin to mud, washing them clean for a while, black. Then, for fun, we make the water come with a rush and spurt it harder, directing it against a buttock or a shoulder, pummelling

their toned limbs like a massage, soaking us as well as the pigs. The water is sparkly in the midday light, cool; it's a fine sport. Everybody loves it: me and Ed, Mo, but especially Little Pig. He stands in the hosepipe shower and laughs with glee. I swear, he laughs with glee. He opens his mouth to catch the water; he shimmies in the flow; he ducks and splashes like a child in a fountain. Long after Big Pig has had a dousing and sauntered off to rummage in the woods, Little Pig is still demanding a soaking. When our visits to the enclosure are delayed, or simply when he feels the heat's getting a bit much, he makes his discontent heard with a low, persistent squawk . *Too dry, too hot; do something.* And often Jean-Claude, who can't fail to hear the full range of pig complaints from his side of the wall, kindly steps in and wields the hose. He doesn't want to approve of it, this indulgence, but he can't resist; no one can.

I understand Little Pig's delight. When the heat crushes us we swim in the river, seeking out the cold pools and currents. Kingfishers slide across us, and damsel flies, equally blue, flick past our arms as we stroke the deep black water. We'll get hot again quickly, almost as soon as we've climbed up the bank, but for a while it's soft and chill, and there's always (always) the momentary tingling bliss of cool water on burning skin as we plunge in. So we treat the pigs to a similar pleasure. When it's too hot and heavy to walk or cycle to the enclosure, and when Mo won't leave the dampish shade of the pen under the house, we fire up our rackety old moped and putter around on the lanes, seated close together, sweaty. The heat hangs silent and the pigs hear us coming, almost before we've left home, and are desperate to be hosed: by the time we pull across the bumpy ground at the edge of the field they're yelping in anticipation. Water in the sun, cool in the heat: holidays.

Nights can be airless and sweaty, breathless, but we and the pigs all bask in the pleasure of the long, balmy evenings. Towards dusk they're always to be found in the woods, among the hot-earth smells, bustling and purposeful, and we dig and prune and harvest long after the night crickets begin their burr. One evening we go into town, where the municipality has organized a *marché des producteurs*, a kind of tasting market, where the stallholders sell plates of food to be eaten at long communal tables set up in the square. Each seller has to raise or make what they sell so everything is local and familiar, but there's enough variety to put together a whole range of impromptu menus: goat's cheese salad, *charcuterie*, or snails, perhaps, to begin; a choice of duck, *veau*, sausage or tripe to follow, cooked under the plane trees on a variety of barbecues and planchas, eaten inevitably with *aligot* – a creamy, cheesy mashed potato – unless the queue's too long at the stall; finish with fruit or cake or ice cream; don't forget the bread and the wine.

We walk through the centre of the town, following the neat grid of medieval streets. This is a *bastide*, a close-knit fortified mesh of straight lanes and passages, too narrow in places for cars to pass. It's a difficult townscape, unsuited to modern living and constantly struggling to attract people to make a home here. Most of the big old merchants' houses have been divided into basic apartments, dark and draughty, let cheaply to families arriving from all over the world – Portugal, North Africa, Ethiopia, Vietnam, Cambodia – who find themselves enclosed tightly in the shadowy streets, battling the testing architecture of a previous age. In winter, the cold lingers in the narrow alleys, unshiftable, but after a scorching day the stones breathe heat on either side of us and we hurry through to the market in a square at the far side, where the buildings give way to the river, running slow and weedy, sliding up occasional currents of welcome cooler, damper air. It feels refreshing, at least for a moment, and we find a place to sit at one end of a wooden trestle table that stretches from the Resistance memorial to the bandstand, a length of perhaps thirty metres. For most of the time, this is a dusty, workaday square, where cars park and *boules* is played in the shade of the plane trees, but tonight there's something soft and romantic, uniquely old-fashioned French, about the place: the stalls around the perimeter glint with colour, the smoke from the fires and barbecues drifts slowly towards the river, families and couples wander hand in hand. There are good smells everywhere.

Ed and I collect our bottle of water and paper place mats from the little wagon run by the town council; we buy a bottle of pink wine and pour some into plastic glasses. Our first course, the *apéritif*, is going to be a *farçou*, a kind of griddled stuffing cake made mostly from breadcrumbs and vegetables, a traditional local filler that acts much like Yorkshire pudding in satiating appetite so that the meat coming later goes further. There's a queue at the stall, with people clustering around the big planchas, so we wait. The band has been unpacking instruments and plugging in wires, but now it strikes up and is on the move. There's an accordion, a trumpet, a tambourine and a singer, and they work their way from table to table playing rousing favourites to get the gathering diners in the party mood. An Occitan classic first, which we clap to; then 'Roll Out The Barrel' in its French incarnation and then '*Y Viva España*', several times. The singer holds the microphone above our table, we sing a bit, the trumpet riffs, and off they go. On the dance floor in the middle of the square, by the bandstand, there are already plenty of couples twirling and swaying, sincere in their dancing.

There are forty or fifty tables, each in turn seating forty or fifty, but there are not enough places; forlorn families squeeze through the makeshift alleys in search of somewhere to sit. We take turns to join the queues for food so that we don't lose our chairs. The band finishes its circuit and settles into the bandstand; the dancers waltz; the evening drifts on. After our *farçou* we have *truffade*, a mountain dish of cheese and potatoes, some duck pâté, a slither of Roquefort, strawberries. It all takes a long time and when we've finished eating it's dark and the heat of the day is finally fading. We give up our seats – only two, not a great prize – and wander with the crowds circulating the stalls. Benoît is here, the farmer from whom we bought our weaners. He has a *cochon*, a young pig, on a spit and is serving paper plates of juicy black-pig pork, each garnished with a nub of meaty sausage. He's sweating with the heat from the fire, and under pressure from the queue waiting for him to carve, but he takes time to wave and greet us.

'How are the pigs?'

'They're fine; they're lovely pigs.'

He gestures at a hunk of meat with the prong of his long fork. 'When they're like this: that's when you know they're worth it.'

On the way home we call at the enclosure, stopping the car some distance away so as not to disturb Jean-Claude and Camille. The sky is high and densely spangled. Noise drifts on the warm air: church bells, owls of several kinds, the creak of a door, a dog barking. We can hear a mouse in the hedge, gnawing. The pigs, though, are quiet. And when we step over the fence we realize that they're not in their shelter. We find them a yard or two into the woods, lying nose to tail along the length of one of their dug terraces, in the relative cool that sinks beneath the trees. They stir a little, but without enthusiasm. We'd all like to sleep outdoors on nights like this.

Our pigs, like Nicholson's, are a summer sensation. Our British visitors find them irresistible. We wander from our house to the enclosure with various combinations of friends and family who cluster by the fence while the pigs perform for them, nuzzling hands, chuntering greetings, showing off. Everyone loves it: they want to tickle Little Pig on the belly, hose them both, feed Big Pig a slice of melon and watch him snaffle the seeds. I'm not sure anyone believes we're really going to kill them.

The pigs, in turn, love the visitors, but they're unpredictable entertainers. They're strong and agile from their forays into the woods, heavy beasts weighing almost 100kg each now; confident, feisty. Little Pig has taken to nipping ankles and fingers and bums, partly for fun and partly to get his way, biting us just as he bites Big Pig when they tussle. He takes no notice if you shout at him and so we've learned to be wary, looking out for a strike on the blind side when we fill the trough or clamber over the fence. But visitors are easier game. Ed's mother insists on coming into the enclosure and both the pigs trot up to her, like dogs might, but then Big Pig crushes against her, she stumbles and steps away into Little Pig's path; Little Pig walks on, over her foot, and as she yelps and tries to pull back, he nips her thigh. The bruises swell and blacken. She hobbles in pain. For the remainder of the holiday she stays behind the fence.

As we exhibit our pigs to our friends and share our pride at such fine entertainment, I enjoy reading more about the success of Nicholson's pig. Since everyone seems immediately beguiled by Big

Pig and Little Pig, I see how their eighteenth-century counterpart might have risen to such fame and popularity. No one, it seems, can resist a nice pig. And Nicholson's tale continues to flounce and preen like a Georgian dandy. Buoyed by the swell of popular adulation, he's found his pig a place in the circus performing at Sadler's Wells Theatre. He's top of the bill; the star. London's pleasure-seeking elite are willing to queue for four hours in the stinking summer dust to catch a glimpse of the famed act, and *London Unmask'd* reports in awe on the pig effect that's sweeping society:

> the proprietor is rapidly amassing a fortune, thro' the sway of fashion, as it would be quite monstrous and ill-bred not to follow the *ton* and see the wonderful Learned Pig: it being the trite question in all polite circles, Pray, my Lord, my Lady, Sir John, Madam or Miss, have you seen the Learned Pig? if answer is given in the affirmative, it is a confirmation of taste; if in the negative, it is reprobated as an odious singularity!

But for all its popularity, Nicholson's pig, like ours, has its moments of impudence. At a special private performance, the pig is put to its counting task as usual and asked to indicate how many honest gentlemen are in the audience. The pig gazes at those circled around it, the dandies in their silks and powdered hair, the scholars in their dark coats, the drunken husbands and sozzled lovers, but otherwise does not move. Nicholson laughs, wipes his brow. He prods the pig between the shoulders, just below his glitzy collar. 'Honest men . . .' But still the pig resists, tired or confused, sulking at some injustice or simply unable to discern an honest man among those gathered, and Nicholson laughs again, makes a small bow to the audience and begins afresh. 'How many, then, are free from mortgages? Count that for us instead. Of all those gathered here, how many are unencumbered?' But the pig can't be bothered. It puts its snout to the floor and snuffles, ignoring the cards, ignoring the crowd, ignoring Nicholson. It will not measure debt any more than it will measure honesty. Nicholson puffs, prevaricates, but is defeated by his pig. He offers a lower bow, an apology, to those who have put such faith in him, but he sees the disappointment in their faces, and the disbelief, and he darts at his stubborn, disobedient companion, flailing with sudden rage and whipping the pig down the stairs.

At Sadler's Wells Theatre, too, the pig is causing disruption. According to press reports, it's honoured with the loudest plaudits from the packed house, but the tightrope performers and acrobats object. They don't mind dancing dogs, they're accustomed to birds of various kinds, but they don't want to be onstage with a pig. The acclaimed tumbler Signor Plácido along with his partner Jean Redigé, otherwise known as the Little Devil, the singer Monsieur Dupuis, the acrobat Monsieur Meunier and the famous rope dancer La Belle Espagnole, march into the office of Richard Wroughton, the theatre's manager, to complain at the degradation, the humiliation, the unbearable ignominy of appearing with such a creature. The pig must go; they won't climb another rope or turn one more somersault until it's been dismissed. But, of course, Mr Wroughton has a drawer full of cash; he can look from his window and see the queue for tickets; he's read the notices in the newspapers and heard the gossip on the street. There's no way he's going to sack the pig. Instead he sacks the company and keeps the pig.

Big Pig and Little Pig may only be the darlings of La Graudie, rather than the toast of London, but they're revelling in their status nonetheless. Jean-Claude and Camille's son, Matthieu, has arrived from the city for a few weeks. He works in a plastic booth in a call centre and so now for his holidays he wants to be outside. He strims, weeds, digs, chainsaws. Most of the day he's coming and going in the garden; the pigs listen for him and he chats to them, hoses them, scratches their ears and their tummies. He sits on the wall and drinks beer while they grub at his feet. On a huge bough from one of the largest oaks in the woods, he sets up a rope swing and in the middle of the night, long after everyone's gone to bed, he sits in the dark and swings. The pigs find this nocturnal attraction a great improvement; they need hardly be alone now at all. I think they believe Matthieu's been stationed in the hamlet specifically for their entertainment, and they accept his company graciously.

A few evenings before he leaves, Matthieu organizes a barbecue. He lights a bulky pile of seasoned wood that he's humped across to a quiet corner of the garden, and we sit while the flames burn down. We can hear the pigs on the other side of the wall. They've come as close as they can and spike our conversation liberally with their grunts. They're not demanding attention, just taking part, and if we fall quiet they snort more vociferously, as if to prompt us. Mo goes back and forth between the barbecue and the pigs, perhaps relaying news. Over the easy weeks of summer, he's become their best friend. Little Pig especially trots across when Mo appears, mumbling happily. They like nothing more than to go nose to nose, a leathery pig snout and soft dog nose; they'll happily stand together in this way for several minutes.

The barbecue is a slow affair. By the time the tree-trunk logs have burned down enough to cook on, it's thoroughly dark. It's a night of lunar eclipse; we've been told to expect a spectacular red moon. At the moment there are only wisps of cloud at the horizon and a normal creamy moon above, but something about the prospect, the strangeness of the event, prompts reflection. I sit to one side of the crackling fire and think, again, about our future here. Back in the UK, my mother has been ill, rushed to hospital out of the blue with acute intestinal pains. Thankfully, it's nothing that can't be cured with an operation or two and a course of pills, and she's recovering now, but there were anxious days at first, a reordering of plans, a surge of battle-stations adrenalin. And with a sudden emergency of this kind, the occasional inconvenience of distance becomes more intractable. Coming and going is expensive and exhausting. But it's also an emotional tug, an unsettling reminder of ties that lie in places other than here. I begin to wonder whether I'm being drawn slowly but inexorably away. There are the uncertainties of making a living, always, but these are niggling and annoying, fretful. Perhaps the greater, though more subtle, force is simply to do with time and natural change, which means the way my family functions is mutating and, with it, my role and priorities. Just as the landscape alters here relentlessly, although almost imperceptibly, from generation to generation so, perhaps, that's how it is with Ed and me. We've been here a long time – longer than any other place I've lived – and perhaps Big Pig and Little Pig are not enough to anchor us, after all. Perhaps they're an expression of something that's already passing. But on this beautiful, balmy, smoky night pitted with flames and the grunt of curious pigs, I'm not at all sure about things. Because if this isn't my place then where is?

Eventually we eat well; drink; talk about the pigs. Camille remembers the woman in their village who went from house to house helping to make the sausages and pâtés on pig-killing day, before the meat – and especially the offal – spoiled. For years, at every house, there was a suspicion that she was stealing. When the meat was all packed away, families found they couldn't find the best joints, but no one had seen her carry anything away – she had no baskets, not even large pockets – and no one could work out how she was doing it. No matter how close an eye they kept, they could not spot anything untoward until, one night, there was music and dancing to celebrate the slaughter and processing of two good animals. It was in a house like theirs, Camille says, but deep in winter, so everyone was dancing in the big barn. The whole village was there, more or less, with an accordionist and a drum, and as one of the farmers took the woman in his arms and twirled her in 3/4 time, a slab of pork fell from her knickers. *Le filet mignon*, literally the 'cute fillet', the best bit of butchery, lying there on the trampled straw, a giveaway.

We laugh, and are suddenly propelled into stories of pig slaughter. Matthieu wanders off to look for the moon, but his parents are intent on recalling the best *tue-cochon*. They try to remember all the occasions they've witnessed, each one ritualized, codified by each village, each hamlet, each community, the men killing and butchering, the women preparing the meat. There are a great many rules about blood: the pig's blood was not to be spilled, not a drop; menstruating women should be left out of the way in the house; stirring the copper cauldron of blood collected from the animal's throat to keep it liquid for the *boudin* was a job reserved for old women, post-menopausal, free of blood. No blood to be shed on a Sunday or a religious holiday; no slaughter during Lent, or on a Friday (a meat-free, blood-free day in the Catholic calendar that each week marked Christ's death on Good Friday). On the morning of the *tue-cochon* a prayer was offered to St Anthony, the official patron saint of *charcutiers*, because he was commonly shown grasping a pig (although the pig was actually supposed to represent the Devil, rather than the prospect of hearty *saucissons*) and the last meat scraps from the previous year were fried up for breakfast – it was the end of one annual cycle and the beginning of the next. In the evening, the other animals and fowl on the farm were fed some of the soupy water in which the blood puddings had been boiled, so that they could show their gratitude to the poor dead pig.

In nearly all cultures, pig-killing day is a momentous occasion, a cause for celebration and nostalgia, a bustle of noise piqued with pungent, unforgettable smells. It's a day of shared excitement, because just as a pig's life was often a communal affair, so was its death. 'When the appointed day came round for the slaughtering,' wrote Edwin Grey in *Cottage Life in a Hertfordshire Village*, in 1935:

> there was a subdued air of excitement and expectancy among the immediate cottagers of which the pig-keeper's cottage was one, for had they not contributed their quota to the wash-tub, and would presently be the recipients of a nice plate of fry or maybe a few pork cuttings . . .

Jean-Claude asks us how we intend to kill our animals. At home, we say. 'Yes, of course, but how?' How are we going to hang the carcasses? Eviscerate them? Strip the hairs? I sense that he'd like to be invited to help us; he's envious of this most historic, most intimate of smallholding tasks, but we don't want to feel constrained by someone else's methods and although we listen well to his advice, we don't ask him to join us. Am I afraid that if something goes wrong – if the whole thing turns into some kind of grotesque massacre – our neighbours will recoil from us, horrified? Or do I suspect I might lose my nerve, after all, and not manage to go through with the killing at all, showing myself up in the end as just another flimsy, urban foreigner who has no place here?

Matthieu comes to fetch us all: the moon is turning red, a proper, deep blood red. We go out on to the lane where there's a less obstructed view and from there we can see the bright slither encroaching from one side as the eclipse passes, already washing away the colour. It's a disappointing spectacle but the night is clear now and glutted with the noise of crickets and nightingales, so that it's a pleasure just to stand here. Beyond the pig enclosure, beyond the woods, we can see into the distance, looking across the valley to where the land rises again; at our feet, the village packs tightly around the church at its centre, the spire softly illuminated and the *fontaine*, too, dappled with light; there's a cluster of lights very far away on a remote hill. Between there is nothing, just fields and woods, dark. Except just tonight there's a paper Chinese lantern drifting upwards, just one, already high in the sky. We don't know what it is at first. It's brighter than the moon, and stranger. We're puzzled by the flickering of the light and the way it bobs and slides; when we finally identify it, Jean-Claude worries that it will fall to earth on parched ground and start a fire. But it floats on up, away to one side. To watch it, Ed and I follow along the lane and then cut back in at the far end of the enclosure from where we can see it finally sailing off over the ridge.

The pigs are delighted that we've come to see them; they truffle contentedly at our trousers and shoes. We scratch them behind the ears and wallow-dust puffs across our hands. The night smells of pig hair and dry grass. I look through the canopy of old oaks to the speckled sky, and my earlier melancholy falls away, like shrugging off a heavy coat. I know there's nowhere else I could really be.

4.

Summer fades, becomes autumn without effort, the days shortening, the mornings cooler and dewy but the evenings still long and warm. A huge soft moon rises at dusk and sits plump on the horizon like a laying hen. Big Pig and Little Pig are putting on weight, maturing with the season. During the summer, their growth slowed: when we measured them in July and August they'd put on little more than a couple of kilos a week – for over a month, Little Pig's figures remained unchanged. But when we measure them during the first week in September, there's been a growth spurt: Big Pig is now a mighty 126kg, Little Pig just behind at 119kg. Little Pig's graph – the thin red line – is spiky, unsteady, a roller coaster of ups and downs compared to Big Pig's regular progress, but they're both shaping up well. And Little Pig's shaky ridge of peaks is less to do with any significant lurches in weight and more to do with the difficulty of keeping him still enough to peel out the string along his back. When we loop it round his tummy to measure the girth he's sure it's tickle time, play time, and he squirms and nibbles and thrusts his head into us. A wriggling graph for a wriggling pig.

On the way back from morning feeding time, early, I call at Solange's farm. It's a hotchpotch of buildings – barns and stables, cottages, stores, sheds, shelters and huts – clustered around a patchwork of yards and gardens. In its time it was another small village, like the Mas de Maury, home to half a dozen families and their animals, but now it's crumbling and only Solange remains. There are three or four similar farms within walking distance of our house, sprawling half-ruins populated by widows. These fragile landscapes of building and field are hardly held together as it is, but when Solange dies, and the other women of the neighbourhood, it's hard to know who will take their place to tend them. Solange's children and grandchildren come occasionally to help pollard the trees or dig over the garden, but they have their own homes, and none of them show any interest in moving here. The farm has looked this way for many years – since long before we arrived – and I suspect it will look just the same for years to come, but the life of it has dwindled. There's little market for such scruffy, expensive heaps of old stone: the boom is in *lotissements*, estates of new-build houses, designed to type, efficient and practical and affordable, with neighbours and streetscapes, a modest suburbia. Fashions will change again, no doubt, but sluggishly: in this forsaken nook of modern Europe, we're too far from the wealth of cities to feel anything but the most dogged of influences as they wade upstream along the slow, wide rivers of the Aveyron and the Lot and the Garonne. In the meantime, Solange lives alone while young families buy up *lotissement* plots to build their dream homes.

The back of the farm is visible from our house and garden, and so I see Solange every day as she goes about her chores. She works every hour of light, except for the siesta; most days I see her with her mattock, bent over, her skirt riding up to her thighs and her wide straw hat drooping over her face. She works through the heat and the cold, growing things. She is well over seventy years old but she chops her wood and stores it in huge stacks in one of the more derelict cottages, piling it up to the rafters on the ground floor, the attic above stuffed with what remains of the furniture; she cooks over a wood fire in another of the old dwellings, using the large room at the top of the stone steps for long, slow cooking in copper cauldrons. She only has a tiny sink and a table in the new farmhouse kitchen and prefers to prepare her ducks here, in the old room, even though it's dark and smoky.

She replies to my shouted greeting as I enter the front yard, but I can't quite hear where her voice is coming from. I try the small vegetable garden, where she grows lettuces, leeks, spinach, a flurry of crisp green leaves, but she's not there so I make my way round, past the large open hangar, scattering the chickens. This beautiful open-sided, oak-beamed, tiled barn is a place of ancient ploughs and tractors, neatly stored; there's a cluster of ducklings squabbling beneath a wooden trailer. Built against one side is the wall of the old well; against the other is a line of double-decker rabbit hutches, shaded by pollarded trees. This is where I find Solange, with a bucket of animal feed.

The rabbits are fat, quiet. The cages are small. We talk while she dispenses the food and water, and then she goes to the end hutch and grabs the rabbit by the ears, hauling it into the open. It dangles from one hand as she flips the cage closed adroitly with the other and picks up the bucket to return to the house. The rabbit makes remarkably little noise; it just hangs there, floppy, heavy, its unblinking eyes fixed on the clear morning distance.

Solange continues to talk. 'I don't think I'll keep rabbits much longer,' she says, 'they're too much work. Just for me. Too much.'

I'm astounded, always, at how much physical effort her day involves. 'You've got a lot already with the poultry and the gardens,' I offer.

She stretches for a moment from her habitual stoop, pleased by such sympathy. '*C'est dur*,' she replies. It's hard.

She places the bucket by a stone trough outside the door to one of the barns, and goes a step or two inside. I follow to the threshold: there are onions laid out to dry all over the floor and I daren't go any further. Solange picks her way in and reaches across to a shelf, putting some tools in the pocket of her apron and coming back out into the sunshine, the rabbit still dangling. Then we make our way to the garage, at the far end of the front yard, where the line of walnut trees begins. This is where her washing sink is, with a large flat stone, a table of sorts, alongside.

She has a story about another neighbour who's had an accident. She tells me that his daughter ran over him somehow with the tractor, and now he's stiff in plaster and can't work. She doesn't like the family much, and picks away at worn grudges. While she talks, she takes the rabbit firmly in her left hand and places it on the stone, holding it with her palm flat on the neck so that its head is sideways, still. Its eye stares up at the sky. 'The thing is,' she says, 'they're first cousins who married.' She takes a screwdriver from her pocket, holds it for a moment about six inches above the rabbit's head, and then with a fluid motion drives it down through the eye. The rabbit convulses under her grip, and makes a noise like the pigs do when they're surprised: a high, anxious screech.

The rabbit kicks. Blood squirts from the wound. Solange keeps a firm hold on the neck, makes a quick movement with the screwdriver and then withdraws it. I can't tell if the rabbit is dead yet.

The body flops, twitching. Solange pushes it to one side and sluices the stone with water from the tap. The edges of the rabbit's fur darken in the damp, but the back and rump shine, rust and silver, fine and soft; the ears lie neatly on the stone. She glances up at the blue sky, perhaps to judge something about the time or the nature of the day, or just to clear her thoughts, and then she invites me into the house for a drink. She gestures at the rabbit. It may or may not be quite dead. Apart from the empty eye socket and a thin dribble of blood, it looks exactly as it did a few moments before: 'I'll leave it here,' she says, 'it'll be fine. I can skin it later.'

There was a time when pigs were slaughtered in a similarly direct fashion. Indeed, some people still consider the old methods the best: the itinerant pig-killer who visited our neighbours simply 'stuck' their pig, in the traditional way. 'Sticking' involves either slitting the animal's throat with a large knife, or driving a spike through its skull: 'while someone held the poleaxe on the pig's forehead, the butcher would take a heavy wooden mallet and drive the spike into the pig's head,' explained a Durham countryman in the early twentieth century. Both methods could involve a slow and painful death, and in fact many people, like Arabella in Hardy's *Jude the Obscure*, believed that this was the only way of obtaining clean, pale meat with the blood fully drained. In general, pig stickers who could achieve their task with the minimum of noise and mess were much in demand, but there are accounts of those who quite openly enjoyed the 'sport' of killing a pig: one Wiltshire cottager recalled that large pigs were 'upended, had their throats slit and were allowed to tear around the orchard, squealing, till loss of blood caused them to collapse'; while in 1813, William Gooch, a Cambridgeshire clergyman, recounted 'a most barbarous and disgraceful way of killing hogs' which amounted to 'a man standing in the middle of a stye, and striking them on the head (by an instrument somewhat like a cricket-bat)'.

We intend to dispatch our pigs humanely. Of course we do. We read as much as we can about how best it should be done, and settle on using a captive bolt which will render the pig instantly and painlessly unconscious (if we do it correctly) so that it can then be killed without trauma for either the animal or for us. We investigate ways of removing the bristles, the next stage after the slaughter. Black pigs: black bristles. Commercial pig farmers prefer sleek pink pigs because their hairs are more or less invisible, so if one or two bits of stubble get left behind, it doesn't really matter: no one notices them sticking out of their roast pork crackling. But our pigs have thick, coarse dark hair which we'll need to take off without damaging the skin underneath. The traditional method is not unlike a high-class man's shave: scald the carcass to soften the hair and then scrape off the bristles with a sharp blade. But with the added complication that a pig carcass is a big thing to dunk in very hot water. A wine vat, a beer barrel or an old bath would do nicely, but we don't have any of these. The best thing we have is a blue plastic tub that we've been using as a water butt. We think it might do.

We'll have to hang the carcasses so we can cool them, clean them and dismember them. We examine beams in the woodshed but they're only a little over head height and when it's hung from its back trotters, a pig carcass will be well over six feet long. A tree branch would probably work, but there are no good solid branches close enough to the house. And there'll be the weight, too. How do we hoick such a weight up high? *You'll need a winch*, somebody says. A winch! *And good heavy chains*. Such things might be an investment if we were planning a full-scale attack on the butchery business, but we can't justify the expense just for Big Pig and Little Pig. So we ask around, forlornly, in the hope that someone might be able to help.

As the evenings draw in, I watch videos of pig butchery, weighing up the subtle difference between one way and another of slicing up animal flesh. I watch English butchers enthusing over hefty roasting joints; French butchers delighting in stranger, more delicate cuts such as the *levure* – from the word for yeast, to rise – a little sliver of marbled meat which puffs up on the griddle or barbecue. When we feel as though we've some kind of understanding of basic principles, Ed and I spend a morning with Benoît, the farmer who sold us Big Pig and Little Pig as weaners. He's converted one of his barns into a workshop for butchering and processing meat. It's stainless steel, cold, very clean, an odd appendage to the rest of the farm which is the usual muddle of old stone buildings and rusting cars and tractors. We watch carefully as he divides new carcasses and cuts them down: joints, chops, steaks. We talk to him about sausage recipes, and about drying out *saucissons* and, of course, about the ham. He suggests we allow him to cure that for us and keep it for a year or two until it's ready to eat: 'Two years is better, if you want real flavour.' We buy an all-purpose saw from the hardware shop, and order a series of specialist butcher's knives over the Internet.

And none of this seems strange. It seems a perfectly ordinary way to spend time. I enjoy the investigation, the discussion, the shopping. It seems largely an intellectual problem: how do you satisfactorily take a bulky living animal and transform it into a state whereby it fits neatly into freezer drawers without waste or damage? The act of processing the carcass is a bit like doing jigsaw puzzles, or the infant's game where you fit wooden blocks into shaped holes, or even Tetris; it's about packing things away tidily, managing a task. It's little more than a question of logistics. So I become thoroughly involved with the planning, and when I've finished watching a video showing me how to winkle the tenderloin from under the ribs with a deft slide of a blade, I wander down to the enclosure to see if Little Pig wants his stomach tickled.

Do I put two and two together? Do I match the butcher's knives with the stomach? The meat with the animal? The live with the dead? Do I *think* about what I'm doing? Or perhaps, more relevantly, do I *feel* it? The moment is nearly upon me; the moment when I'll have to decide and then act; when I will have to know, for sure, whether or not I can kill my pigs and make that knowing count. Because just now I don't think I do know, not certainly. I think I've shimmied and waffled; I've shunted away unpleasant thoughts and left them to wither. I've been having too much fun. But Big Pig and Little Pig are supposed to die at my hand. That's their destiny, preordained. And I'd better face up to it, sooner or later.

One of the pigs' new favourite games is pear chase. I stand at the top of the slope with a bucket of windfall pears from the tree in our garden. The fruit are too small and grainy for us, but the pigs love them, and in particular love foraging for them, so I hurl them one at a time as hard and as far as I can. The pears bounce off in all directions, ricocheting from trunks, rolling down the terraces, splatting hard against stones; the pigs follow after, galloping down the hill, slipping and sliding, stopping to find a pear, hearing another one fall close by and setting off after it, barging and wrangling, snuffling through the dug earth after the scent of fruit. When I've emptied the bucket I watch them for a while and then leave them to their search; they'll be at it a long time.

Pears. Apples. Plums. Blackberries. There's more fruit than they can eat, and still plenty of produce from the garden, still more courgette mush, still pumpkins and spoiled tomatoes. As the nights begin to draw down damp, conditions are perfect for growing, and we begin to come across sprouting tomato plants all over the enclosure, courgette plants, too, cucumbers, all poking through now where the pigs have 'processed' the seeds in their dung. They eat these seedlings, too, and chomp through clumps of lilac-flowering lucerne, a high-protein food crop which has seeded from fields far away and taken root amidst the grass in shadier corners. All this, and still the acorns to come, and chestnuts, and walnuts, too, from some of the trees at the edge of the woods. The perfect way to fatten up the pigs. Well-fed pigs with a good layer of fat will be in perfect condition for the cold weather at the end of the year – and for slaughter.

Our farming neighbours are fascinated by what we're feeding our pigs. It's always the first question, even though they've asked us several times before. Where do we get the grain? What quality is it; what's in it, exactly? Are we supplementing from the garden and kitchen? We run through the details and they nod in approval. We go to great trouble to fetch the sacks of dry, soft, organic grain from Benoît. He's agreed that we can go along and help ourselves from his store, keeping count of the sacks and settling up later. We go once a week or so and stand beneath the silos, manoeuvring the sacks on to the tricky spouts, holding them firmly so that the floury cereal doesn't spray everywhere when the catch is released and the contents hurtle down the metal pipe in a burst. Benoît's pigs hear the rumble of the feed in the tubes and come careering hopefully to the fence, keeping a close eye on us, barging so energetically and so close to the single electric wire that every time I'm sure they're going to pour forward in a mess of heavy black pig and overwhelm us. I'm used to two pigs – this scrum of twenty or thirty squealing animals is alarming. But it's no wonder the grain is such an attraction. The roaming herds have cleared great swathes of Benoît's forested land, digging out the undergrowth and leaving just the oaks standing in the rocky earth, and there are dried peas in the mix, and beans and corn; good things.

What are you feeding them? It's an obsession that goes back a long way. Most of us now are interested in what we feed ourselves: we're bullied and cajoled until we're simply forced to take an interest in it. Fat? Salt? Sugar? *Really?* How many portions? But in the past, it was what you fed your animals that mattered because this, in turn, had a direct effect on what you ate: if your pig was healthy and stout, with plenty of meat, then you ate well for a long time. If it was ailing, or the meat was poor, then you and your family might just starve. So it was worth taking note of what food made your animals thrive.

By the seventeenth century there was already recognition that husbandry – the cultivation of animals and crops to elicit the best possible yield – was a 'science' which demanded close attention to detail, as well as enterprise and experiment. In 1612, the significance of adding peas and other high-energy legumes to foodstuff as a valu-able source of protein was championed in a husbandry manual written by Gervase Markham, a soldier, horse breeder and poet who also found time to urge the housewife to acquire the 'inward and outward virtues' of a 'complete woman', and to tackle modern farm-ing methods. But cereals and pulses were (and still are) expensive, so most cottagers or pig farmers continued to rely largely on forest grazing, known as pannage, to fatten their animals. Wooded land, and access to it, however, declined steadily from the Middle Ages onwards, as trees were cut for timber or charcoal, populations grew and towns expanded. Particular conditions in some areas also had an effect: the increase in demand across the world for high-quality English wool, for example, meant that trees were felled and forest cleared as more farms were laid out to grass – sheep were more profit-able and much less labour intensive than pigs. In the early nineteenth century, the fortunate inhabitants of the New Forest had rights to pannage from fifteen days before Michaelmas, at the end of September, until forty days after: around 6,000 pigs were let loose to feast on the nuts and acorns. This right to graze, called the 'Common of Mast', still exists, although fewer pigs are given the opportunity to fatten in this way. But in general, by the 1900s, unless you were rich enough to own your own stretch of woodland – or fortunate enough, like us, to borrow some for a while – it could be a struggle to find good land for fattening your pig. While cottagers in the New Forest might have been able to feed their animals conveniently right throughout the autumn, in many areas, acorns, beech mast, hazelnuts and chestnuts were becoming a scarce commodity.

The reduction in forest grazing meant fewer and fewer big herds of pigs, and more emphasis on the family pig fed from scraps and scavenged hedgerow titbits. And the pig's natural ability to fatten on all kinds of waste products was put to good use in some places with inventive reciprocal arrangements between pig owners and local industries. The nutritious leftovers from distilling and beer making were particularly popular: brewer's grains, sweepings from the barley stores and general beery sludge fattened some 9,000 pigs a year around the large London breweries at Vauxhall, Battersea and Wandsworth. Dairies, too, were a good source of food; the mutual dependency of the pig and the dairy endured well into the last century and led to the establishment of an important droving route taking pigs from Wales to the dairies in Wiltshire and Gloucestershire and eventually on to the London meat markets. Pigs loved the whey skimmed off during cheese making and, in turn, they supplemented the income of the dairy farmer for no additional cost: during his *Tour through the Whole Island of Great Britain* in the 1720s, Daniel Defoe stopped to admire the pigs in Wiltshire and Gloucestershire, and the system which sustained them. 'This bacon is raised here by their great Dairies,' he remarked, 'as their Hogs are fed with the vast Quantities of Whey, and skimm'd milk, which the farmers must otherwise have thrown away.' Even today, here and there, the long-standing link between the dairy and the pig remains intact: Big Pig and Little Pig, when they were very young, had their diet supplemented with the *petit lait* (whey) from the goat's cheese farm just down the road from where they were born.

The acorns are beginning to fall, pattering through the undergrowth on breezy days like intermittent rain; plums and apples are still in abundance. The pigs spend almost the entire day eating, taking only occasional breaks from foraging to wallow, rarely dozing. They don't look fat. But they're beginning to seem heavier, more cumbersome: it takes them longer to puff up the slope to the field; Little Pig sometimes pauses halfway up the climb, gazing mournfully towards the summit. They're no longer sprightly youths; in their black skins, they have more of a studied air about them, like portly Victorian gentlemen. This new bearing suits Big Pig perfectly. He's growing firmer of flesh and character. He's begun to separate himself from us a little, responding less urgently to our calls, measuring his place in this haphazard herd of humans and dogs and pigs; his calm self-reliance is not yet aloofness, but admits more and more a wary distance. Little Pig is just burly. He still wants company, entertainment, attention, and presses for it more vigorously.

The harvest from the garden is almost finished. There's little more to be done now except the usual clearing of dead plants and sorting of stakes and nets and ties. Since the pigs have so much food in the woods, and are so busy foraging for it, we decide to take the opportunity to have a couple of nights' holiday. Jean-Claude agrees to keep their water topped up, and dole out the grain rations; we walk the perimeter of the fence with care, slowly, checking for any possible glitches that might cause problems while we're away. I'm struck again by how successfully the pigs have opened up the land and swept the forest floor; I watch Big Pig snuffling methodically along one of the terraces, turning up the soil, crunching his way towards the big oak with Matthieu's swing, where the acorns are gathering. It's all orderly, calm, disciplined. There seems no reason not to take a holiday. Ice cream. Swimsuits. No pigs.

When I was young, one of my mother's many reasons for not allowing pets was the work involved in keeping them. It's a tie, she always said. Having a pet, she maintained, would mean a loss of freedom; it would mean not being able to do things. And in part, of course, this is true. Most people these days have some free time and choose to spend it *doing* something, usually away from home, in town with friends or travelling, unconstrained by the routines of animal feeding. Keeping pigs is a reminder of a different age when families didn't expect to go anywhere and there was not much room for leisure. It made no difference if you had to be home to feed the pig because you would be at home anyway. Solange has been away once in her life, on her honeymoon: she and her new husband took a couple of days to visit the shrine at Lourdes and pray. Since then, for fifty years or so, she's been at the farm, every day. But, like other things, this compact world view is changing: young families around us go off on holiday, professionals fly abroad for meetings, couples take weekend breaks in the cities to go to concerts or theatres. Farming is no longer, by default, associated with the patch of land on which the farm stands – many expansive barn roofs are newly cloaked in solar panels, growing energy as a crop, supplying homes and businesses far distant – nor is it assumed that cultivating fields and keeping livestock has to be all-consuming: there are vegetable gardens kept for pleasure, chickens too, ducks, sheep, a few cattle. Even in this ancient heart of agriculture, farming is losing its hold, its constriction, on living – the daily professional devotion to livestock is much loved and respected but is no longer considered a natural, inevitable occupation.

But slipping from the old ways perhaps has more impact than is immediately obvious. The apparent timelessness of the landscape belies the pressure on farmers to expand and diversify. Gradually, in an almost invisible, piecemeal fashion, old field systems are nudged and tweaked to make them easier, larger, more profitable. Stone-walled paths are pulled out quietly – by the time someone notices a track marked on the map is no longer where it should be, the land has been flattened and evidence concealed. Around our house, several of the smaller fields have been melded together, hedges uprooted and trees felled, small fallow meadows replaced with larger plots that can be ploughed and harvested by tractor. This does not seem, on the face of it, a terrible thing. Farmers need to make a living; the landscape has to be shaped to new demands. The fields are still fields, flickering with butterflies and bright with flowers, only they're larger now, and the view has opened up between them, one from the other. But look more closely and even in this place of apparent permanence you can spot the effects of these changes. When we first came here, a summer twilight bustled with hedgehogs; glow-worms sprinkled the verges; barn owls perched on the fence posts and swooped low when we passed. There are glow-worms still, sometimes, glittering here and there like tiny splinters of neon, but there are fewer of them; I hear a barn owl chuntering occasionally, or screeching, but it's a long time since I've driven home late from town and caught the beautiful pale swoop of them in the headlights, one after the other, many owls like puffs of ghosts; it's several summers since I've seen a hedgehog.

There must be a decline in other creatures, too; in things I haven't noticed – bugs and insects, mice and moles, unspectacular and uncountable little birds – and in the plants that thrived in the tiny sheltered meadows.

Perhaps I'm saddened by these tiny shifts in the environment because my own place in it is so uncertain; because Ed and I force ourselves to peek now and again into the future to see whether we can picture ourselves here or whether we've been carried far away by economic forces and family loyalties. Perhaps I want this place to remain the same, timeless, unchanging, because that would indicate something reassuring about my own position and even the state of the much larger world beyond; it would suggest that, yes, there are places where small lives flourish quietly and undisturbed as they always have done. But I don't think my observations are merely sentimental. I realize that they're not scientific record either, but they are carefully and thoughtfully made over time. It may be a very small decline in this very large tract of land that makes up the natural treasure chest of south-west France, but it's a lessening, nonetheless, a sign that nothing is what it once was, and my fear is that too soon, as in other rural landscapes, the balance will lurch and the hedgehogs and glow-worms and owls will be fully lost, as the old pig-keeping ways have been lost, and only the widows will regret them; and then the widows, too, will be gone.

In this poised moment of the not-quite-ancient, not-quite-modern Aveyron heartlands, the life of the land is still just about held in balance with the pressures of farming but it's clear that small-scale agriculture is struggling, and we're fortunate that we've been able to keep pigs as an interlude, a hobby. We haven't needed them or their meat to ensure we won't starve; we haven't had to fit their care around the exhausting demands of working the land. We haven't had to calculate overheads per kilogram of meat in order to turn a profit. It's been an indulgence, a treat. We've been tied to them but this has been our choice; we've welcomed the bond. It's not meant missing out. Rather, it's made new things possible, and has forced new things upon us: I now know, for what it's worth, how to put in a proper electric fence; how to mix animal foodstuff correctly; how to inject a pig. But more than this simple process of learning, it's also brought a kind of freedom quite different from the ability to go away for the night or take a day off. Tramping round to the enclosure three times a day, every day (sometimes more), caring for and simply watching the pigs, has gifted me what I can only describe as a 'freedom of being', a kind of licence to be nothing other than this, a person with pigs. This sense of liberation is unexpected, and I'm not entirely sure how it's come about. It has something to do with connection and repetition, but also with new experience abutting tradition, and the physical sensations of mud, dust, grass, grain. It's as much about grubby, tiring, welly-boot tasks as the brief interludes of walking with the pigs or showering them under cloudless skies; the daily interaction with the pigs and the land they're inhabiting has become like an extended meditation, each moment, each experience incubating the next, serenely but certainly; it's allowed me to place myself in time – here we are with weaners; here they're too big for their enclosure; now they're moving to the woods, growing, fattening – and this is comforting, freeing, because it's a definite chronology, unequivocal: I remember when it started and I know when it's going to end. It's going to end with the death of the pigs.

For now, though, I'm taking a trip. The mornings are already heavy with dew; the hoopoes and orioles have flown, the last of the swallows flit and twitter on the telephone wires. The evenings have emptied into quiet: no frogs, no crickets. Soon it will be difficult even to remember, accurately, the heat of summer, and it will be too late for this kind of beach holiday. So, for the first time since they arrived in January, I'm leaving the pigs. Perhaps this is part of the process of withdrawal, of estrangement, that will need to happen over the next few weeks and months if we're going to kill them. I find myself wondering if they'll notice our departure at all, or if they'll simply continue in the woods, as they always do, their ears, eyes and snouts fixed on the fall of acorns. Big Pig and Little Pig, getting fat without me.

Fattening a country pig is about working with the seasons, taking full advantage of the abundance of fruit and nuts in late summer and autumn. But if you're in the middle of a town – no orchards, no acorns, no trees at all – where the seasons are blighted by smog, and uniformly fruitless, and you still want to raise a pig, then you have to think again. While farmers and cottagers found it increasingly difficult to fatten a country pig as rights to pannage were curtailed and forests denuded, those who moved into the growing industrial towns discovered new ways of bringing up hogs among the terraces and in small backyards. Nicholson's pig was not the only pig accustomed to urban living. As far back as the 1690s, husbandry manuals were including 'Instructions to Fatten Swine in Towns' but it was during the nineteenth century, as the Industrial Revolution took hold, that pigs began to be a common sight in the domestic streets that were packed around the mills and factories. By 1850, as many as 3,000 pigs were recorded in the potteries district of North Kensington, in London, while during the 1860s, the parish of St George the Martyr, in Southwark, launched a campaign to discourage the keeping of pigs in such a built-up area: 'their condition and surrounding were filthy, as negligence and want of convenience could make them,' noted the parish Medical Officer. 'There were also public sties in which from ten to forty pigs were huddled together, and the smell from which the winds carried far and wide.'

In France, measures to ban pigs from the street were first introduced in the thirteenth century but proved ineffective and impossible to enforce. Frequent trials took place in which wandering urban pigs stood accused of causing damage or accident. What strikes us now as the bizarre custom of putting pigs in the dock – and often sentencing them to death – arose partly because there were just so many pigs loose in the towns, and their activity quite often conflicted with human interest. Horses, donkeys and cows, rats and even insects were also subject to lawsuits but pigs were the serial offenders, simply because they were so common and so boisterous: from the Middle Ages until the eighteenth century, pigs were executed for offences ranging from sacrilegiously eating consecrated hosts to chewing off ears or killing children. The public executioner in Paris was permitted to seize any loitering pig and cut its throat unless its owner paid a ransom of 5 silver *sous*.

On the other side of the Atlantic, New York City passed its first law banning pigs from the streets in 1648, but this was largely ignored and almost two centuries later, in the 1820s and 1830s, there were riots against the 'hog carts' sent to round up some of the thousands of animals still free ranging. An early nineteenth-century aquatint of one of New York's smartest areas, Broadway and the City Hall, shows pigs roaming among the elegantly dressed couples and expensive carriages enjoying the spacious streets and tree-lined parks. But while this demonstrates that wealthy districts were not pig-free, pigs in towns, as in the country, were generally animals of the poor, and they quickly became associated with the worst of the slums. Working in the squalor of Manchester's industrial neighbourhoods in the 1830s, James Kay-Shuttleworth, a doctor and politician, recalled how common it was to find destitute families sharing their yards and alleys with their own pigs, and even with those being raised commercially:

> The houses of the poor sometimes surround a common area, into which the doors and windows open at the back of the dwelling. Porkers, who feed pigs in the town, often contract with the inhabitants to pay some small sum for the rent of their area which is immediately covered with pig-styes and converted into a dung-heap and receptacle of the putrescent garbage which is now heedlessly flung into it from the surrounding dwellings. The offensive odour which sometimes arises from these areas cannot be conceived.

For many of those clamouring to watch Nicholson's sleek black pig, it was the contrast between his lovable animal and the sad, reeking creatures of the city slums which came as such a surprise. They were accustomed to associate pigs with the dirtiest habits and conditions: a print by Thomas Bewick, for example, made around 1797, shows a man sitting in an outside toilet, with his trousers down, defecating energetically into a pig enclosure. Such works suggested that pigs were fit for nothing more than feeding on, and living in, waste and excrement. But here was Nicholson's pig, rising above such assumptions and showing itself to be – well, human? In Sarah Trimmer's *Fabulous Histories* for children, one of the ladies watching the pig perform finds the disparity between her expectations and what she actually sees upsets everything she thought she knew about animals:

'I have,' said a lady who was present, 'been for a long time accustomed to consider animals as mere machines [. . .] but the sight of the Learned Pig, which has lately been shewn in London, has deranged these ideas, and I know not what to think.'

If a dog or a cat or a horse had displayed such talent then it would not have become a sensation (indeed, as we've seen, talented dogs and horses and cats were frequently paraded on the stage to lukewarm receptions) but a pig, *a pig*; it was its very pigness which was both the attraction and the repulsion, causing enough of a stir to thoroughly 'derange' the most settled of ideas.

Writers, cartoonists, artists and those in pursuit of any kind of celebrity picked up on the strange attraction of Nicholson's pig, and decided it was worthy of attention. In addition to those queuing for tickets to see the act in person, there was a remarkable flurry of references to it in prose, poetry and print: 'the learned pig was in his day a far greater object of admiration to the English nation than ever was Sir Isaac Newton,' noted Robert Southey, the Victorian Poet Laureate. Following the death of Samuel Johnson, *The Morning Post*, among others, compared the age's portly figurehead of wit and wisdom to Nicholson's show pig, running a poem that claimed 'Another hog is come / And Wisdom grunts at Charing Cross'. The poet William Blake referred to the Learned Pig in his notebook, and William Wordsworth included reference to it in his long poem *The Prelude*, as an example of the 'out-o'-the-way, far-fetched, perverted things / All freaks of nature' which were entertaining London society and pandering to 'man's dullness, madness'.

Poking fun at the absurdity and vanity of the crowds who gathered to watch the pig seemed to keep the intelligentsia more than comfortably entertained. The caricaturist Thomas Rowlandson drew Nicholson's protégé hard at work picking out alphabet cards surrounded by fat and grotesque spectators displaying many hog-like features of their own; his friend Samuel Collings drew a chaotic scene of a pig leading a cavalcade of carnival performers to overthrow the classical muses in 'The Downfall of Taste and Genius'. Even the prime minister, William Pitt, was frequently referred to, and drawn, as 'The Wonderful Pig' or 'The Learned Pig'. The best British traditions of art, debate, theatre and learning, the satirists suggested, were being ignored or debased – and what better illustration of such calamity, of such popular ignorance and degeneracy, than a pig.

Nicholson, however, seems delighted to derange people's ideas. He's astutely silent on any controversy surrounding the act. I find no comments from him about its place in cultural life or even about its unexpected popularity. He simply goes doggedly about his business, performance by performance, thriving on the debate his pig is causing. The more received opinions are crazed and disordered, the more his black pig is talked about. Satire, caricature, poetry: it's all the same to him; it's all publicity. Fame. Soon the faddish gaze will shift; before long, the *ton* will tire of him and his animal and he'll be returned to obscurity. The pig will have to be fattened for lard. But for now he has poets and philosophers ridiculing and berating him, which is all he needs.

But the pig in all this, the patient black pig that once slouched below Samuel Bisset's Belfast bar, a reluctant pet, has begun to fade. Physically it's much the same as ever, thinner than it once was perhaps, older, though still a good-looking, polished pig. But we don't hear much of it; it's begun to vanish from its own story. Since its refusal to perform to order, counting honest gentlemen or those of its select audience without mortgages, it has become little more than a poster pig. There it is, right enough, unmistakable in newspaper clippings and cartoons, but it's come to be something else, a symbol, a cipher, with the disillusion of a dying century piled upon its sinewy shoulders. It no longer seems to me a real pig, with piggy traits: we see nothing of its impudence, its spirit, its cleverness. We don't know how it lives, or what it does when it's not performing. No one is interested in the mundane habits of a metaphor.

After more than a year at the heart of the London scene, Nicholson takes a break, keen for some country air, perhaps, or wary of exhausting the capital's attention. The pig tours again: Banbury, Oxford, Bath. It's autumn in the Cotswolds, crisp and appley, but the pig passes through those grassy pastures without pausing; it belongs entirely now to the towns. There, it does what it's supposed to do – tells the time, reads thoughts, picks out maidens – but the tricks are worn now, too well learned to entertain a curious pig; the crowds are the same all over, brash and noisy, apt to poke it. The pig performs; repeats; performs again, over and over. You can almost sense its weariness from here, two hundred and fifty years later.

And in the winter of 1786, quite suddenly, the pig disappears. It does not perform; the newspapers are free of it. No matter how hard I look, I can't find any news of Nicholson or his travelling menagerie. There are reports of other spectacles, and plenty of interest in the ubiquitous Sarah Siddons, playing the tragic muse in a Shakespearean pageant at the Theatre Royal, Covent Garden, but nothing about the pig. There are not even questions about its fate. No posters, no reports, no bookings. I begin to think something must have happened. Has Nicholson retired? Has the pig run away? Died? I discover that it was a severe winter, one in a series of bitter winters, with heavy snow falling as early as October and the Thames freezing over. Not good conditions for an itinerant performing pig. But still I'm surprised that news of its sickness or death did not reach the papers. How can such a famous pig just vanish?

At the seaside, the weather is dry and hot. We loll in the sea, like pigs in wallows, and we get some good news. I've sold another novel. I had a hopeful email from my agent a few weeks ago; that turned into a more hopeful phone call; a long wait. And now, at last, a contract on its way. This is hardly the kind of deal you might read about in the newspapers – my advance is small; the whole negotiation low-key – but for Ed and me, it's momentous. Even modest amounts of money can be life-changing, and the windfall has bought us another few precious months here at least. It's an uneasy, impermanent solution but we're becoming skilled at evading the future, and instead of worrying about the long-term, we revel in the relief of an escape. The income from my novel will trickle through in instalments over the next eighteen months or so. We do the calculations and come to a decision: we'll put aside all thoughts of moving, all job adverts, all family negotiations for another full year. During that time, we'll treat everything as certain. We'll not allow ourselves to doubt or fidget. We'll just enjoy being here. One more year will give us time to see things through properly with Big Pig and Little Pig; it will allow us to make the best use of the meat and to benefit fully from a store cupboard of home-raised pork. After that – well, who knows?

As we drive back inland, we're buoyed by our new certainty, eager to see the pigs again after the break, looking forward to making plans. The verges brown and crinkle. It's been unusually warm everywhere, an illusion of summer, and when we go round to the enclosure, the field is dusty again; the pigs have pulled the shelter apart, opening the flaps of plastic to allow more air to circulate, and loosening the straw. Jean-Claude is in his vegetable garden, crouched in the dirt, running the parched soil through his fingers.

Where are the pigs?

He shrugs: 'In the woods. Keeping out of the heat.'

But the pigs are not in the woods. We've called them and they haven't come. We've gone down the hill, pushed through the trees to the very bottom of the slope, checked in their favourite spots under the tall oaks. There are no pigs.

Jean-Claude is sanguine. He mentions something about boar. About the start of the hunting season. *La chasse* was out around here on Sunday, he says.

La chasse. A powerful local force, the seat of an old-fashioned, much-respected authority, it meets twice a week, occasionally more often, from late summer through to spring. A trail of muddy 4x4s, ancient vans and assorted trailers rattles around the lanes, announcing its arrival. The vehicles peel off along the tracks until they've encircled a stretch of woodland, and the men – it's only men, here – unlatch the cages to let out the hounds, which don't bark or bay but just trundle through the trees, purposeful. The hunters lean against the bonnets of their vehicles and smoke, their fluorescent caps and jackets the only real disturbance to the landscape. For long stretches of time nothing very much happens. It's an amiable way to pass a bright Sunday.

But mobile phones have stacked the odds. A hound, some distance off, perhaps a mile or more away, begins to bay; an animal has been spotted, a deer or a boar. Phones buzz; one huntsman calls the next; the circle of vehicles is pulled tight by the voice on the end of the telephone: *here, over here, this way*. What used to be a sport of skill and signals and stealth is now a full-on show of force: the cars race towards the sighted prey, throwing up mud and stones, the phones still ringing. One of our neighbours, a boy of eighteen, has a gun which can shoot a boar at a distance of over a kilometre. 'I have to aim down, towards the ground,' he says, 'otherwise, you know . . .' and he gestures vaguely towards the houses to suggest stray bullets.

It's not unusual for Mo to find deer carcasses when animals have been shot but have escaped *la chasse* to die later, perhaps days later. I once traced a trail of blood along a series of tracks, following the steps of a wounded boar. I traced it for a long time, perhaps an hour or more. What began as a drip, drip, drip became a steady deep red line and then a Pollock-esque study in violent mark-making. I eventually lost the trail as the animal cut away from the path and into thicker undergrowth. I presume it died there, among the brambles and wild strawberries.

Could Big Pig and Little Pig have got caught up with *la chasse*? Could they have been mistaken for boar? They're the same colour, after all, and the same shape; they don't move with quite the same erratic, high-shouldered shuffle as boar, but in the woods, from a distance, they might have seemed the perfect game. Even if they weren't targeted, they would definitely have taken fright at men trampling through the trees, at the sound of gunshots, at dogs. They bolt in panic if we surprise them in the straw or when they're head-down in the earth, snuffling for bugs; how much more terrified would they be if they were caught up in a huntsman's ambush?

We've discussed before the risk of getting the pigs tangled up with *la chasse*. Why hadn't we done more – somehow? We're angry now. With ourselves and with the men with guns. And how do you begin to look for two lost pigs? I remember the morning I found them in the Mas de Maury enclosure, spooked and frantic: if they'd found their way out on that occasion, I'm sure they would have just scattered, wild, instinctive; skirted open ground and buried themselves in deep thickets. From here at La Graudie panicked pigs could run in all directions: along the stream and into the valley, then up on to scrubby dry hills; or away behind the village, climbing through the woods and across the main road, breaking free on to the endless stretches of oak *causse*; or back through the hamlet and into the scruffy farmland fields with their dense hedges and copses.

The phone rings just as we get back to the house.

We've got your pigs in our garden.

They're near the lane. Eating the damsons.

As breakouts go, it's a modest one. Little Pig and Big Pig have made it only as far as the next hamlet of houses, Mas del Sol. From their enclosure, if they retraced our worn trail through the field to the lane and kept going, it was the first place they'd come to.

And it's right next to the Mas de Maury. From one corner of their early walled pen, you could see the roofs of Mas del Sol, hear the chickens and the dogs. I begin to wonder: was it an escape with a purpose? Have they been curious all this time about what went on in this cluster of houses? It seems more than a coincidence that this is the first time we've ever left the pigs, and also the first time they've bothered to break out of their enclosure – it's possible that they were scared by *la chasse*, I suppose, and were reacting out of instinct, but it also occurs to me that they might have been trying to make a return: since we'd abandoned them to go on holiday, perhaps they were unsettled, lonely even, trying to find their way home, to the safe place they remembered, the first place – to us.

Of course, there's no way of knowing what might make two black pigs wander off; it's quite possible that Jean-Claude was slow filling their water and in the hot weather they mounted an expedition to find refreshment for themselves. But it's a relief to track them down so quickly, and it's useful to know that they can obviously walk free of their enclosure and its flimsy wire quite easily if they want, or need, to – it's just that most of the time, they don't bother. Most of the time, they have everything they need; they're happy.

We grab our buckets and sticks and rush off to Mas del Sol. Big Pig and Little Pig are strolling along the lane, waddling round a bend that hugs the sagging wall of a stone barn, their black haunches sashaying, their tails twirling and whirling, their grunts going back and forth between them in quiet conversation. They seem to be enjoying their outing. There are the damsons, wild and plentiful, blackberries still, elderberries, walnuts. There's water, too, and perhaps even the possibility of a whole new wallow: the man who called us, Raymond, had woken from his siesta to find the pigs kicking over the tub of water he'd left in his yard for the poultry. When he'd gone out to find out what was going on, the pigs were sloshing in the puddle, the ducks squawking alongside. They'd seemed pleased to see him, he said. New places, new people, new friends.

They're pleased to see us, too. They hear or smell us as we approach and immediately thrust their heads up, listening intently. Little Pig turns first; he trots towards us, and Big Pig comes, too, catching up quickly, so that they arrive together, a scramble of pig. They don't seem to feel 'captured' in any way; there's no defeat in the reunion. Instead they seem keen to return to their enclosure and to rummaging in their own woods. They nudge us forward;

want to follow. Raymond and his two grandsons encircle us, creating a kind of cordon, and we try to organize the pigs and the buckets into an orderly livestock procession of sorts, but in the end we all go back to the enclosure together in an untidy scuffle: me and Ed and Mo, Raymond and the boys, Big Pig and Little Pig, sauntering in the late afternoon sun.

It's chestnut season. The end of autumn. While we live firmly in oak country, just a couple of miles up the road the soil changes, and the dips and valleys in the land are filled with chestnut woods. Some of the villages, bounded on every side by chestnut trees, take their name from the fruit – *Castanet*. For a few weeks, the woods are carpeted with huge, shiny nuts, so densely scattered that you're walking on layers of prickly green casings and crunching the nuts underfoot. The chestnuts are beautiful things with their grained mahogany shells; they cry out to be stroked; just the look and feel of them promises something special. And the pigs love them – more than perhaps anything they've eaten so far, more than acorns or melons or sweet pumpkins – so we collect bucket- and bagfuls, spraying them down the hill as we did with the pears, watching pigs and nuts bouncing together down the soft slopes.

Rich and mineraly and nutritious, chestnuts are perfect for 'finishing' the pigs and giving the final meat a good flavour. They have been used for centuries to plump up the best pigs – it's the chestnut woods around Parma in northern Italy, for example, which give the renowned *prosciutto* its quality and taste. In the middle of the nineteenth century, the Royal Agricultural Society of England was urging its members to seek out chestnut groves because 'hogs fattened with chestnuts have fine-flavoured flesh'. But people love chestnuts, too. Just as they give the pigs a boost of protein, so traditionally chestnuts have provided villagers with a 'fattening' before the lean times of winter. Starchy and high in vitamins, chestnuts provided an important staple in many parts of Europe, ground into flour, preserved, roasted, as sweet delicacies. But the three weeks or so of collecting were hard labour, breaking the prickly shells by hand, sorting, peeling, drying and grinding: it's been estimated that a family would need to put in 110 working days between its members over the short season to gather enough chestnuts to live on, usually amounting to 100 days of work from the women and children and 10 days from the men.

Not surprisingly, the gathering of such a harvest was cause for celebration, and in the chestnut areas local to us this late-season abundance is still fêted with enthusiasm. With Big Pig and Little Pig snuffling contentedly through the woods in search of the nuts we've scattered, Ed and I take a short drive into the valleys south of our house, to the annual *fête de la châtaigne*. It's a Sunday morning of church bells and Keatsian mellowness, but as we approach the village there's a surprising amount of traffic and bustle – small white vans, groups on foot, a line of men armed with metal poles, a municipal police car – and we park at a distance, walking into the central square on foot. It's a wide marketplace of trampled earth, symmetrical and pleasing, with medieval arcades on all sides and low stone-and-wood houses clustered above, a well raised in the middle. But the attraction today is not history or architecture; it's the chestnuts. Ranged across the square are half a dozen or more big wire tumblers, like barrels of sturdy mesh, each one propped over a huge wood bonfire, each one being turned by hand by a red-faced man, a chestnuteer (most wearing the colours of the local rugby club). Inside the tumblers are thousands of chestnuts, rattling and spinning; behind are sacks overflowing with more gathered chestnuts; clustered around are crowds of people to watch. Many, many people standing on a Sunday morning watching chestnuts roast.

The smell, of course, is delicious, a heady concoction of woodsmoke and charred chestnut, enough in itself to keep us all transfixed by the tumblers. It's a smell that promises good things, satisfaction, satiation, and it's easy to see how such a festival has survived so long; in the grip of such a smell it's possible to understand how important chestnuts were to a community facing a long freezing winter with meagre stores. With the weather turning heart-sinkingly cold and the days shortening, here were great piles of fire to recall the warmth of summer and armfuls of rich, soft nuts to help you put down a layer of insulating fat. Pigs and people preparing for winter.

Ed and I stroll from fire to fire. They're all more or less identical except for the man wielding the crank and the slight change in tone of the chestnuts rattling against the wire. There's an accordion playing jolly tunes, Beyoncé piping out equally cheerfully from one of the first-floor windows. Under the arcades, there's a makeshift bar, cobbled together from wooden trestle tables and a plastic awning; we wait in line for glasses of sweet wine. Then the bells toll the midday angelus, traditionally a call to prayer, but for now, today, a dinner gong: the first of the tumblers has been stopped and pulled back from the fire, the little 'window' in the wire opened. With a flick of the crank, the chestnuteer lines up the gap with a bucket and the blackened, crispy chestnuts pour out. There's a murmur of appreciation from the crowd, an inevitable movement forward towards the bucket, an expectation. We've been gathering chestnuts for weeks for Big Pig and Little Pig, putting handfuls aside for ourselves, bagging up boiled nuts for the freezer, slipping a couple on to the fire at the end of meals, but this is a crackling, smoky surfeit of chestnuts, a rite of gluttony, and we jostle with the crowds, as excited as everyone else, as eager for our share. Later in the afternoon, there's a meal in the *salle des fêtes*, five courses of chestnut dishes with dancing, but for us this is enough: we dip our hands into our carton of nuts, and with burning fingers begin to peel.

It's not yet perfect pig-killing weather – the daytime sunshine raises the temperature so that it's warm enough to sit outside for lunch, with a jumper on – but it's heading that way. White egrets arrive at the lake at the same time as our wood delivery arrives in the front yard. We spend two full days stacking the logs along the walls of the old barn, piling them neatly: good, dry oak logs. Fires are lit all over the neighbourhood, all burning the same *causse* oak; the air shimmers with the unmistakable musk of winter. Mornings are suddenly frosty; the garden ponds freeze lightly, trapping water lily leaves; some of the hens begin to moult, scattering feathers everywhere, becoming shy and grumpy and scraggy.

We want to kill the pigs close to the house – we'll need access to water and heat, tools, YouTube. We decide to fence off the vegetable patch at the end of the back garden and move the pigs there briefly, just for a week or so as we make the final preparations for the slaughter, long enough for them to clear and turn the land for us so that we won't have to dig it ourselves for the following year. There'll be plenty of buried seeds there left over from the summer, shoots, gnarly beetroot, thick overgrown clumps of chard and lettuce. Once again we begin to poke plastic stakes into the ground, unravel spools of wire. In the meantime, we also reduce the size of the enclosure in the woods, narrowing it at the sides, snipping off a few yards at the bottom, making it more difficult for the pigs to evade us at the far reaches. Big Pig and Little Pig potter alongside us snuffling, occasionally nudging. Their hair is growing dense again with the colder weather, filling up the ridge along their backs, thickening over their haunches and matting on their stomachs. We're getting towards the end of the 'finishing' period now, when the pigs' muscle should take on its final marbling and the last layers of fat are being laid. What they eat now will seep into the flavour of the meat: all those pears and acorns from the autumn will round out and deepen the taste; we're still feeding them extra chestnuts, rich, sweet, pungent. As we work our way round the enclosure, Big Pig wanders away, sniffing, finally plunging his nose into the soft loam at the base of an oak tree. He digs, throwing the soil from one side to another. Little Pig, inevitably, barges in to see what the attraction might be. They dig together diligently for some time, determined, energetic; we move away from them, post by post, winding the wire back on to its spool.

It's only later that we wonder about truffles. The oak woods of the *causse* are truffle country: the ugly, brown-black lumps, like dried dung, are on sale through the winter in the local markets, nestled in lined baskets, a prize. It's usually female pigs that are used to hunt for truffles – dogs are popular for this, too – but all pigs seem to love the lingering, earthy, mushroomy flavour. When we go back the next day, we're no longer absolutely sure which tree Big Pig stopped at but we take a guess and crouch among the depressions where the roots tangle close to the trunk. We've never come close to finding a truffle before; we have no idea what we're looking for, but we search anyway, rather half-heartedly, throwing aside the leaves and scraping through the soil. Bits of twig; stones; more leaves. There's nothing out of the ordinary. We soon give up the quest. But we wonder, nonetheless, if the pigs have been feasting. Pigs finished on truffles: that would be fine meat.

As we work, stumbling through the woods and rifling for truffles, we talk, inevitably, about our plans. This is our last chance to change our minds. If we're going to kill the pigs ourselves, at home, then we have to be sure; we have to know we're doing the right thing. It's obviously not something we can back out of halfway through. And we're nearly sure. Nearly. But just now, almost at the end, there are doubts, niggles of uncertainty. Even Ed, after so many months of confidence, begins to hesitate. Have we made a mistake? We run through everything for the final time and we reconsider the alternative: should we think again about sending Big Pig and Little Pig to the abattoir? Are we absolutely certain we want to kill them at all?

Confronting the realities of what goes on in an abattoir, even a good abattoir, is not easy. We don't want to think about terrified animals, poked and prodded, herded, gassed, hung, bled; the noise of the machines clattering; the cold, wet, bloody environment; the concrete, the metal. This is not the intimate, almost sacrificial death of a pig at home. This is efficiency, industrialization, distance. When abattoirs started to take over from home killings at the beginning of the twentieth century people didn't quite know what to make of this new system: the French belle-époque postcards that had once shown photos of happy families posing with their pigs in their arms now focused on the huge bleak slaughterhouses. They featured walls, gates, guards suggestive of prisons; one card, from 1905, entitled 'Lyon-vaise. The bleeding of pigs' shows a high-ceilinged concrete barn with tiny windows and harsh electric light, rows of pig carcasses on either side dripping blood, and the workers standing to attention in the middle of the room, doing nothing. Everything is seen at a distance; the workers are tiny, no more significant than the hoists and vats; the view is orderly, inhuman.

One of our neighbours has a cousin who works at the local abattoir, and by chance he's at the house when we call by. We don't ask him specifically about our pigs, but we show interest in his work. He's a fat, unreflective man who doesn't like to talk. He doesn't tell us, he perhaps can't tell us, about what he does every day but he says bluntly that he hates his job, the cold mostly, and the discomfort, the smells and noise and dirt. It's a factory job like most other factory jobs: boring, monotonous, repetitive. We struggle to hold a conversation. He shrugs a great deal.

There's nothing essentially wrong with a small, well-run abattoir like the one we have in our town. It's an efficient, clean way of turning live animals into meat for sale. Most pigs have to go to an abattoir. There's no alternative. But for us there is an alternative, a choice. We want the pigs to have a good death; we want to honour them in this. We want to avoid fear or confusion, unnecessary delay. It makes sense, then, to go ahead with our original plans and kill them at home. So why are we hesitating?

The days are short now, the sun hardly rising above the tall trees in front of the house. In the enclosure, leaves fall fast to cover the last of the acorns; sharp morning frost silvers the meadow and the pigs hunker low in the straw. We set a date for the slaughter. Assuming the weather's cold enough, we'll do it in a few weeks' time: mid-December. We've got visitors coming for Christmas and don't want to confront them with the sight of dead pigs. But if we stick to the timetable, that would give us enough time to kill the pigs, do all the butchering, pack away the meat and clear up. Cover our traces. As if nothing has happened.

We no longer bother to 'weigh' the pigs with our trusty piece of string. There doesn't seem much point. They're fully fattened, hefty; we can see by looking at them that there's going to be plenty of carcass weight. Their graphs have each reached an impressive summit at around 170kg – Little Pig's red line an Alpine ridge below Big Pig's – and the only important measure now is one of freezer space. They're probably still putting on slow growth, little by little, but winter feeding will have slowed this down and it doesn't seem to matter like it once did. It's hard to contemplate them continuing to grow and preparing to die, at the same time; if they're maturing still, developing, then there's life in them, potential, unfinished business. It might make death seem untimely.

We begin to amass the equipment we need. We've got our hands on a captive bolt which operates on compressed air to stun an animal before slaughter. It looks disturbingly like a gun, some kind of police handgun from American cop films. It's black, weighty, glossy; a serious weapon. But when you pull the trigger it thrusts a metal bar from the barrel instead of shooting bullets. The bar whops the animal in the forehead and instantly fells it. From the same man, a local farmer, we've also managed to borrow two lengths of heavy chain, each with a pulley. Bring them back clean, he says; if there's any rust on them they're as good as useless. Finally, Jean-Claude solves the problem of how to hang the carcasses. He takes us round the back of his barn. Leaning against the wall are racks of scaffolding. There are six or eight pieces, which would form a block tall enough to loop the chain about eight feet above the ground and winch up the pigs. The scaffolding is old and rickety but seems sound enough. We load it precariously into the back of the car to carry it the short journey home, the open boot spewing rusty metal poles like a mouth full of Twiglets. Over the following days we fit together a basic tower alongside the woodshed, out of sight of the road, hidden. We try out the chains. A scaffold. Hanging. Death.

I spend half a day constructing a shelter on the vegetable patch. I rake over the old stalks, pull out the last tendrils of the pumpkin plants and level out an area for the straw. I don't take a great deal of care with it; I don't bother taking apart the current shelter for materials, making do instead with what I find around the house, some plastic sheeting, planks. Even propped against the stone wall it has a precarious air, but it doesn't have to last. The pigs won't be there long.

I collect an old upright freezer from a couple up the road. They have a new model, and offered us this cast-off for free. It takes a lot of puffing and heaving to get it into the back of the car and even more to unload it at the other end. It's immediately clear why they wanted to get rid of it: it rattles and groans when I plug it in, its motor going full tilt into the night, devouring electricity like Pac-Man on speed.

Good, then. Ready. We move the pigs for the last time. It's a fine crisp morning, frost lying in the shadows and the sun slanting low and pale over the ridge at La Graudie. The woods sigh out a thin mist; below, in the valley, light and shade criss-cross the fields around the stream, making them uncertain, unsteady. Jean-Claude has a bonfire, wispy and slight; the dribble of smoke seems melancholy. Everything seems melancholy. There's a sense of parting, of rupture.

But that's all in my head, of course. The pigs charge towards me, entirely un-melancholy. I drop the wire from two of the posts near the ash tree and immediately Big Pig is striding out of the enclosure, head high, snout twitching; Little Pig passes him, runs ahead. They're eager, excited. There's none of the wariness of the first move; there's no fear in crossing the line of the fence. They want to be out and about. The chance to explore is a thrill.

It's all I can do to keep up with them, rattling the bucket. But they're not much interested in my stash of grain and chestnuts, nor even in what's on offer on the verges and in the hedges. They browse the winter pickings nonchalantly, more curious about the experience than the food. We progress at a brisk trot. They know they're going somewhere; that's enough. Big Pig hardly pauses, falling into a steady pace; Little Pig can't help being distracted sometimes but catches up, follows. And so we go: the path from La Graudie, the left turn on to the lane, past the stone cross that marks the track to the Mas de Maury. Do they pause here? Remember? If they do, it's fleeting.

There's a long stretch of lane from here to Solange's farm, uphill, bending, thick hawthorn hedges on one side and open fields on the other. This is new territory. After a moment, Big Pig stops to sniff, holds his head still to listen; he seems satisfied that everything's as it should be, and we go on. The procession is more intermittent now. I have to haul Little Pig from the ditch by stuffing the bucket under his nose. Big Pig tacks across the lane right on the bend, his trotters clipping on the worn tarmac, and I have to call him back towards the verge. Just before the entrance to Solange's farm, they both slow, linger: they seem weary. It's a long walk on new ground for fattened pigs.

Solange hears us as we pass, straightens from her work in the garden, waves. I wave back. There's only a field's length to go now, and then we'll be off the lane, safe from any traffic. There's the rumble of a tractor somewhere, but distant. We're progressing more slowly. Big Pig has his nose close to the bucket which swings at my side; Little Pig is dawdling, dropping back. He has his eyes to the ground, his ears flopping over. Even the puff of floury dust as I shake the grain hardly causes him to lift his head. This is quite different to the sharp, clippity-clip pace of the spring walk when we brought the young pigs to La Graudie. It's not only more pedestrian, but somehow, too, more solemn. It's the beginning of an ending, after all. It's shadowed by the knowledge of loss to come: a parting from Big Pig and Little Pig; perhaps, in a year or so, the leaving of this place and this life. It's not a sad walk – surely a walk with pigs can never really be sad – but it's a sedate, thoughtful one.

We've taken down some of the wooden railings that surround the back garden so that the pigs can come straight through from the lane. We cross the grass close to the pond. Mo is standing at the ground-floor window of the house; he starts barking as soon as he sees us. Both pigs respond to this: they're looking round for their friend, sniffing hard, suddenly curious again. They cut away across the open ground, heading towards the house. Little Pig makes it as far as the gravelly terrace but is confounded by the odd surface and the abrupt proximity of high walls; he continues to listen out for Mo, but from a standstill, and when I go to him and place my hand on his neck, he turns with me and allows me to draw him back on to the grass where Big Pig has begun to graze.

When I close the fence around their new enclosure, the pigs stare at me in disbelief. Is that it? Is the outing over? What are they doing here? They plant themselves resolutely at the wire, unmoving. I step over and walk behind them to the shelter, talk to them, pull out some straw and show them the feeding trough, but their protest continues.

They're not used to such a small space, nor to such openness. There's the protection from the wall, but no trees of any size and certainly nothing like the sloping woods at La Graudie. I get the distinct impression that they're disgruntled. They want to go home.

Almost as soon as we move the pigs to the garden, the rain begins. I can't remember it raining ever before for any length of time in December; December is cold, bright, clear. Always. But this, quite clearly, is rain.

It means a delay to our plans. We can't kill pigs in this. There's good reason why stories and pictures of slaughter day tend to be snowy, frosty at least: traditionally, as for us, the task required the natural refrigeration of the coldest weather, since if temperatures were too high the meat would not chill properly, and there wouldn't be enough time for processing hams and bacon and sausages. Pig-killing days were the dark, bitter, short days of midwinter. Look, for example, at *Winter Scene with a Man Killing a Pig*, painted in the middle of the seventeenth century by David Teniers the Younger. The killing is going on almost out of sight in the bottom left-hand corner of the painting, the animal obscured by the gathering of the extended family. The focus is on the freezing dusk: snow lying thickly on the village and fields, and more promised by the ominous clouds; the pond iced up so completely that boys are skating on it. The houses are dark: there is no flicker of a fire (although thick smoke pours from the chimney), nothing comforting; the palette is cool, the landscape stretching away greyly to the bare distance. This is winter at its harshest, when signs of spring are a long way off and every daily chore is made harder by cold hands.

The tough, dirty, meticulous work of processing pig meat was more taxing in cold weather – it demands dexterity and energy and stamina, all easily drained by freezing temperatures – but the celebration which followed was, like other seasonal feasts, a bright moment in the bleak monotony of midwinter: here was the anticipation brought on by the smell of meat cooking; the joy of a job well done; the comfort of knowing you would not starve this year. But we're edging towards Christmas. At this rate, our pig-killing feast threatens to crash into Christmas lunch. We watch the rain disconsolately as it puddles on the grass and fills the pond to overflowing. The hens congregate under the table-tennis table and sulk. I walk with Mo down to the Mas de Maury and find the well there gushing over, the water running in quick rivulets down to the lake, a pair of mallards paddling on the path. Not pig-killing weather, not at all.

Big Pig and Little Pig make the most of their new pen. They find sunflower seeds in abundance, pumpkin seeds, roots, wintry stalks. But in such a small space, with two grown pigs trampling and rummaging and the rain steadily falling, the clay soil of the vegetable patch quickly becomes mud. A lot of mud. Thick, heavy mud. There are soon pits and hollows around the shelter that fill with water, unintended wallows. Along the perimeter where the pigs loiter, hopeful, there is a slosh of sticky ground. Plant roots hold the soil firm in places, but the pigs are eating these, or digging through them, and bit by bit the entire area gives way to mire. When I step over the electric fence my wellies sink immediately; the clay holds them so tightly that I'm thoroughly stuck. It's takes a great deal of yanking to pull myself free with a slurp, only to get stuck again as I go forward. For the pigs, the problem is the same. Their trotters slide deep into the mud. They move heavily, with great effort, sucked into the ground at every step. They're accustomed to the friable dry soil of the woods, running up the slope, moving freely. This glutinous mess is a misery.

There's nowhere solid to put the food trough. The bedding straw is damp. The shelter lurches under the weight of water. The fence posts skew in the mud. We can't keep the pigs here much longer in these conditions, but while it's raining we can't kill them either. We'll have to wait. We watch the weather forecast anxiously. Will it turn colder? Soon? Little Pig glares at me accusingly, mired up to his knees. Just beyond the pen, the grassy garden must look like a haven of firmer ground and grazing, but this is death row now, there are no concessions. The pigs remain in the mud.

And just as the rain eases and the temperature drops, a chill wind bringing crisp air from the mountains, a packet of knives arrives in the post. There's a small weighty cleaver and a clever butcher's knife with a slight blade, turned up at the end, for delicate work. Both are so sharp that even resting them gently against my hand lifts away a light sliver of skin. There's a longer knife with a wider blade, a kitchen knife, for basic work on cutting up joints. And then there's the knife we'll use to kill the pigs. When I take it from its box I'm astounded by its size and weight: it has a long, heavy blade, at least twice as long as a kitchen knife. It's bulky, unwieldy. When I try it out, it swishes through the air. It is, as far as I can see, a sword.

The size of the knife brings home the size of the task. A big knife to kill a big animal. A weapon of power: accurate, brutal. I have never wielded such a knife, never had any need to. It's too big to carve a Sunday joint or slice a pumpkin or cut through rhubarb stalks. I replace it in its box, afraid of it.

Lives moving towards deaths; stories working towards conclusions. Narratives playing out, inevitably. The pigs, of course, know none of this. They're not interested. They heave through the mud, sticky pigs, the clay coating their hair thickly, like a beauty treatment of some sort. I can't see them from the house but I can hear them, grumbling, tussling, not able to settle under these new conditions where every step is an insult. Do they wonder why their luck has changed? Do they have some kind of animal presentiment of where it all might lead?

But perhaps there's a happy ending. It's not impossible. We all like happy endings, after all. And for the first black pig of our tale, Nicholson's pig, things are looking up. Just when I'd lost all trace of him, when he'd disappeared from sight and must be presumed bacon, I find a report from a London newspaper which brings him back into the spotlight. January 1787: 'the Learned Pig of Charing Cross is one of the rarer monsters of France,' it declares delightedly. 'It has fed its owners fat through Calais, Boulogne, Montreuil, &c., &c.' For a moment I'm taken aback by this unexpected expansion of the pig's horizons. A metropolitan career seems one thing, but an international one quite another. I check again. But it seems true enough. A British pig in France. On the eve of revolution, at the very moment English frigates are fighting French ships off the coast of Brittany, our performing black pig has crossed the Channel in search of new admirers. I can't find any accounts of how he got there; I can only imagine the discomfort of the crossing, the waist-coated pig back on a boat in a January swell, but there's no doubt that he's here all right, being 'fed fat' by new audiences, spelling out strange words in an entirely new language, telling French time, counting *francs* and *sous*.

I read more, astounded by the bravado of the pig's timing. Nicholson perhaps thinks himself above, or below, political matters: he perhaps does not care for talk of war. He's making money from the pig, and that might seem enough. But whether he likes it or not – whether he knows it or not – revolutionary politics is fanning the flames of stardom. By the later 1780s, there's an edginess to life in France, discontent and uncertainty, anger. Much of the anger is directed at first at the Queen, Marie-Antoinette, but in time it's the King himself who becomes the focus of popular fury, and how better to bring the godlike Louis XVI down to earth than to reimagine him as a pig? In the years running up to his execution in January 1793 thousands of caricatures appeared showing Louis as a pig, or some-times as a hybrid monster, half man and half hog. Deformed. Bestial. The cartoons revelled in the very worst of 'pigness', emphasizing dirt and squalor, showing the Louis-pig defecating, wallowing, vomit-ing. The aim was to make him grotesque and despicable. A popular stamp, for example, showed him crawling along through the sewer of royal life while being defecated on from above. The once sacred body of the King was being roundly rejected, trashed. Pig pamphlets, pig cartoons, pig prints, pig stamps: pigs everywhere, and loaded with meaning, a visible expression of revolution.

How timely, then, for our black pig to embark on a French career. 'Calais, Boulogne, Montreuil, &c., &c.' say the papers. This is a well-trodden route, the same route taken by Arthur Young, an agriculturalist whose travel writing became enormously popular for its social and political observations. His first visit to France, like the pig's, was in 1787 and the news reports seem to have enjoyed the idea that the learned writer and the learned pig tracked each other, road for road, from Calais to Boulogne to Montreuil. But I'm struck by the way these accounts seem to fade away without conclusion, drifting into a vague &c., &c. Etc., etc.: leaving us to fill the gaps. In fact, the London journalists are being shy. Many English men and women are fearful of the French, terrified in case the taste for revolution finds its way across the Channel, eager to keep a distance, and the papers don't want to turn popular opinion against their favourite pig. So they're careful to suggest that the pig is dawdling in the coastal towns of Normandy, perhaps taking some sea air, hugging close to his British roots in a landscape which Young praises for 'strongly resembling England'. But Montreuil is only a few kilometres from the centre of Paris. And so, &c., &c., what the papers are glossing over is that Nicholson and his pig are progressing to the heart of things, to the seat of power both royal and revolutionary. In a January of unrest, of wintry discontent and tense grumblings, the performing pig is making a name for himself in the capital. Is he pandering to the perfumed elite or rousing the revolutionaries? It's likely that at this time his audience is a strange mix of the rich and the raucous, as it had been in London, and of course, you can't start a revolution with an itinerant pig – but I'm fascinated by the knowledge that shortly after our Learned Pig's successful performances, pictures of Louis begin to appear as a hairy black pig. An erudite pig and a pig-king, both entertaining the crowds.

By summer of 1787, Nicholson has brought his pig back to Britain. They tour again: Retford, Newark, Lincoln, Stamford. They make a foray into Scotland, performing to great acclaim at the Grassmarket in Edinburgh. The pig, the papers claim, has made more money in its distinguished career than any of the period's most acclaimed actors or actresses; it's a genuine star, welcome everywhere, fêted, fawned upon, loved. A national treasure, perhaps. But by the end of 1788, the picture begins to look bleak again. The pig loses his grip on the headlines, fades in and out like a Cheshire-cat grin, and in November, the bad news finally comes: worn out by its labours, the pig has died. Old black pig. Too decrepit and weary. I find several reports of the pig's death and, worse still, perhaps, one of the papers notes that Nicholson, too, has succumbed to the effect of his heroic endeavours and has been shut away in an Edinburgh asylum to end his days with the insane: 'Too much learning, we suppose, had driven the pig mad, and so he bit his master.'

But can that be it? The reports seem strange to me, and confused. Has the pig died, or gone mad? Why would Nicholson be confined as a lunatic just for being bitten by his star performer? Or has the pig, finally fed up, attacked Nicholson and paid the price for its pique? I root around for more information, for something more, a happy ending. Perhaps because I know it's the last days for Big Pig and Little Pig, pacing the squelchy pen until the weather turns cold, I'm unwilling to leave the story unfinished. I've followed this dapper eighteenth-century pig, this fashionable phenomenon, from Belfast to Dublin, across the sea to Chester, over the Pennines to Scarborough, to country fair and city theatre, to revolutionary France and back again; I've seen Bisset killed in defence of his pig and Nicholson revelling in riches. I can't leave it here, uncertain and sad. There must be more.

With my own pigs' story dwindling to a close like a dark December afternoon, I'm increasingly desperate to keep this one going. I want just a hint of life, a glimpse of a future. And at last, in a batch of old news reports, here it is. A year after its supposed death and Nicholson's incarceration in an Edinburgh madhouse, the Learned Pig makes the papers again. Alive. A number of accounts in October and November 1789 agree that the pig is topping the bill in Hereford, Monmouth and Abergavenny, performing as well as ever on a journey along the Welsh–English border – on his return from an arduous tour of France. Not dead, then, not mad, but, in the summer of 1789, back with the French: 'from his frequent interviews with the French patriots, he is almost enabled to hold a discourse upon the Feudal System, the Rights of Kings and the Destruction of the Bastille,' one newspaper claims. July 1789: the fall of the Bastille, one of the most iconic moments of European history. I feel an odd buzz of excitement. Can it be true that Nicholson and his pig were counting cards in a French theatre at the moment the Paris fortress fell to the crowd?

There seems little doubt that it's the same pig. If something had really happened to the original black pig, back in Edinburgh, at the end of the previous year, Nicholson would not have had time to train another to take its place. Besides, the papers are adamant that this is the one and only Learned Pig that for four years or more has 'afforded such amusement in most parts of England'. They've followed his story this far every step of the way, like diligent drovers, and they probably know the unforgettable wise pig when they see it. It seems certain that it's our black pig back from the dead and, better still, tangled up with one of the great events of revolution. There will, in time, be other performing pigs. There will be imitators and successors, more sapient hogs, more ambitious owners, more attention and controversy. But this, for now, is the original pig, Bisset's pig, sagely bringing out its tricks in a France of crisis and insurrection.

After this, there are no more reports. After a balmy autumn in the Welsh Marches, the pig finally disappears. But this seems to me like a good enough place for him to end. I'm content with this. I imagine the old black pig picking its way through rural France during a season of riots and unrest, making its final appearances in Paris during a summer frenzy of protest, standing onstage with its worn-out antics while the world reconfigures about it. The usual audiences falling away; new ones taking their place. Everyone drawn in, everyone fascinated by a pig that can read minds from a set of alphabet cards even when the city is a place of violence and chaos. What a highpoint on which to finish; what a long and gruelling journey; what a remarkable expedition for a pig. It seems only right that a quiet walk in the Welsh hills should follow, a return to ancient drovers' paths, to peaceful lanes and untroubled country crowds. The poor, weary, old pig has been performing for over five years; it's been attacked, whipped, prodded, shouted at and harassed; it's been hot and baffled and thin. Can it have a happy ending? Is this one: a stroll through the cool shadows of a Welsh market town? Will this do?

It will have to. It's the best I can manage. And for good measure, there's even a romantic postscript. Some time after first reading about the black pig and his adventures, I come across a marriage notice for the parish of Banbury, in Cheshire, in 1812. It's no more than a sentence, just an ordinary note on the routine list of parish business for the year. But it catches my eye: it's a name I know. My black-pig story has a twist in the tail. Here, tucked away among baptisms and deaths, is proof of a wedding, a celebration: 'At Banbury, Mr John Nicholson, 89, proprietor of the well-known learned pig, to Miss Eliz. Smith of Malpas-hill, 23.' So, a young bride for an old man who's been made very rich by a pig, and the traditional conclusion to all good stories: a marriage. A happy-ever-after?

5.

A winter night. Cold fizzing in the air. Stars, lots of stars, but still thoroughly dark; a broad, bitter silence.

Tomorrow is the day. For now I can't sleep.

Ed and I go over the plans, one more time. To do this properly we have to be sure, unblinking, and we are: we're prepared; primed. There's no place for doubts or second thoughts – that would only unnerve us and unsteady our hands.

Ed is quiet, organized. And me? My squeamishness, my hesitation, my fears? In the dark of the night they've slunk away to hide. I don't allow myself to visit old memories, to unearth old piggy joys. I feel as though I've grown a shell. I test it, tentatively, tappity-tap, as if looking for a patch of hollow wall beneath a plaster veneer: I imagine snippets of the slaughter, form speculative gory pictures in my mind, sneak a look at them – and sure enough, it all bounces off and I'm intact inside my defences, calm and collected, untraumatized. That's all right, then. *I'm* all right, the soft part of me hidden away, protected. I'm ready. I can do this.

Now it's come to it, we're keen to get on. We bustle. It's still night, still dark, but it seems important to be doing something. And amidst all the activity there remains a taunting, uneasy dread. Our fear is not that we won't or can't kill the pigs, not now. What we're afraid of is that we'll do something wrong. The point of this home slaughter is that Big Pig and Little Pig are assured a humane end, but if we mess up somehow then it could be worse than any factory death: frantic, painful, slow. Ed takes the killing knife from the box and practises: a long thrust forward, a turn of the blade, a brisk, upward flick. He does it again, and again, a sword exercise. I watch the clean lines cut in the chilly air, the repetition mesmeric. I watch it without emotion, the knife click-clacking against my crisp, impenetrable shell; watch it as nothing more than a show of dexterity, although I know that with those fluid movements we need to sever all the major blood vessels around the heart, the carotid arteries and the jugular vein, slicing the animal's life into pieces so that it dies quickly without any risk of it regaining consciousness or suffering in any way. I know, too, that stabbing a live, moving pig with such accuracy is not an easy task. It's nothing like as effortless as the deft flick of the knife suggests – which is why the village pig-killer was traditionally so respected, of course; in the mass of dense muscle packed into a pig's body it's not easy to be sure exactly where the knife is. It's like slicing a grape in a bowl of treacle, blindfolded.

Big Pig and Little Pig in the dappled dawn. They stir from their shelter as they hear us approach, greet us as usual with soft grunts. Mo scampers ahead of us; a small family of deer – a buck and two does – skips across the bottom of the garden and bounces over the adjacent field in a bob of white bottoms. The pigs heave through the mud to meet Mo at the wire. They stand with him, nose to nose, offering a sniffly 'good morning'. Then Mo slips away and the pigs focus their attention on us, expectant. But we don't feed them. There's no last meal. Instead they're on a fast, water only, so that their stomachs and intestines will be reasonably empty when we kill them. One of them – whichever is left behind – can have a meal later, to tide him over until his time comes. But for now they must both stay hungry.

They don't understand this, of course; they're indignant at the lack of breakfast and the change to routine. Little Pig chews at the top of my wellies, in hunger or protest; Big Pig seems to think he must be mistaken: surely there must be food. He checks behind us for evidence of a bucket, sniffs hard, snout high, wades a step or two through the gloopy mud to make sure there's no telltale tub on the other side of the fence. He slurps back, ruffles through my pockets and then, finally convinced, raises his head and glares at me. The long summer of pears and pumpkins and acorns and chestnuts tumbling down the slope in the woods, abundant, juicy, a game, has come to this last morning: a hungry dawn of hard frost, the cold grip of mud, disappointment. We do our best to settle them and to ease their discontent – we talk to them and scratch the tufts of hair between their ears; I tickle Little Pig on the tummy as he likes – but perhaps they sense our nervousness, because they soon slink away.

Which one, then? Which one first? We reckon we can kill one pig today and butcher it tomorrow morning, then kill the other pig and finish butchering it the following day if need be. Three days in all. If we stick to that timetable we'll be neatly finished a few days before Christmas, with time to collect visitors from the airport, hang tinsel and baubles, bake mince pies. Because of the mild rainy weather we've been forced to wait longer than we'd hoped – we hadn't meant to run this close to the festivities – but we can just press on with the slaughtering, back to back. And we've got an early start. So now all we need to decide is which pig to begin with. Which one first?

We choose Big Pig. No particular reason. Random fate, perhaps – and a nagging sense that his more placid nature will help us do this calmly, this first time. He's also closer to us, which decides it. Little Pig has gone off behind the shelter; it's Big Pig who's stuck at our side and it's this, in the end, this proximity – or loyalty – which settles it for him. I take a piece of white chalk from my pocket and mark a cross on his forehead, smack in the middle. A dusty white cross on a dusty black pig. Then we go in for breakfast.

It's a bright day, as the coldest days are. The sun rises in a smear of reds and oranges, the frost hard and white on the trees and fields, the sky hard and blue. When we've eaten (what do we eat? I can't remember) we check the equipment again – the knives, the captive bolt, the scaffold, the chains – and stride out across the grass, crunching the ice underfoot. The cold and the damp-wood smell of winter and the unmistakable twitter of my excitement shut down thought. This is physical now, sensual; nothing else.

Is there doubt now? Right at the very end? If there is, I can't feel it: I'm tucked down in my shell.

I distract Little Pig with a handful of old chestnuts, letting him snuffle for them in my pocket, drawing him away towards the wall, heaving through the mire so that Ed can drop one of the fence posts and let the wire fall. He has a bucket of grain. Big Pig, hungry, doesn't bother with me and Little Pig at the back of the pen, hardly glances at the collapsed fence, just pulls himself through the last few feet of mud towards the food. I let the nuts fall for Little Pig and squelch back as fast as I can to reconnect the fence. One pig in, one pig out.

There's a surprise now. Big Pig moves out across the grass, takes a few steps towards the middle of the lawn, pauses – and then gambols. Liberated from the horrible heavy mud that's held him tight for days, his feet and legs suddenly light again and his body free, he gambols. Out over the crisp grass, a dance of sorts, clumsy but sprightly too, trotters flailing, head bobbing. I've never seen this before. I've seen the pigs scamper and shove, run and skip, but not this, this romp. It looks like happiness. He circles, cavorts. He's forgotten the grain for the moment; forgotten everything but this agility and weightlessness. He prances like a show pony; his ears flap, his tail twirls. In the early light he steps out a gavotte, a big old pig about to die and dancing.

It takes us a minute or two to attract his attention. We rattle the bucket, call, flap our hands at him. Eventually he calms and is more the Big Pig we know, stately, imperturbable. He stands still again – I wouldn't be surprised if he's out of breath – and in this more usual pig state he remembers his hunger; he's pleased now by the scent of food, another pleasure, and after a moment he comes hurrying for the bucket. I let him bury his head in the grain, so that I can be sure of him, and then I lead him a few yards to the sheltered dip of land alongside the woodshed. He shuffles against me, grunts contentedly and puffs flour through his nose, snorting it in a cloud into the cold air.

I empty the grain in a soft pile on the ground. Big Pig leans forward, his head down, his snout low to the ground. He's motionless, for a brief second or two, while he eats. This is the moment. Quick now; this is it. The chalky white cross. Ed stands up close to Big Pig's head, steady, feet apart. Big Pig takes no notice of us. He's snuffling through the grain. I watch him eating; I watch the flop of his ears and the gentle roll of thick hairy skin at the neck, but out of the corner of my eye I can see Ed, too, gathering himself, and the minute seems to stretch on, everything brilliantly clear, suspended in the winter morning.

Aim. Ed presses the pistol end to the chalk cross.

Fire. He shoots the bolt.

Big Pig falls. He just keels over heavily on his side without a sound and lies completely still.

The recoil from the bolt surprises Ed, catching him hard in the shoulder; he staggers backwards, pained. But there's no time for this. The bruises can come later. We have to carry on, now, while the pig is out cold. We have to keep our wits about us and act promptly.

There it is, the sword. Ed picks it up and flexes his arm. I don't see him hesitate. 'Hold the legs,' he says. I hold the legs, gripping hard just above the trotters, and he pushes the knife through the skin at the base of the neck, just above the dent of the breastbone. He drives in deep and jiggles the blade as he's practised, dropping the handle so that the knife rises.

Blood streams from the wound. Hot, deep red. It floods through the frost, melting the ice, sinking into the earth. And the pig kicks. Convulses hard. Thrashes like a live beast. I'm not expecting this. I expected death to be motionless, I suppose, serene perhaps, a quiet slipping away. But this is frantic, as though Big Pig has woken at the last moment and is battling to save himself, flailing against oblivion. I think I cry out; I certainly recoil and let go of the legs and they flail uncontrollably, catching me several blows in the stomach and arms.

The convulsions ease. Slow. It's a shudder, a twitch. Then nothing.

I've watched an animal die for the first time. It was alive and then I killed it. Inside my shell, I think I hear part of me screaming.

'He didn't come back, he didn't feel it; that wasn't him, was it, waking up?' I throw my anxieties at Ed who mops them up.

He appears calm, certain: 'It was involuntary. He didn't feel it.' Ed has done it all correctly, the stunning, the sticking, keeping his nerve when I lost mine to the thrash of death throes.

'So the last thing he knew, then, was being out in the grass and getting grain – being happy?' I ask this question several times, and afterwards I think about it a great deal. I believe it's true: Big Pig's final minutes were content, free of anxiety, even joyous. It was a good death, the kind we'd planned for. I think of him dancing across the grass, his last moments filled with pleasure, animal pleasure in food and freedom, and I'm pleased we went through with this, with killing him here at home.

Ed stands back, rubbing at the ache from the captive bolt, the knife beside him on the ground. He watches the blood seep away. 'We should have saved that,' he says mournfully. 'It's a waste.'

Take a breath. It will be a little while until the blood drains through. There's nothing to be done. It's quiet, calm. The pig's wound steams in the cold. In the bare trees alongside us, pigeons flap for a moment, like plastic bags caught in a breeze. That's all.

We've elected to do this alone. Paintings like Teniers' *Winter Scene*, accounts from the past, snippets from nostalgic literature like *Lark Rise to Candleford*, the stories told to us by Jean-Claude or Solange – they all agree that this is a job for a family, a team: friends and neighbours working together. But there's just the two of us, hidden from sight behind the wood store with a dead pig. And when we come to try to move the carcass, we suddenly realize what we've taken on. This thing, this dead weight, is massively heavy. We take it by the hind legs, one leg each, and attempt to drag it the short distance to the scaffolding frame and the pulleys, but it hardly shifts. A warm, black stone, immovable. We try again; heave. But in the end all we can do is slide the body round and roll it slightly so that it has its back to the frame, edging it forward just far enough so that the chains can reach it.

There are two big metal hooks on the end of the chains. We have to slide these through the hind legs, just above the trotters, right through from one side to the other, hooking them round small bones and sturdy tendons, making sure they'll hold and not just rip straight out. It feels like unnecessary violence. I remember a lesson from school, a long time ago: *how was it, Miss, that Jesus didn't just slide off the cross? How come the nails were strong enough to keep him hanging there?*

The hooks have strong sharp points. They push through the legs with surprising ease, like driving tent pegs into soft ground. We take out the slack in the chains and begin to winch. It's clanking, mechanical; it seems more to do with fixing cars or loading trailers than animal husbandry. But the pig carcass moves, sliding steadily through its own blood, feet first across the crimson-frost grass, its bare grey stomach skywards as it inches towards the sheltered leafy ground that supports the frame. We winch rhythmically, one of us on either side.

Wait. Ed calls. We stop. There's a thick metal pole across the top of the scaffolding tower which holds the structure tight and to which the winches are attached. It's begun to buckle under the strain. There's a disconcerting curve, a sly smile, in what had been a perfectly straight bar. We stare at such evidence of pig weight, not quite believing, and unwind the chains a foot or two to loosen them; the carcass slides back down on to the ground. We climb up to examine the scaffold. Even without the load, the top pole remains bent. Prod. Sigh.

We're acutely aware of the potential physical dangers of what we're doing. Knives; thrashing animals; heavy lifting; boiling water; slippery ground. We'd whispered to each other in the dark of the night: 'Be careful; above all, be careful.' But this is a new threat: the collapse of a scaffolding tower along with 170kg of animal as we work below. What a way to go, crushed by a dead pig. We don't want to take the risk. We decide we can't go on. So we unhook the carcass from the chains and there it is, again, flopped.

Well, then, it doesn't matter. It's not important. We'll get on with taking off the bristles. That's the first job, anyway, and it can be done just as well here on the ground, surely. How hard can it be? In 1911, Beatrix Potter reminisced with pleasure about her early experiences of scraping 'the smiling countenance of my own grandmother's deceased pig, with scalding water and the sharp edged bottom of a brass candle-stick'. The author who encouraged us to fall in love with Peter Rabbit and Mrs Tiggy-Winkle was matter-of-fact when it came to the practicalities of country living and believed that shaving a carcass was good family entertainment. Protesting against legislation which aimed to prevent children taking part in the slaughter process, she was disgusted: 'The present generation is being reared upon tea – and slops,' she huffed. So, then, all it needs is an old candle-stick and a kettle; child's play.

Because we're short of a scalding tub, and it's a long way from the scaffold behind the wood store back to the house to a source of boiling water, we've actually eschewed candlesticks and the like, and decided instead on a modern method of stripping the hairs. The shops sell a powdery white concoction that claims to make it simple to pluck the feathers from fowl and the bristles from pigs. You mix it with water and paste it on, like a beauty mask, and – *swish* – a quick pass of an old wallpaper scraper, and off come the hairs. The packet shows a smiling old woman holding up a perfectly plucked goose; there's no sign of a shorn pig, but the message is clear: a tiresome chore made swift and simple.

Winter-thick, wild black bristles. A dense, outdoor-pig coat. We slap the gunk on to one of the pig's flanks and we scrape. Nothing much happens. There's a nasty chemical smell, and some of the hairs break; there's a sludge of them attached to the scraper, it's true, but after ten minutes or more of energetic work the coat looks much the same as ever, only more scraggy and matted. Here and there we can see patches of elephant-grey skin, but nowhere have the hairs fully lifted. It's an ugly mess. Perhaps with a nice, sleek pink pig, raised indoors so that its coat is thin, the gloop might be enough to do the job, but this just looks as though Little Pig has nipped out mouthfuls of bristles in a scrap. It won't do.

We chuck away the powder, cursing the unnecessary expenditure and the delay. The morning is already advancing more quickly than we'd imagined and we've not managed either to hang the carcass or even to begin stripping the hairs. Today is the winter solstice, the old-fashioned St Lucy's Day of John Donne's poem that 'scarce seven hours herself unmasks'. We need to get a move on.

Ed lights the blowtorch. It hisses and spits. We've been warned against such a brutal attack on the bristles in case we scorch the skin or, worse still, the flesh beneath. We don't want to raise the temperature of the carcass, obviously, and we don't want to damage the meat. But it's only a small blowtorch, not unlike the kind chefs use, and we're hopeful it might speed things up. We let the blue flame steady and then swipe it back and forth over a section of the rear leg: a bony, hairy bit close to the knee; a trial run.

But pig bristles, it turns out, are not crème brûlée. Our poor specimen of a blowtorch is not up to the job. There's a bitter stink of burning hair as the ends of the bristles brown and melt, but we're left with long obstinate stubs spiking from the skin which discolours and singes. We work on the patch of carcass for a while, just in case there's a technique to it and everything comes right in the end, but it's just smelly, messy, unsatisfying. At this point in the day we still have a vision of clean, smooth pigskin and a neatly stripped carcass, and this isn't it.

And so we're left with scalding. The traditional option; Beatrix Potter's delight. But for this to work in loosening the hairs, the water has to be as close to boiling as possible, and in such freezing temperatures and with the house a hundred metres or more away, this poses a logistical problem. We set big pans of water to simmer on the cooker in the kitchen, and organize a rudimentary shuttle system: one of us brings the water across while the other scrapes, keeping the supply coming as quickly as we can, keeping scraping.

We do this for hours. Back and forth. Up and down the stone steps. The kitchen fills with steam; we wear a muddy path from the house to the scaffolding tower. We scrape.

It's not quick or efficient or pleasant. It's difficult to get the water to the carcass hot enough: when we pour it over we have a minute or so during which the bristles tend to scrape off, but as soon as the water cools, the hairs stick fast. So we end up bringing across smaller and smaller pans – which, in turn, means more journeys. The bristles are most dense along the ridge of the back, around the neck, in the nooks behind the legs; we keep at these thickets, over and over, but the folds of skin and the contours of the body make it difficult to get a clean scrape and in the end we begin to ignore these areas and concentrate instead on the flanks and the shoulders, which are broader and firmer and so easier. In time, patches come cleanish. Each of us develops a technique which works: mine involves gripping the hairs between the fingers of one hand so that they're pulled tight against the skin, and running the scraper over the muscly curves with the other. This effects a reasonable shave; the hairs come off, with effort. But each bristle is coarse and wiry, and before long they lacerate my hands. I put on a pair of thick blue fleece gloves: my movements become clumsier and my hands still smart and bleed beneath.

It's slow, painful, exhausting. We have to manoeuvre the carcass so that we can clean each side of it, but even turning it is a struggle – and we still have to work out a way of hanging it. The sun, low in the sky, is already on our backs and will set in a couple of hours. We can't leave a half-ready carcass lying around on the ground through the night. Animals will come for it, for one thing. More importantly, we need to eviscerate it today so that there's no risk of the innards turning bad and so that we can hang the emptied pig for the flesh to cool and harden, ready for butchering tomorrow. That's a lot to do; we still haven't finished with the bristles. We never thought it would take this long.

It's not going to be clean and smooth, we see that now. Just clean enough and smooth enough, or nearly. We decide to leave the trotters and the head as they are: the hairs there are too matted and the bony contours too difficult. We'll work on one or two areas on the main part of the body – Ed has future crackling in mind – and we'll just have to make do with the rest as it is, still black in places, patchy, riddled with stubble.

Do I think about what I'm doing; about any of this? Not really. Not yet. I just work.

Live pig, Little Pig, needs looking after. He needs feeding, until his time comes. I take a break and wander down to the vegetable-patch pen. He's standing in the mud, halfway between the shelter and the fence, still. He squelches a heavy step or two as I arrive, but nothing more. He has his face to me, his big ears drooping, his eyes bright; his tail twirls. But as far as a pig can be, he seems expressionless.

He could not see the slaughter or any of the work on the carcass from where he is; there was no particular noise when Big Pig died, no squealing, nothing more than a quiet thud. But I have no idea how much Little Pig may have sensed or understood. What would the smell of blood have meant to him, so much blood? The stench of chemicals, or of burning hair? Can he smell death; the death of a pig?

He's bewildered at being alone, that much is clear at least. When I step over the wire with the bucket of grain, he makes more of an effort in the mud, stumbling over to me, nudging, trying a nibble at my overalls. I stand with him while he eats. In the field beyond the garden wall there are half a dozen pale cattle. I hear them breathing heavily, snuffling. A robin flits and bobs on the brambles. Little Pig snatches at the grain, fluffing it on to the ground where it lies, sticky and browning, until he noses at that, too, digging it more, making more mud. He eats diligently, with determination. His appetite is unaffected by the day's events. But I can't stand here with him much longer, and as I leave he looks up, stops eating and tries to rush towards me. Until he's held by the mud, marooned, and in the end sinks to a halt in the middle of the pen, in no-man's-land. He lets out a quiet grumble. I don't turn as I walk away. I know what I'll see: a surprisingly small pig, half-coated in clay, alone.

We have to get on. Winching; gutting; butchering; Little Pig still to come; Christmas. There are no more than a couple of hours of daylight. The sky already has a whitish sheen as the cold gathers for night. We stand and look at the scaffold one more time. We examine the bent crossbar again. Will it take the weight? We swing on it; pull down hard, and decide it will have to. There are no alternative places to hang the carcass. Briefly, we consider sawing it in half on the ground and taking the pieces inside overnight, but even though the house is cool in this weather, impossible to properly heat, it's nothing like cold enough for storing freshly killed meat for fifteen hours or more. So what had seemed an unacceptable risk earlier in the day is redefined as a minor hazard. By now it seems wimpy to make a fuss about a flimsy crossbar.

Gently we winch the pig. The chains ratchet slowly, loop by loop, the carcass begins to lift, hairy trotters first. The legs wave in the air, its back peels from the ground, twists slightly; the whole thing continues to rise until just the head is resting on the trampled grass. The ears are skewed; I don't look at the eyes.

The crossbar has bent some more but is holding. We keep an eye on it and winch again. The head slides, lifts; it's only the snout now, finally, snuffling in the grass, and then it, too, is pulled up and the pig is suspended. The scaffolding creaks; the crossbar has a wide, low curve. A few more turns bring the carcass well clear of the ground, and we lock the pulleys. The pig swings ever so slightly, side to side; it's upside down, half stripped of hair, legs splayed, a wretched thing.

We take off the head. A decent all-purpose DIY saw is fine for this. It's a simple, brutal task, and once it's done and the head hauled aside out of the way, the pig is much less a pig. It's not yet quite meat and nothing more, but it's losing its pigness all the time, losing its familiar shape and colour, forcing attention from where we're used to look-ing – the head and face, the shoulders – towards the stomach and the legs, which are unremarkable, unprepossessing, just undefined ani-mal. Without the head, the body is lighter, too, of course, which mitigates some of our concern about the state of the scaffold.

Eviscerating the carcass, however, is more tricky than you might imagine. It's not just a case of emptying the insides. For one thing, the intestines can be tasty and useful, cooked up as chitterlings or made into sausage casings; we have plans for the liver and kidneys, the heart, perhaps the lungs. Everyone knows one thing about pigs: you can eat everything but the squeal. Traditionally, nothing was wasted. The bladder was dried and used to store tobacco; the stom-ach was sometimes blown up for children to play with, a pig-balloon. We may not be quite that thorough but we do know not to be care-less with the middles. More importantly, a slip of the knife and we would puncture the gall bladder, spilling bitter yellowish bile which will seep into the not-yet-cold flesh and taint it. This would be a dis-aster. All these months of work raising a good pig, lost with a moment's clumsiness.

I'm the dexterous one, so the gutting job is mine. The way the pig is hung, the rump is just above my head height, so I stand on tiptoe to begin. I have to cut around the skin at the anus and then carefully through the muscle to release the rectum. I've been told to pull this and tie it off, so that none of the faecal matter can slip back into the innards and contaminate them. This sounds straightforward enough, but I've never pulled a rectum before, and it's more stub-born than I'd anticipated. I'd imagined something like those pop-up plastic tubes that come on top of cans of oil and tins of varnish, but of course it's nothing like that: it's slippery and fleshy and isn't designed to be hauled into the open. It fights back; resists. I have to use more brute force than I'd have liked; I have to tug and lever. A black oaty slop of pig poo slides on to my hands. When the rubbery tube of the rectum finally eases clear of the body and Ed leans across to make the tie with string, I'm breathing hard, sore from standing on my toes and pulling at such an uncomfortable angle, slightly taken aback by what it actually feels like to be doing this. It's the difference between watching someone dive into deep, cold water and actually diving in yourself: the physical sensation is unimaginable unless you're there, immersed. I suddenly feel winded. And we've only just begun.

Next I slit the body through the stomach from top to bottom; or more accurately, since it's inverted, from bottom to top. The knife moves easily and lightly: swish; unzip. It's nothing more than a basic kitchen task. I've got a clean straight cut and I begin to open up the carcass. I work very slowly but gradually the slit widens, deepens. I cut deeper still, but there's not as much flesh here as you might think, and before long I've revealed the abdominal cavity as far as the ribs. I'm inside now. Pig middles are here en masse in front of me: a neat, complex new world folded inside the skin and muscle. There's a slight membrane to cut, here and there, a few places where the flesh sticks tight, but mostly the innards reveal themselves without fuss and I'm faced with a dissected body, like a Vesalius anatomy drawing.

I somehow expected mess of some kind, sloshy liquid, blood even. But it's clean and dry. The organs have a patina to them: some of them gleam like pearls in a shell; some have the fine, worked shine of good leather shoes or brushed racehorses. There are pleasing shapes, a concoction of textures. The cavity is tightly and cleverly packed, like a stuffed but orderly suitcase, layered and tucked and tidy. The inside of a pig is a beautiful thing.

But it's difficult now, up close, to be absolutely sure of what's what. It's bitterly cold, the dusk is beginning to settle in the trees, we've been working outdoors all day and we've never before had to identify the nuance of pig innards. We're a bit bamboozled. *Are those the lungs? Where's the heart? I think that must be the liver – isn't it?* What I thought I knew about pig anatomy is disconcerted. Organs don't look the same as they did in diagrams, or even as they do on a butcher's slab; some are concealed, at least in part, by twists of intestine or folded behind other things. I'm not sure where to put the knife.

We're slow again, picking our way through the physiology. Concentrate; think! A few things become clear. At the top there are the greenish spirals of the large intestine; the richly coloured, meaty organ below, partly obscured, is the liver. We want that out, for sure.

The lungs are easiest to identify because of their spongy texture, and because there are two of them, but they're huge, far bigger and broader than I'd imagined, and I doubt what I'm seeing. We can't find the heart at all, for the moment, and the kidneys are hidden; the stomach bulges to one side, the only thing that's smaller than I'd expected. This is nothing like the frog we dissected in school.

The innards will just fall out into a pan. That's what you read. *The intestines will fall away, and then the rest of the insides will release in two parts.* It sounds simple and unequivocal. But these innards stay where they are, intact, gleaming. I reach round and behind, cutting through the diaphragm where it's attached to the bony wall of the chest, but it's difficult to see exactly what's attached to what and I'm still not quite sure where the bile sack is hiding, so I work warily with the tip of the knife: *snip, snip, snip.* This seems to go on a long time. I'm patient; slightly mesmerized by the deft nip of the blade. So when the abdominal cavity suddenly and completely slides its contents towards me I'm taken by surprise.

The whole lot empties forward in a solid mass of heavy organs. I should let it all just tumble into the tub below, but there's a strand or two of tissue still attached, and remarkably this is strong enough to prevent the innards coming completely free. So they dangle, making the carcass lurch on the scaffold, and before I'm quick enough to move away, they've piled against me and I'm cradling them against my body, trying to support them, taken aback by the enormous weight of this intestinal mess in my arms.

It's no more than a few moments. Soon Ed comes and steadies the carcass, hoisting the innards to allow me to cut through the remaining slivers of tissue; the organs fall free into the tub, their dense tangle loosening, everything sliding apart so that it's easy to see each element clearly, separately, offal on a butcher's slab. But for those moments I'm overwhelmed by the physical surprise of the pig guts against me: the clean, fresh, slightly salty smell of them; the not-quite-utterly cold; the huge, slippery bulk, unforgettably heavy, like cradling an armful of wet beach stones.

Step away. Take a moment; we're nearly done. We'll be finished before dark, just about; there's only the clearing-up to see to. Put down the burden of innards, shake out the soreness, step away.

We rummage through the intestines in the tub and bag up the offal for the fridge and the freezer. We're picky. We'll buy skins for sausages; we decide against keeping the lungs; we don't bother with small, springy bits we can't identify. But there's plenty, nonetheless; more than enough. With another pig to come.

The carcass, slimmed down now, has emptied the last vestige of pig.

We hose it down. Cold water on a cold evening. The ground beneath the scaffold becomes sloppy but the meat shines, dark and new and lustrous. With so much weight removed, there's no danger now of the crossbar giving way and we hoist the empty body a little higher, checking the grip of the hooks in the legs, settling the thing for the night. We've got some sheets of clear plastic which we wrap around the scaffold and tuck over the top of the legs, letting it flap down below. The structure takes on the odd ghostly appearance of something from a TV police drama, but it feels like the proper thing to do, a covering of some kind, a shroud.

We're too tired to do anything more, and it's too late. A moon is rising; stars breaking out low on the eastern horizon. The chickens have roosted, fluttering up into the cover of the conifer trees. Little Pig is in the shelter, a black shadow against the pale hay, alone. We check on him, quietly, and then scurry into the house to warm up as best we can. We do ordinary things: cook, drink wine, watch television, play with Mo. Not much is said about what's happened that day, not much at all. Perhaps we're just too tired to talk.

★

A kestrel hunts in the early light, a copper cut-out against the mauve sky. It hovers, flicks down over the garden, cuts away. A bevy of small birds tumbles in its wake, twittering; from the bare damson tree behind the pig pen, a flock of long-tailed tits scatters. Little Pig dozes, eyes open, deep in the straw. Now and again, his ear twitches, but otherwise he's still. The ice has set hard on the puddles in the mud around his shelter; it's a morning for lie-ins.

The original plan had been to slaughter Little Pig today. Finish butchering one pig; start all over again with another. Two pigs, three days' work; that's what we'd said. And then Christmas. But we know now, this second morning, how naive and foolish – how plain laughable – such an idea was. We can't go through all that again today, we can't; I can't imagine scraping hairs again, over and over, or hoisting innards or watching, again, a thrashing, dying pig. Not now; not yet. And besides, we can't rely on the scaffolding.

So where does that leave Little Pig?

Alone in the straw, dozing.

We close our eyes to the problem and rub our hands in the cold. Let's just get on. For now, at least, let's get finished. A few hours and we'll be done; then we can think more clearly.

We lift the plastic cover: the no-longer-pig hangs there exactly as we left it, except there are teeth marks now and some torn flesh, at the bottom of the carcass where the cavity opens up just above the dangling right leg. Something has been gnawing at the bare meat in the night. It's not done a great deal of damage: it's chewed away a dent, cleaned up against one of the bones, that's all. I can cut out the spoiled bits with a knife. And probably we shouldn't be surprised that we've left a chunk of prime pork swinging in the open and something's helped itself to a tasty takeaway. But it must have been an animal of some size to reach high enough and to leave such marks. This isn't mice, or rats, or even polecats. Most likely a dog or a fox, perhaps even a hungry winter deer. It's natural, of course; it was probably inevitable. But in the chill of the new morning, with the blood from the slaughter still staining the ground around the scaffold, there's something unsettling about the thought of a good-sized predator feasting on this suspended flesh; there's a kind of horror-film element to it, a whiff of *The Silence of the Lambs*. I take off a layer of meat around the chewed wound, tidying it up carefully with the point of the knife. I try not to think too much about what went on here but concentrate on removing the evidence. There: good as new. Pristine.

After this, the first real job of the day is to split the carcass. Ed does this, sawing through along the backbone from top to bottom. The two halves swing apart. Each is still hefty, muscle packed against the curve of ribs, the heavy back haunch and leg hooked to the chain and the front shoulder and leg dangling below, but each one is manageable at least, light enough to handle between us. The meat has firmed up during the night. We're ready to butcher.

We set up a table on open ground in front of the house. We've bought a thick, bright yellow plastic cover for it, like a picnic cloth, and when we've pinned this round and laid out the knives and bowls and bags – blues and greens, more yellow – the whole thing has the air of a party. I'm wearing a scarlet coat and woolly hat, a stripy apron; we've cracked through the winter greys: it could be preparations for a summer barbecue.

We unhook the first of the sides and lug it round together from the scaffold, across the front yard to the table. We begin: the hacksaw for dividing the half-carcass into sections; the cleaver for breaking through bone joints, separating ribs; the large knife for the heavy mass of flesh; the small knife for delicate work. We pore over the meat for hours like the most intricate of surgeries. It's fascinating; frustrating. *Where do the chops end, then, and the ribs begin? What about the belly? What's this big bone here?*

All the meat is for our own use. We don't need to be exact about the butchering cuts: in principle, anything will do as long as it fits into freezer bags. But having got this far, we'd like to end up with something approximating good-quality pork, rather than hacked roadkill. And I'm enjoying the complexity and propriety of the task. I like the way the texture and colour of the meat changes as we work through the carcass: darker here at the shoulder and dense, paler and looser at the rump; threaded with fat in places, lean in others. I like the milky translucence of clean bone. I like the feel of the knife carving out sharp lines without effort. This is not like yesterday's thrashing pig and heaving innards. This is a puzzle: you can stand back and scrutinize it, work it out, explore bit by bit with the tip of the knife. It's neat, cold, precise; un-animal.

But it's time-consuming, too, and we don't finish butchering the first side until after lunch. There's still the other to do, and already we've got a great deal of meat in bags: lots of big joints from the leg, chops and ribs, many piles of scrappy offcuts. The trotters are wrapped, stewing bones bagged, slabs of thick, white back-fat put aside for rendering into lard, and kidney-fat stripped off for suet. In places where the hairs were still too dense and spiky, we've peeled off the skin and discarded it; some of the larger stripped bones will be thrown away, too. But almost the entire half-carcass has been divided and subdivided on the party table, identified (more or less), and transformed into a state for storing and eating. This seems like an achievement of sorts. But it's only half a carcass. Now we have to do it all again.

It's the last Sunday of Advent, a few days before Christmas. This evening I'm singing in a concert at one of the local churches; at three in the afternoon there's a rehearsal. I have a solo part and can't miss either. We sloosh down the table and bring round the second side of meat from the scaffold, just as the clock strikes two. We'll work more quickly this time, now that we know what we're doing, and we'll be less distracted by the magnificent physiology of the animal we're dissecting, but there's absolutely no way we'll get this second side done together. Almost as soon as it's laid out and trimmed, I have to go. 'Just take out the fillet before you head off,' Ed pleads. And so I ease the tip of the knife along the bone one more time and draw out another handful of flesh.

I'm late; the last to arrive in the village. The church is on top of a hill, the houses clustering down the slope around it, a network of narrow alleys, cobbles and steps. There's nowhere to park nearby and I leave the car some distance away on the road and clatter up the deserted street, my footsteps echoing in the cold. When I turn under a stone arch on the flagged path that winds up to the church, there's a huge bough of mistletoe above me, stuffed with berries. It makes me pause. Christmas. I'd completely forgotten. In an instant I'm transported from close work on a dead pig to the anticipation of celebration, with all its memories and associations and nostalgias. I'm unsteady on the steps.

The church is small, austere, beautiful. There are one or two pieces of artwork in the recesses along the vaulted nave and some stained-glass windows in the apse, but mostly it's plain, a repetition of local stone, a larger version of the *caselle* huts in the fields. The walls are worn and patched, discoloured in places, evidencing centuries of use and poverty. Above the hewn altar there's an Occitan cross constructed from fluorescent light tubes which, when the church is fully dark, glows yellow, casting the entire place in lovely light, but in the winter afternoon it hangs, grey and dated, like something in an abandoned electrical shop.

The choir is moving benches. There's discussion about where we should stand; someone has made droopy red fabric flowers to pin on the black-and-white of the usual uniform but some singers don't want a part in such foolishness and a clique of malcontents is plotting in the corner near the vestry. I find a seat on a wooden chair on my own. I take off my gloves and stare at my hands. The skin between the fingers is rubbed off to leave raw red weals, a result of yesterday's battle with pig hairs; on my palms and index fingers there's a busy network of bleeding cuts and fluttering wisps of skin: each time the sharp blade of the small butchering knife has so much as brushed my hand it's left a small, clean wound. I hadn't really noticed the pain but I begin to now, as the cold and the adrenalin subside and as I look at the mess. A friend from the tenor section comes up to me and stands alongside for a moment. He, too, looks at my hands. 'What on earth have you been doing?'

Do I admit to it? I look around; we're alone. I wasn't going to tell anyone. I didn't want to talk about this yet, and not here. But I can't help myself. 'I've been killing a pig,' I say.

Almost immediately we're called to our places. I give him a few whispered details. I tell him about the scaffold, about the butchery, about the cold, dirty skirmish with the bristles, above all about those last moments of Big Pig's life, those moments of happiness that vindicated our decision to undertake such a task. This way, making a sensible account of a justifiable act of violence, I hope he won't think I'm mad. But I've been busy all day, for two days – not thinking, hardly talking – and it's only as I begin to wrench this thing I've done into a conversation that I'm struck by its odd other-worldliness, its brutality and visceral power, and I realize that I probably sound mad, after all, because I'm whispering in church about the quick plunge of the knife and my hands are covered in blood. I pull on my gloves again. I ease the slaughter from my thoughts and put it to one side, tuck it into a niche somewhere in one of the side chapels. I can't think about it; I wish I hadn't talked about it. I examine my shell for cracks. Then I follow the line of sopranos along the length of the nave to the altar. We start to sing. I concentrate on the sound as it rises in the old church, filling it, fading into the battered stone, lingering in the raft-ers where the vaulted roof leaks damp. My throat and chest are tight; my hands tremble; my mind seems to have dislodged itself, prised out on one of the high notes and drifting away with the echo. Here it is, then: I'm about to cry. But I don't, not quite, not now. I sing instead.

When I arrive back home, dark is falling and Ed is clearing up scraps from the table. He looks pale and weary but the carcass has been butchered. I take Mo with me down the garden to check on Little Pig: he's standing as close to the fence as he can, his head pushed out over the top, grunting at us with attitude. Mo sniffs with him for a while. I step over the wire to fill the food trough and break the ice already forming at the edges of the water tray. The mud clogs around my wellies. It's a bleak place to be; I can't help thinking of First World War trenches. Smoke from our chimney sinks towards the garden and drifts across as Ed goes inside to stoke the fires, and for a moment the impression is stronger. Mud and cold and death. I spend a while scratching Little Pig on the head, on the tuft of thick hair that sticks up between his ears. He nudges me. I scratch some more. He seems utterly lost, forlorn. He's never been on his own, ever: always he's had the reassuring grumble and scuffle of at least one other black pig. Lonely Little Pig makes me sad.

There's little more than an hour until I have to leave again for the concert. Ed and I spend the time labelling bags of meat and trying to arrange them so that they'll freeze quickly. Bits of pig slide away into drawers and pack into Tupperware; the final disintegration. All that remains is the head. 'We should use it,' Ed says. 'We should butcher that, too. Or boil it up.' There's good meat on the head, especially in the cheeks. Pigs' ears are a delicacy at the Thursday market, both raw and cooked, piled in trays with flaps of unidentified skin and roasted hearts, or chopped into glutinous casseroles. But the head is still in the state it was first thing this morning. We haven't touched it since rolling it away from the rest of the body under the scaffold. It's still lying there in the scruffy grass. And we can't face beginning again; we don't even know where to begin again. A head. A black hairy head. Slicing into such a thing seems a step too far at the end of an exhausting weekend of slaughter and butchering. The thought of it makes me squeamish for the first time. And so we make a decision: we'll just throw it away.

We make one other decision – or rather, it's forced upon us. We give Little Pig a temporary reprieve and decide to postpone the slaughter. We haven't done it this afternoon, as we first proposed, and now it's only a matter of days until Christmas. We have family arriving tomorrow evening at the airport, expecting a cosy quiet celebration, and we can't do it while they're here. Besides, who slaughters a pig on Christmas Day? We're also frazzled by the work so far; the thought of another two days of pig-labour is too much. We'll wait a week or two. He'll be fine. One dead pig, one live pig. It's not ideal. It's not what we'd planned, but it seems the sensible thing. We don't foresee any problems.

And so I drive back to the concert with a pig's head wrapped in black bin bags on the seat alongside me. At a point in the lane where it sweeps down across open land, I pass a small white stone slab which marks the boundary between one *commune* and the next; in this case also between one *département* and the next. On one side, where we live, we have weekly bin collections from the house; on the other there are large communal bins lined up in the lay-bys and at junctions, and residents have to take their rubbish to one of these for disposal. I drive to the first of these depots, which is tucked away under some trees, deserted in the dark, the litter of frosted cardboard and broken glass twinkling in the car headlights. There are five or six containers, some for recyclables and some for other refuse. I push back the plastic lid of one of the all-purpose bins and chuck in the head. It flips free of the bin bags and lands upside down. I hurry away.

I'm ashamed of this act of profligacy; I know how my neighbours would shudder at such waste. And I feel I've betrayed Big Pig. It's the head, after all, the recognizable part of him; the big, solemn, dignified head. I'd rather have boiled it in a pan for hours and skimmed off the scum and cooled the gelatinous liquid for stock and picked the meat from the bones and let Mo have the ears for a treat; I'd much rather have *used* it, all of it, as proper recognition of his Big Pig-ness. But I've been beaten by time and tiredness, by choir concerts and the sting of my hands and the inglorious, queasy realization that I don't want to meddle with brains and eyes and snouts and the too-familiar shape of the skull.

The concert happens. We sing. Christmas sweeps in on familiar melodies. I have to breathe properly to make the notes come right and it makes me wonder whether I've breathed at all since the moment I drew a white chalk cross in the middle of Big Pig's forehead. It feels as though my breath has been trapped inside me, festering.

Afterwards there are cakes and mulled wine in the draughty *salle des fêtes* but I slip away and drive home. I pull the car into the front yard and park. When I get out, I walk round to lift the boot to take out my music and bits and pieces in a carrier bag; I place my hand on the latch and I stop.

I look up at the huge black sky, the stars piercing in the cold, and my poor illusory defensive shell explodes into a million little pieces which fall away from me and leave me soft and small and bewildered. I begin to cry. I cry painfully, tightly, not able to take my eyes off the stars. The church bells strike the hour, carrying clearly in the chill air. I continue to cry, wrenching out strangled sobs. I'm not sure what I'm crying for. I don't think I'm mourning Big Pig; I'm not actually remembering the death; I'm no longer reeling from the work on the carcass. But I've rarely broken down like this, with such sudden passion, and I feel alone and tiny in the unforgiving bitterness of winter.

Ed has the fire roaring in the living room and Mo is curled under a blanket and there are lovely smells in the kitchen. The shutters are closed to keep out the cold. Everything is cosy and safe and warm. This, then, is the end to the weekend, not standing outside weeping at the stars but sitting at the table, sharing a meal.

We're eating roasted tenderloin fillet, *le filet mignon*. It's one we butchered earlier today. I remember the struggle to take it out from under the bone and the anxiety about trying to ease it out whole. There are cuts all over my hands from the knife work. They still sting. Normally, this is one of my favourite pieces of meat, but this evening it tastes strange. We both eat for a while without mentioning it. I wonder if my mind is playing tricks on me; reacting to the weariness, perhaps, and the upset, the associations. Yesterday this was Big Pig, today it's a slice of pork on my plate. Perhaps it's no wonder it tastes strange.

But it's not just me imagining things – in the end we look at each other and confess: *the flavour's a bit odd, isn't it?* Not off, as such, or even particularly unpleasant, but just odd. We've read that such fresh meat can have an unfamiliar taste, and it could be simply that we've never eaten anything so recently taken from a live animal. The enzymes haven't had much time to act on the tissue, working on the proteins and carbohydrates, releasing the familiar flavour. And it could be that we're unaccustomed to such dark, gamey pork. On the plate, the meat could be mistaken for beef. Perhaps the chestnuts and the acorns and the pears have infused the meat with this flavour and we're just not accustomed to it. But I'm recalling the weight of the pig innards in my arms and the battle to release them and the anxious, delicate work with the knife in and around the intestines and the implacable warnings: don't, whatever you do, don't puncture the gall bladder. And so there's another doubt which we finally admit. We look at each other across the table and whisper it. Could it be that we've messed up somehow, and the meat has acquired a taint? Could it be that Big Pig is spoiled, after all? An entire carcass ruined, after everything? We brush the idea away. It's too miserable to contemplate. It'll be fine, just fine, we're sure of it. We're being foolish. And besides, what can we do? We'll just have to wait and see. There's no way of knowing yet.

6.

We move Little Pig out of the mud. He's plastered in clay: as his legs sink into the mire, his tummy flops into the squelchy ground until the entire bottom half of his body is caked hard and brown. It must be heavy and uncomfortable, and I can't help thinking how much more difficult it will be to scrape such a filthy carcass.

He can't stay on the vegetable patch. It's already cratered and bare; now that we've postponed plans for his slaughter, we'll have to move him somewhere better for a couple of weeks, with solid ground and new foraging. But everything's been dismantled back at La Graudie and I'm anxious about trying to walk him too far on his own, without Big Pig's steady influence, so we simply fence off the bottom half of the garden, an uneven grassy strip dotted with molehills and mouse holes, divided by a rickety wooden fence from Solange's rocky land which abuts it. Our visitors have arrived and we enlist their help to create a new pen in the shelter of the mature pines and conifers which pack the corner nearest the lane. It's an original way to prepare for Christmas and we all pile in to help. In the flurry of activity, I try to forget my distress after the concert, the sudden tears that took me by surprise. But I find myself thinking a lot about that moment under the stars. And the more I think about it, the more special it seems to me. It was prompted by tiredness catching up with me, of course, and relief at having got through the physical challenge of the weekend, and no doubt the so-familiar carolling, a brush with sentimentality. But it was also the point at which I came to understand deep down, in a way without words, what it was I had done and how it was to take a life; it was a genuine, non-clichéd moment of truth; the culmination of the many things I'd thought and read and experienced about the pigs, the year-long effort and deliberation and anxiety and play, their significance to our small territory here and my place within it, all this distilled to nothing, to tears-without-thought which were, in fact, everything. Even now, especially now, sloshing through the mud of Little Pig's shabby enclosure, it's a moment I treasure, and which I understand will stay with me for the rest of my life, one of those rare, beautiful, disturbing, fleeting crises that will somehow affect who I am and what I do and how I think about the world.

But my feelings are still too recent, too not-quite-exposed, for me to understand in any meaningful way and for now, there's a shelter to be dismantled and rebuilt. Me and my dad, in woolly hats and thick gloves, take down the old structure on the vegetable patch and heave planks and corrugated iron back and forth to the new location. We choose a sheltered corner among the pines and conifers, where the ground is reasonably dry, and we begin the task of stacking and balancing and buttressing. The plastic sheet is holey, torn ragged at the edges where the pigs have chewed and rummaged, but it's serviceable. We use the tree trunks to support and wedge. In an effort to give Little Pig a more desirable residence – perhaps to make some amends for such a miserable situation – we drag the heavy wooden picnic table from the front of the house and use this to create a solid central den. Another shelter: the fourth. Like a *Blue Peter* presenter, I'm adept now at turning scraps, debris, rag-and-bone into something useful. There's clean, dry straw; a draught-free nook. Practice makes perfect: it's perhaps the best shelter yet.

But Little Pig shows no interest. No interest at all. He ignores us as we demolish one shelter and lumber across the grass with the planks to another. We have to take down the electric fence: he seems to regard such a move with disdain. He makes no effort to bolt. When we walk him across to the new pen, he doesn't seem to notice the crisp fresh grass under his feet; he steadfastly refuses to acknowledge the bundle of straw waiting for his housekeeping. He's not even particularly bothered about the bucket of grain. What he likes is to stand with us, right alongside us: nudge, nudge; barge. As I crawl into the shelter on my hands and knees to pull down the plastic sheeting and lay out some of the straw, I see him standing with my dad, the two of them just idling, ambling along the length of the fence at the back of the garden, pausing often, as though to take in the view of the bare winter fields or to watch the crows rising from the tall oaks around the lake at the Mas de Maury; my dad, who's never touched a pig in his life, guides Little Pig with a soft hand on his head. A light stroke is all it takes to guide him one way or another, to prevent him going on too quickly: Little Pig responds immediately, sticks close, doesn't want to risk losing his new friend.

But the wind has whipped up, freezing, and it's a steely, raw day of dim light, and my dad has not come all this way to babysit a pig, so we finish the shelter as quickly as we can, reset the electric fence and go inside where the fires are burning and Ed is making soup. I can see Little Pig from the windows at the back of the house. He's not moved since we left him. He's not gone anywhere near his shelter, nor investigated the limits of his new enclosure; he's not so much as nosed the soft dry soil under the pines, which I thought he would love, new, leafy soil, perfect for rummaging; he does not grub or dig, he doesn't eat. He stands still, his head raised towards the house, and he looks towards us with small black eyes.

★

Never keep a single pig, we were told, right at the beginning. Always two at least; more, if you like. A pig needs company, stimulation, interaction. A pig needs to be part of a herd. A drift of pigs, it was called, in the Middle Ages. There are other evocative collective nouns for pigs, too – a drove, for example, and a sounder, from Old French and Old English – but I like the sense of 'drift': it captures the way pigs move together en masse when they're ambling forward. If they're alarmed, or eager to reach food, they simply bolt in an ungainly gallop, but when they're quietly grazing they drift, one animal taking the place of another, the group swelling and retreating, carving a shape into the landscape. We don't often get the chance to see large numbers of wild or free-range pigs moving freely now, but it's a good, honest sight, rhythmical, mesmeric, not unlike the pulse of murmuring starlings or a Grand Tour peloton of cyclists, only slower. A drift of pigs. Pigs together in number, hearing, feeling, touching each other; not alone.

And in the early nineteenth century, as if to prove the point, our one black Learned Pig becomes many; he metamorphoses and multiplies until there's a veritable drift of learned pigs. When our first exhausted sapient pig had given his final show, and John Nicholson retired from business to enjoy a quiet life with his young bride in rural Cheshire, there was a rush to fill the gap in the market and to capture the attention of a fond paying public. Suddenly performing pigs were appearing on playbills all over the country. Pigs. More pigs. More black pigs. Nicholson's back-and-forth from city rooms to country fair and from France to England has done little more than whet the popular appetite, and for the next half a century, the Learned Pig becomes a common sight, imitators and imposters taking to the stage with a set of alphabet cards and a well-turned trotter.

In its new incarnations, one significant improvement is made which immediately sets audiences in a frenzy. It's the simplest of things but a brilliant moment of marketing: the pig is given a name. In fact all the pigs are given a name – the same name – and so the idea of the Learned Pig becomes inextricably associated with a single pseudonym: Toby. 'To be, or not to be': Toby. Apparently borrowed from Hamlet's existential soliloquy, the choice was a joke of sorts, and a nod to the questions raised by a sapient pig – to be animal, to be human, to be a success.

When Ed and I started with our own pigs, we'd been careful not to give them names because that was one way, so we thought, to keep them at a distance. Not pets, not companions, but animals raised for meat. Nameless. In the same way, giving the sapient pig a human name, making him more familiar and homely and recognizable – transforming him into Toby – brought him instantly closer to his public, gave him personality and identity, and provided a striking focus for the advertisements. 'Toby: The Greatest Curiosity of the Present Day' claims a poster from 1817. This is, perhaps, the first Toby, making his debut at the Royal Promenade Rooms, Spring Gardens, just off Trafalgar Square in London, not far at all from the Charing Cross rooms where Nicholson had first shown his learned pig, thirty-two years earlier. For four performances a day – 'precisely at the Hours of 1, 2, 3 & 4' – Toby does those things we now expect from a clever pig: he spells and reads from cards, adds up accounts, tells the time, guesses the ages of his spectators and reads the minds of those assembled in the crowd. He is, the advertising trumpets, 'astonishing', 'surprising', 'extraordinary', although from this distance, of course, we are less impressed: Toby is an old black pig reinvented, a repetition of tricks, a worn act with a new name.

This Toby is owned by Nicholas Hoare, a magician. And it's quite possible that this Toby is already, in fact, several Tobys: some accounts note that Hoare exhibited more than one pig, and it's not unreasonable to suggest that such a demanding programme of shows was fulfilled by two or three Tobys taking turns to delight their audiences. Unlike John Nicholson and the first pig, Hoare has serious competition and training two or three near-identical Tobys gives him a margin of error. After all, who could tell one black pig from another? Who would look that closely? Hoare needs to keep his tricks fresh and his pigs on their toes because a mere stroll away, at 23 New Bond Street, twice every afternoon, a Parisian with an Italian name, Signor Castelli, is exhibiting Munito, 'The Learned Dog'. Munito, a highly manicured and modish white poodle, is expanding the repertoire to make a case for canine superiority, not only counting and spelling and telling the time, but also answering inquiries on botany and natural history, and playing a mean game of dominoes. Both the Prince Regent and the Duke of York are said to be overcome with enthusiasm for this new doggy marvel: 'the doors of the exhibition room are daily thronged with the carriages of the Nobility and Gentry who go to view his extraordinary performances,' enthuse the newspapers.

Pigs and dogs head-to-head, not to mention performing geese and the lure of exotic animals shipped from overseas: tigers and crocodiles and snakes. With so much at stake, other Tobys soon join the battle to uphold the pig's supremacy in a crowded marketplace. Taking up the London challenge under the guidance of William Pinchbeck in 1818, one Toby boasts the wisdom of the Orient, acquired from a Chinese philosopher, while local fairs are awash with other Tobys who, for a penny, will attempt some basic spelling. American audiences, too, want to see a pig of such talents, and a new iteration of Tobys goes to work in the growing cities of the United States. A poster for the Barnum & Bailey Circus advertises a 'Troupe of Very Remarkable Trained Pigs [. . .] Showing Almost Human Intelligence' and William Pinchbeck leaves London for Boston where he sets up with a Learned Pig, only to find his show pirated by charlatans and chancers who tarnish Toby's good name by exhibiting pigs 'not by any means competent'.

Our old black learned pig without a name has become Toby, an international brand, but not everyone adheres to the original rules of the franchise: there are pink pigs now, and brownish ones; pigs with shorter ears and longer snouts; clever pigs and dunces. It's a free-for-all of pig tricks and cute goings-on. Some audiences are known to come away disappointed. Toby lingers on, but the panache and excitement of the early days has been lost. Charles Dickens, an amateur conjurer when time allowed, goes so far as to unpick the mystery of such performances and lay bare its mundane mechanics: 'It was clear he chose by smell [. . .] the waistcoat had an aniseed scent,' he claims. In fact there is more to it than that – a combination of sound and scent, a complicated series of signals – but Dickens's investigation is a sign that the new audiences of the nineteenth century are wary of ageing spectacles and less likely than their eighteenth-century counterparts to take a wise pig at face value. In an age of invention and discovery, tastes are changing, and by the 1850s, some poor pig, a shadowy Toby, is merely an afterthought in the tawdry, run-down chaos of Savile House in Leicester Square: 'Acrobats in its drawing-rooms, Spiritual Rappers in its upper rooms, the Poughkeepsie Seer in the entrance hall, and the Learned Pig in the cellar,' notes a writer for the Victorian magazine *Household Words*.

Like the pig in the Savile House basement, Little Pig has been left behind. And he doesn't like it. Less than half an hour after leaving him to come inside the house, I look out of the window to see him striding purposefully up the garden towards us. A Little Pig waddle, his stomach swinging, his tail twirling, his ears flapping. He's coming quickly. By the time Ed and I have pulled on our boots and coats and rushed outside, he's made his way up the side of the house as far as the stony terrace and is tramping across the flower bed, pushing through prickly clumps of winter-grey lavender.

He seems pleased to have found us. When Mo skids round the corner and comes scampering after us, he seems even more pleased. Everyone's here, playmates and comrades, a drift of sorts. He slows down now, stops. He has a look around. Now he's no longer on his own in the middle of a big field he seems quite content; this will do – he nips at my trousers in celebration.

He walks with us back across the grass to the enclosure. There's no sign that he's explored his new home in any way. The straw bedding is still outside the shelter; there's grain in the trough; the grass is untrodden. But the fence is down. Little Pig has pushed through, collapsing a couple of the poles and flattening the wire. 'We must have forgotten to switch it on,' Ed says. But the little green light on the battery is blinking away and the wire is giving off a telltale *click*, *click* where it's lying on the grass. We shrug; an oddity. My dad comes out and walks with Little Pig while we work on the fence. They stroll companionably as before, along the perimeter of the garden, back and forth under the trees. Little Pig is calm; he pauses here and there to forage. My dad pulls his woolly hat lower over his brow and clasps his arms about him. Mo runs round them.

We add extra poles so that the fence is tighter and we uncoil more wire to add an extra layer. Three strings: we haven't bothered with this much fence since the pigs were weaners, since the first days on the Mas de Maury enclosure when we were frightened of them getting out, or things getting in. We're careful, thorough. My dad brings Little Pig inside the pen and we turn the dial on the battery so that more current circulates. The green light blinks furiously.

With Little Pig safely confined, again, we turn our attention to one of the last outstanding butchery tasks: sausages. We've bought a meat grinder at one of the local hardware shops, a bulky beast with a heavy handle and a choice of three grinding plates, all of which might be labelled 'coarse'. It's supposed to be screwed to a table, but since we don't want our dining table drilled with holes or clamped at the edges with hefty fastenings, we've attached it to a plank of wood and it balances rather precariously on the work surface below the kitchen window. We've also bought natural sausage casings, which unpack from their box in a long coil, fragile and slippery, difficult to manipulate. We could have used the intestines from our own carcass, cleaned up and dried out, but as beginners we thought it was safer to let someone else take charge of the process in a small concession to commercialism. Now that we've seen the transparent delicacy of the final thing, this seems a good decision.

We've put aside shoulder meat, scraps of this and that from the legs, a few chunks of good belly and some slices of hard fat for the basic sausage. We recruit the unfortunate Christmas visitors in the task of cutting this up into rough cubes and feeding it into the grinder. It's a slow, unfestive process. It's only possible to stuff a handful of meat at a time into the funnel at the top of the machine, and grinding is tough work; the handle is hard to turn, forcing the meat through the narrow cylindrical body and then through the plates, like pushing plasticine through a colander. Eventually a thick pasty sludge of sausage mix emerges from the other end and squeezes into the casing.

A few years after arriving here I watched a very old man cutting hay with a scythe. He was alone. He began just after sunrise and worked the length of the field through the day, slicing through the long grass in a narrow strip – the width of a man's arms with a scythe attached – until he reached the far hedge and then turning to work his way back. He was in the valley, alongside the stream, but the sun is high and hot in early summer and the field shimmered in the heat, without shade. I didn't stand and watch: I passed instead, time and again, and each time I passed he was working with the same steady unforgiving cadence. If he paused to drink or eat, I didn't see that. I didn't see him rest. I remember him because I was astounded by his strength and determination and concentration, by his skill and by the pure doggedness of the *paysan*. Peasant – a word we use as an insult in English but which the French around me employ with much respect, often love. *Paysan*: a man of the *pays*, the land. A man who can scythe all day because the hay needs scything. A woman who can wield the heavy wooden handle of a grinder over and over, round and round for hours, accepting the pain that sets in around the shoulders and along the arms, because the meat needs grinding. How important is it that people still know how to scythe a field or grind meat by hand? Not very, I suppose. It probably adds nothing to life except toil. But the very fact that the practices of the *paysan* still linger here, out of date or newly relevant, is at least enough to make us pause for thought, just as I paused by the stream in the valley to marvel at an old man's rhythmic labour.

We set up a relay: chopping, feeding in the meat, grinding, manipulating the casings. It's companionable. The smell of freshly ground pork gives the kitchen the clean, heady scent of a real butcher's and there's a definite pleasure in such shared exertion. Neighbours and friends congregating for the *tue-cochon* – I can see how this worked. Coming together around a dead pig. There was always *eau-de-vie*, Jean-Claude once told me, towards the end, when only sausages and *boudin* and the pâtés remained to be made. The men had mostly finished by then, the heavy work done, and they knocked back slugs of spirit while they watched the women wielding the grinding handle. His father always warned him against drunkenness after such cold, tough labour, and against eyeing up the women while they were working: a tipsy uncle had lost the tip of a finger in the meat grinder while he was leaning in to flirt. The girl, flustered, had not acted quickly enough to disentangle him, and the family had spent several months trying to make out the taste of human flesh in their sausages. Sober and unromantic, we manage to get by without any such disaster, but I still doubt it's what the visitors had in mind for Christmas entertainment.

I've watched a video about tying off sausages and it looks easy, like sculpting balloon dogs at children's parties. But when it comes to it, the deft flick of the wrist that transforms a single length of meat-stuffed tube into a string of lovely sausages proves tricky. You're supposed to be able to twist along the length, so that each individual sausage holds in place, but the slippery skin likes to unwind itself and there's a surprising bulk to this much-ground meat, and it quickly becomes one of the games of the season. Our skein is uneven: some are short and bulging, some long and skinny. But eventually, it holds together, one sausage twisted into the next, a pleasing meaty paper chain.

In the past, sausage knowledge was passed down among local families, along with recipes for making soap from fire ash and the secret locations for picking mushrooms. All our neighbours, I suspect, know how to make a good sausage, without fuss – although Solange and Camille are pleased not to have to do it, and prefer to buy in bulk at the supermarket. But to outsiders, especially those from towns and cities, butchering and processing were a mysterious, rather disconcerting art, a skill acquired from a dark past and practised with knives and grinders and cleavers. It was a trade associated, inevitably, with blood and gore, and all kinds of myths sprang up giving butchers – especially urban butchers – a particularly ambiguous place in traditional communities. These were important men (almost uniquely men, of course) who provided an essential service. But they were often viewed with suspicion, or even repulsion. The influential urban elite of the growing towns didn't like to be reminded of the horrors of animal slaughter taking place not far from their doorsteps, nor of the workers steeped in blood. Butchers were outsiders, transgressors – they were seen as violent men, not just because their daily work involved chopping up carcasses but because this was simply the way they were, by nature.

Louis-Sébastien Mercier's eighteenth-century chronicles of Paris suggested that butchers couldn't help being savage ruffians. Living with the sights and sounds of slaughter, he claimed, inured them to brutality and death, and transformed them into some kind of man-beast monster prowling the stinking abattoirs in search of a fight: 'ferocious and blood-thirsty with their naked arms, a thick neck, blood-shot eye, dirty legs, bloody apron; a knobby and massive baton arms their heavy hands and always ready for a brawl which they enjoy.' Other eighteenth-century writers in Paris readily agreed, continuing to promote butchers as 'violent undisciplined men' – 'If one could gather eleven to twelve hundred in three or four places, it would be very difficult to contain them and to prevent them from beating each other to death,' one learned article noted grimly. And it wasn't just Paris that housed such desperate hooligans: London's Victorian cattle market at Smithfield was also a place renowned for lawlessness and violence, reputed across Europe for its filth, 'drunkenness, confusion and riot'; the workers there – drovers and butchers – were commonly described as 'savage'.

Under the influence of such real-life examples, folk tales and fictions delighted in the butcher as a figure of darkness and violence. The French equivalent of the bogeyman, *le croque-mitaine*, is a butcher who cuts up and devours small children, while a distinctly menacing character from traditional French Christmas stories, Père Fouettard (Father Whipper), accompanies St Nicholas in his search for good children, punishing miscreants along the way: in several versions of the story, Père Fouettard is a butcher who kidnaps three wealthy, plump young boys and eats them. The fear that butchers were only a good meal away from cannibalism crops up time and again, and is still a powerful undercurrent in popular culture: the 1991 French film *Delicatessen* features a darkly comic butcher-landlord called Clapet who lures the poor and unemployed to his lodgings, prowling around the staircases with a large knife and neatly filleting human bodies in the basement.

Without too much undue butchery violence, we finally end up with beautiful long strings of sausages. Three recipes, each a different colour and texture: a Lincolnshire-type sausage, with dark scraps of sage visible through the casing; a basic pork sausage which is soft and fat; and a peppery, spicy version, reddish, rusty from plenty of Spanish *pimentón*, and grainier to the touch. It seems like good work. But holed up in the kitchen with the grinder cranking and the evocative scent of crushed herbs, we've been cocooned in our own world and it's only when Mo barks that we're shaken out of our sausagey reverie.

He's barking excitedly; it's the high, eager bark he gives when someone he knows comes to the house. He wants to get out; he wants to leap and greet.

I look out of the window next to the front door to check for visitors. I see Little Pig. He's on the path between the lawn and the steps, looking around as if in search of something. He's listening to Mo, following the sound, trying to unpick the mystery of a dog indoors, a bark behind walls. Has the fence failed again? We pull on our outdoor clothes and head out into the cold. I'm weary, a bit fed up of pig in all its forms. Little Pig clatters into us and I grab him by the loose skin of his neck in an attempt to haul him down the side of the house and off my front garden. He's stubborn for a while; he digs in, pulls away, grumbles. It's only when Mo goes running past, delighted at this unexpected outing, that Little Pig brightens. Ah, just the dog he was looking for. Mo comes back and they waggle together, nose to nose, as they used to do at the fence. And then Little Pig comes with me, trotting happily alongside, allowing me to guide him across the terrace and on to the grass at the back, his tail swishing contentedly.

We take Little Pig back to the enclosure and repeat the fence operation: drive the poles in, tighten the wire across, check and recheck, click on the battery to run the current. 'The battery must be draining a bit,' Ed suggests. 'We'll ratchet it right up and it'll be fine.' We set the dial as high as it will go, check the water in Little Pig's bucket in case it's beginning to freeze, and step over the wire to make our way back to the house. As we do, we hear a noise behind us. We turn to see Little Pig barging the fence. He's trampling through all three wires, bringing down two plastic posts at the same time, disentangling himself from the wreckage with a kick and heading towards us with brisk determination.

He's fixed on going back to the house. It takes us several minutes to get him under control, talking to him, standing close, offering a handful or two of grain. Eventually, he calms down. Since my dad, sensibly, has given up the pig-droving business after a short but glorious career, it's my turn to lead Little Pig backwards and forwards across the grass and keep him happy while Ed mends the fence, again. At this point we still believe – we have to believe – that there's some kind of malfunction with the equipment. But I've only just begun steering Little Pig awkwardly back towards the bottom of the garden, pushing against him with my legs, tacking sideways in a clumsy loop like a lopsided supermarket trolley, when I hear Ed squeal. He stumbles back, rubbing his hand and arm. The electric fence is working.

With the dial turned up so high, there should be enough current running to shock a much bigger animal even than a large fat black pig: a horse or a cow, or a man. But we saw Little Pig barge through. Without hesitation; without making a sound. For another minute or two, as I work Little Pig back in the direction of the enclosure, Ed checks the flow of electricity around the complete circuit and we discuss the possibility that there's some kind of 'dead zone' where the current is reduced or not flowing at all. We don't quite know how this might be true. Even with my rudimentary grasp of the rules of physics it seems far-fetched, but we cling to the idea because we don't want to believe the alternative explanation.

The alternative explanation is that Little Pig is so lonely and distressed that he's willing to push right through a live electric fence.

We try just one more time. The usual routine. Posts, wire, battery; the clicking green light. Current running; all round. But Little Pig knows the routine, too, and even before we've left him this time, he's off. There can be no doubt. We watch as he simply walks through the fence, steadily, without pause, without the slightest flinch.

Big Pig and Little Pig, together, respected their enclosure because there was no real reason not to. There was no incentive to break out. Now Little Pig has a reason: he doesn't want to be on his own; he wants to be with us, at the house; he wants to leave this place he doesn't know, with a shelter he's never claimed; he wants to find Mo and stand with him, the two of them waggling, doing their dog–pig thing.

We let him walk. What else can we do? But it's the afternoon before Christmas Eve and we've got a 170kg pig that we can't enclose and can barely control. A sad, frantic, disorientated pig. This feels like a disaster, and an emergency.

Mo stands inside the house at the front window. Little Pig stands outside, a step or two away. They keep an eye on each other. Little Pig shows no desire to roam; he's apparently quite content to loiter in the front garden with a Dalmatian for company, and we leave him for a while. We attempt to solve two impossible conundrums: how to clean the squishy gunge of meat from the mechanics deep in the body of the sausage grinder, and what to do with Little Pig.

We briefly discuss ways of securing the enclosure or creating some kind of pen in the woodshed. We face the prospect of walking endlessly with Little Pig, up and down through the Christmas holidays, finding a way to pass the nights. We take heart from the fact that he's not rampaging through the neighbourhood, but we know that he's becoming more and more unpredictable and unruly.

We ring the abattoir.

We've got a pig. We need to bring you a pig.

We don't stop to think whether this is really what we want. I've read horrible stories about slapdash abattoirs and cruel practices;

I've been told that the stress of an abattoir death can affect the final quality of the meat; I'd dismissed the idea of our pigs going anywhere near the municipal abattoir a long time ago. But things have changed. We can't go on with Little Pig as he is, and we can't come up with an alternative. We feel cornered, desperate; we need to find a solution, and this appears to be it.

Hello? Yes? Can you tell us what to do?

Because we've made all the arrangements at home, we don't know much about how the abattoir works. The man on the phone is very helpful but he warns us straight away: tomorrow is the last slaughter day before a long holiday closure. It's Christmas Eve; after that there'll be no one at work until the New Year has passed. Everything's easing down. They might not be able to accommodate us.

It's only one pig. A big pig (a Little Pig), but only one. It's urgent.

There are set days for things, the man explains – days for taking large numbers of commercial stock and days for taking one or two animals from *particuliers*, smallholders. In addition, there are days for different animals: cow days are the most frequent, this being cow country, but there are designated sheep days, too, and pig days. Yes, there are pig days.

There's no flexibility in the system. French bureaucracy doesn't allow it. Certain animals on certain days; that's the rule. But, the man says, you might be all right. Tomorrow, the last day before Christmas, is a smallholders' day, *and* a day when they can take pigs. A lucky 1-2. A godsend. 'But you have to get your animal here this afternoon. It has to stay in overnight.' How long do we have, then? 'You have to be here by four thirty,' he says. 'Absolutely no later.'

We can't afford to miss this deadline. We can't be stuck with Little Pig for two more weeks and don't want to spend Christmas slaughtering and butchering a pig. But it's only a little after 2 p.m. and the abattoir is no more than twenty minutes' drive away. That leaves us about two hours to find some kind of transport and to devise a method of capturing free-roaming Little Pig to put him in it. Surely that's possible; surely.

★

Sapient. Knowing. As I watch Little Pig pressing his snout into the gap under the front steps, I wonder how much animal instinct can look like human thought or emotion. We've killed one pig and we're about to send another to its death but Little Pig is concerned with nosing up grubs from the mossy slime that clings to the stone in the damp shade. He's apparently untroubled by memories of the weekend slaughter; he seems to have completely forgotten a morning spent pining for company and barging fences. He cannot know what might happen next. No past, no future, just hunger and curiosity, grubs and stone, and the occasional itch that needs vigorous attention on the door frame.

I think about my other pig story, the tale of Learned-Pig-turned-Toby, and I wonder what clue, if any, it might give me to the real nature of a pig. The distance between my pigs' lives and the singular experiences of performing pigs two centuries ago seems enormous. It's easy to think there can be no connection at all between Little Pig, waiting for a ride to the abattoir, and the glory days of multiple stage-struck Tobys. But Toby's story forces me to return to the puzzle of anthropomorphism, and it's here that Little Pig's life collides with the older history; it's here that I'm forced to consider, again, what it is that Little Pig perceives or understands or feels; what it is that makes Little Pig a pig and only a pig.

We're so accustomed to slipping across the boundary between the animal and the human that it's perhaps only moments like this with Little Pig that force us to confront the strange and unpredictable intimacy of our relationship with the beasts around us. The earliest of stories from around the world endowed animals with human qualities: Aesop's fables from Ancient Greece; the fourth-century Buddhist Jātaka tales; fairy tales and Biblical stories of all kinds. The modern pigs of *Charlotte's Web* or *Babe* have been made at least partly human, as have lovable, family favourites, like Piglet in *Winnie-the-Pooh* or Peppa Pig, and Orwell's memorable allegorical pigs in *Animal Farm*. We habitually think of animals in human terms. But keeping my own pigs has made me think more closely about this tradition, and why it has such a hold on us, and at this moment, with Little Pig's fate in the balance, the problem of anthropomorphism seems to me more complicated and personal than ever.

And stepping back into the early nineteenth century, I catch sight of anthropomorphism run wild: the flurry of Tobys set light to something of a craze for pigs with human qualities and humans with piggy features. In particular, it resulted in a revival of the fascination with the pig-faced women of folklore. A learned editorial in *The Times* in 1815 brought readers up to date with the history of pig-faced women in general while it became popular knowledge that just such a young lady was living right under readers' noses in London's Marylebone. Reputedly young, of Irish noble birth and possessed of an excellent fortune, she had only been spied briefly, heavily veiled, and it quickly turned into something of a sport to spot her in a passing carriage and send a letter to the press describing her snout or her hairy pig's head. In February, *The Times* carried an advertisement from a 'young gentlewoman' who volunteered to be the pig-faced woman's companion in return for a 'handsome yearly income', and a month later George Cruikshank published a cartoon of 'The Pig-Faced Lady of Manchester Square' playing the piano, her svelte body and shapely legs turned to the viewer and visible under a scanty dress, her pretty pig's face covered with a flimsy lace veil. Several would-be suitors and members of elite society were rumoured to have seen the woman in the flesh in her refined London home, while pig-faced women of less obvious gentility became a staple freak-show attraction at country fairs until the middle of the century.

This rather prurient appetite for a not-quite-human, not-quite-pig hybrid prompted Toby to step off the stage and make a foray into literary circles, where he presented himself in distinctly human terms. 'The Life and Adventures of Toby the Sapient Pig: with his Opinions on Men and Manners. Written by Himself' was published sometime in 1817 and sold for a shilling. It begins with a dedication to 'great persons' and a moralizing paragraph espousing the virtues of '*time, assiduity,* and *patience*'. Then it plunges into a new Learned Pig story, the black pig reinvented, his history retold for a new generation and his celebrity reaffirmed: 'I was born,' it begins, 'in a place, if I am rightly informed, called *Aversall*, or *Avershall*, on the *Duke of Bedford's* demesnes.'

This is Toby presenting an autobiography in the tradition of rambling, conversational eighteenth-century adventures such as *Robinson Crusoe* or Henry Fielding's *History of Tom Jones*. This is a pig relating its history and its career as though he were a man; a pig giving itself the airs of the aristocracy, a famous pig pandering to the curiosity of its audiences and laying claim to an entirely new readership. This Toby is well above the squalor of the sty: 'I have never since been suffered to mix with any of the family,' he snorts dismissively. This Toby teaches moral lessons about 'irreproachable conduct'; he praises his 'purity' and the brilliancy of his own intelligence which 'shone like a constellation'. He looks down on the bestial, uncivilized behaviour of some of the human louts who come to watch him perform: a drunken man, he notes primly, 'outsteps the brute creation, in his thoughts, words, and deeds'.

The slim pamphlet, which claimed to be 'literally the truth', was 'published and sold by Nicholas Hoare', Toby's trainer. It's playful and eloquent, sly and celebratory, a fine piece of advertising, a final flourish in the uneven story that has brought a sapient pig from a country pub in eighteenth-century Ireland to a sophisticated late-Georgian reading public. At the same time as readers were relishing Jane Austen's novels, poems by Byron, Keats and Shelley, historical romps by Walter Scott, the 'Songs' of Robert Burns, Hegel's philosophy and logic, and Malthus' political economy, Hoare was bringing us this new piece of literature – the tale of how a humble black pig had become 'the topic of the day'.

The pig with a human name, Toby. The pig as human, or like a human. Toby talking with a human voice, recounting our hopes and fears, laughing at our vanities, sharing our sensitivities, judging our lapses, marshalling our sympathies. An anthropomorphic transformation, from the ambiguous, unnamed performing pig, an entertaining animal that in time became less animal, to a fully functioning, emotional, intellectual being with a family tree, a grasp of etiquette and a thorough belief in its own genius. Woman, man and pig, side by side, companions, adversaries, equals.

★

Is this how I view Little Pig? Like us? Feeling things as we do; sharing a human grasp of life? A Toby? I don't, surely. I'm thoroughly aware of him as animal. I've been clear about that, all along. An intelligent, sentient, unique animal, but an animal, nonetheless. But in that case, why do I worry about the abattoir, a place designed for the efficient dispatch of animals? Why does it seem such a big step?

We only know one person with a working trailer that's big enough to take a fattened pig. There are such trailers all over the neighbourhood, obviously – all the farmers have them – but we only know one person well enough to ask him to help us at short notice the day before Christmas Eve when we've made a mess of managing our pigs. His name is Claude. He's a dairy farmer. He's been kind to us before: he's lent us his JCB and had us round for dinner and taken us cycling with his children and helped us locate our septic tank. He sells us our wood every year and Ed has sometimes worked with him, splitting logs. We call him as calmly as we can and explain: we have to take Little Pig into town before he runs amok. We have to take him this afternoon before the abattoir closes; we'd like to take him now.

Claude is in the middle of something. He, too, has chores to finish before Christmas. He's bound by milking hours, morning and evening, and he presses all the other farming jobs in between, so he's always busy, even in midwinter, and today he's mending a barn roof. He speaks to us on his mobile from a perch on the rafters. We can't let this distract us. 'Please, can you help?'

We give him the deadline. He puffs. It's perhaps for the best that we can't see his face. In the spirit of negotiation we promise to have Little Pig ready when he arrives. All he'll have to do is drive us to the abattoir in time for the 4.30 curfew. He can leave immediately after we've delivered Little Pig and be back in time for the evening milking.

Claude is a very nice man. He agrees to help us. He'll come at four, he says.

We take a moment to savour our relief and then go outside to Little Pig. The afternoon is already dusky. There's a chainsaw burring close by, a field or two distant; a harsh, lonely sound. We saunter up to Little Pig and pay him some attention, caress the flop of his ears and run a hand under his muddy stomach. We want to lull him: we have a plan.

There's only one place we can think of in which we can secure him in anticipation of Claude's arrival with the trailer. It's not a place we usually keep animals. Under the stone steps that rise to the first storey – the main rooms – of the house, there's a kind of cubbyhole, tall enough to stand up in, about the size of a small bathroom. It's a cold, stony nook where Mo likes to lie in the heat of the summer. At the back of it, there's a glass door that leads into the lower rooms of the house, old workshops and stores, animal byres in the past; at the front there's a wire-mesh panel that can be pulled across to close it off. I'm not quite sure what purpose the mesh panel serves: it was a feature we inherited from the previous owner and never bothered to change. When Mo was a puppy it was sometimes useful for penning him in so that he couldn't jump up and knock over elderly visitors. Now it's our pig trap.

We need Mo's help as bait. Ed takes him inside on the ground level, into the scruffy room behind the glass door, and closes him in. Predictably, he comes to press his nose hard against the pane and to whine in protest. We hope this will lure Little Pig, tempt him into the pen out of sympathy or curiosity; for extra enticement we scatter a good dollop of grain on the concrete floor. We open the mesh panel as wide as we can and stand back. Little Pig sniffs, listens. I turn my back on him; pretend it's nothing; no trap here, nothing to worry about. He comes to the threshold. Mo is quiet now, looking at him through the glass, wagging. Can Little Pig's small beady eyes see a dog behind glass in the dark recesses under the steps? He can smell the grain, though; his snout flicks and wiggles with delight. He takes a small step into the shadow, a slow, wary step, and then in a rush, nose to the ground, stumbles forward for the food. Mo shuffles on the other side of the glass door; Ed and I push the mesh across and slip the bolt to fasten it. Little Pig in his final enclosure.

We go inside and prepare the meat for supper: a joint of pork belly. A slab from Big Pig, heavy and hearty. We've set it aside to share with the visitors, dark red flashes of flesh buried deep in layers of lard. It will need long, slow cooking so the fat renders down and the meat pulls apart, soft and moist. Almost as soon as it's in the oven it fills the house with the gorgeous rich smell of roast pork, making our stomachs rumble. It's something to look forward to, after this is all over.

Claude comes at four, as he promised. I hear his van and trailer rattling along the lane to the house before I can see them and I'm full of relief, again, and gratitude, but also anxiety now – and something else, duller, a sadness. The trailer is backed across the front garden so that the rear of it is as close as possible to the wall and the mesh panel. The heavy tyres cut ruts in the wet lawn as Claude edges backwards and forwards trying to position the vehicle just right. In the end there's a gap of a couple of paces between the back of the trailer and the wall. Ed and I make human barriers so that Little Pig can't bolt through this space, this small portal to freedom – we stand either side with old doors, blocking any route except one: the one to the trailer.

But this leaves Claude to guide Little Pig and Little Pig doesn't know Claude and doesn't trust him. There's a stand-off. Ed and I coax Little Pig from behind our barriers but he's not listening to us – he's glaring at Claude and, just beyond, the step up into the trailer. He doesn't seem to like the look of either. This is all strange to him, and frightening. He's on his own again, trapped. He can surely hear the impatience in our voices. The summer days on the oak wood slopes of La Graudie and playtimes under the hose, making sunny rainbows, have come to this: a man he doesn't know shouting at him and yanking at him and a metal crate of some kind looming above him, huge and high, and nowhere to go. He doesn't have to be a clever pig – a Sapient Pig – or an anthropomorphic Toby to realize that this is not a good situation. Animal instinct can tell him that at a sniff and a glance.

Claude hoists Little Pig's front legs on to the step of the trailer, and in a flailing, kicking, puffing skirmish of pig and man manages to force Little Pig inside and close the back flap.

Snap – bolt. Done.

But I don't watch.

★

The abattoir. From the French verb *abattre*, to beat down, to fell. One of the busiest municipal enterprises in an agricultural town such as ours, a much-valued local service. It hunkers down in the industrial estate in the valley, with the rubbish dump and vehicle workshops, a collection of low concrete-and-metal buildings in a very large car park that can accommodate cattle wagons and articulated lorries but this evening is deserted and bleak.

As night falls, we unload Little Pig into a corridor. It's bare, dark in places, harshly lit in others, leading nowhere; stained greyish concrete walls sucking us inevitably into a place we can't see. It's the kind of place Kafka might have imagined. We slosh through a thin film of brownish water. Now he's here, Little Pig trots on quite happily, following Ed and Claude; I can hardly keep up with them. The man in charge – the man we spoke to on the phone – emerges from somewhere dressed in full whites and a bloody apron, a net cap on his head and his feet in yellowish-white wellies. He welcomes us like old friends, with a broad smile and an enthusiastic handshake. He slaps Little Pig on the rump and eyes him up professionally. He's admiring, fond even. 'He's a beauty,' he says, 'you've done a great job here.' He runs a hand down Little Pig's back, around his shoulder and down a leg: 'This is fantastic meat, this is.'

He has to ink Little Pig with a number. He allows us to choose – anything from one to ten. *Pick a number, any number . . .* It might be the start of a conjuring trick but, of course, it's not as magical as that: we choose 6, randomly, and he whacks a heavy stamp into Little Pig's side. The noise of the blow makes me open my eyes wide. It feels as though it should be reverberating throughout the entire building. He's hit Little Pig with a squarish paddle that's spiked with thick wires like nails which drive the ink into the skin. He holds it to one side for a moment while he checks the mark; it looks brutal, a medieval weapon. But Little Pig hardly seems to notice. He's truffling in Ed's pocket, a thick-skinned, solid-sided pig that doesn't seem to mind the tattooing.

We trot on again. The corridor spits us into a holding pen, large enough for perhaps six or eight good-sized cows. It's the kind of pen you find at cattle markets: solid enough but with metal fencing that rattles and shifts. Little Pig is the only animal here. The entire abattoir seems empty; there are no noises or smells, no evidence of work or death or distress, just all of us standing around under a low ceiling with Little Pig bumping and barging from one to the other.

Through an opening at the end of the pen, I can see a couple of other men, dressed again in whites. One is slooshing the ground with a hose, the other is bent low and awkwardly over some kind of metal equipment as though he might be mending something. The abattoir was opened in 1960; thousands and thousands of animals have ended their lives here in the last half-century. What was once a state-of-the-art facility is now battered and draughty, grubby. For years there's been talk of building a new slaughterhouse with modern equipment, a more pleasant place for workers and customers and beasts, but the finance has never quite been found and there's been political squabbling, and for now we're left with this unforgiving bunker. As we slip out of the pen and head to the small office alongside, Ed nudges me: we can see another man now, manipulating a huge saw in place to cut a carcass in half. When he lines the saw along the backbone and presses the button to switch on the power he receives a shock: he starts back and the power cuts out. He swears loudly. Then he lines up the carcass and the saw again, presses the button, starts the power and gets another shock. He jumps back, swearing. Carcass, power, shock, expletive. Repeat over, as if it's a joke in some sadistic children's cartoon. What a place to work.

Claude goes home to see to the milking while we contend with the paperwork. The man senses our discomfort and tries to reassure us. 'We'll look after your pig,' he says. We ask him to make sure Little Pig is killed as soon as possible in the morning, so that he doesn't have to wait longer than is necessary, so that he doesn't have to endure hours in the gloomy pen with the conveyor belts cranking and the saws screeching and whatever other things we can't imagine here this evening in the calm of closing, a day before the Christmas holidays. 'We'll do him first thing,' he says, 'I promise.'

And that's it. Nothing more to be done. Little Pig will spend the night here, in this hard-bitten, grisly place. A Little Pig in a large, empty barn designed for death. He will be further from home than he's ever been; in the morning strangers will come and manhandle him, not bad men but ungentle ones with a job to do; they will kill him without thought, efficiently and anonymously. This is not a place for sympathy or sentiment. It's a cold place. There's no sign that Little Pig is anxious or discomforted, or in any way prescient of what the morning might bring. He seems settled. But perhaps he's just bewildered and exhausted from a day crushing electric fences and trampling the garden in search of company; perhaps he's got this far, to this, lost his companion and his freedom and his view of open land stretching away to sky, and simply given up. There's no way of knowing. How much can a Little Pig feel? How much can it know? Here in the abattoir these questions are not asked. It's an animal in a pen, that's all. An animal inked with a number and ready for processing. Good meat.

The manager files the paperwork and shakes our hands. We make our way out through the concrete corridor. Earlier, I'd followed the trailer in the car, and we head without speaking to the corner by the entrance gate where I've parked. Above our heads a red plastic sign reads 'Abattoir Municipal' in plain capitals. It's unlit, but in the pulse of the floodlights outside the building it seems bright and draws my attention. I wonder how I've come to this place, after all, how Little Pig has finished up here. It feels like a defeat.

This was not the end I imagined. It's harder, much harder, to contemplate this abattoir slaughter for Little Pig than to face up to killing a pig at home. It's far more upsetting to abandon him here than to help Ed drive a large knife into Big Pig's throat. I understand that most people have to use abattoirs; I know that they're not purposely cruel places. They're practical, effective, accountable businesses. That doesn't mean I have to like them. I feel we've been lucky: the pens are much quieter than usual; the men under less pressure to process the animals; the atmosphere calm, almost peaceful. Little Pig, as far as I know, is not stressed or suffering. But still I wish things had not fallen out this way. I wish Little Pig could have endured a stay in his grassy enclosure, learning to dig the soft soil under the pines, unearthing winter grubs and lolling in his straw for a week or two until Christmas was over and the visitors gone and we were able to give him a respectful death. But his animal fear and loneliness and confusion were too strong, too instinctive, for such compromises. He couldn't be sensible – how could he be? – and so we brought him here, to this. As I start the car and take the turn towards the road home through the valley, there's a lumpen stone of sadness lodged in the pit of my stomach. I remember Big Pig in his final minutes, contented and comfortable, dancing in the frosty sun, and I consider Little Pig abandoned in the dripping, shadowy purgatory of the abattoir holding-pen, and my thoughts cloud over, obscured by guilt and sadness, and I can't find my way through to think clearly about what death should be, could be, because Little Pig is left behind and I have let him down.

7

The roast pork belly that's been in the oven for hours comes out on the table in a magnificent pile of crackling and soft-pulled threads of dark meat and puffs of white meat and sticky, crunchy nubs and rich, velvety dripping. We eat with our fingers and celebrate – celebrate Christmas, celebrate the sausages, Claude's intervention, an end to the work with the pigs, the loaded freezer; we celebrate the conclusion of another year here and more months to come, eating the meat and tentatively rooting ourselves. After all, who knows what might happen by next summer? We might never have to give this life up, after all. And just now such a thought seems hazy and unreal, ungraspable.

After the trip to the abattoir I'm hungry and cold and giddy. I almost forget Little Pig in my greed for the hot tasty meat. And this time, there's none of the doubt that niggled with the first fillet joint from Big Pig: this belly doesn't taste tainted or strange, it tastes delicious. Something else to celebrate: we haven't botched the butchery.

The next morning, Christmas Eve, we collect the carcass from the abattoir. It comes in two halves, wrapped in polythene, with pink papers which give us all kinds of detailed information about body weight, fat-to-meat ratio, fat thickness, the healthiness of the internal organs – and the time of death. 5.30 a.m.

The manager was as good as his word. Little Pig must have been the very first animal killed that day, long before it was light, before the noise and stench of other slaughters could distress him. This seems a very good thing. I think of the man's kindness to us – his attempts to ease our fears and his admiration for our work with the pig – in such an environment of daily ugliness and physical discomfort, and I admire his fortitude and resilience. This is not the savage butcher of urban myth; this is a gentle man doing a brutal job. Little Pig's death was perhaps not ideal. It wasn't the fairy-tale ending imagined by the romantic smallholder. It wasn't how I'd hoped it would be. But it was humane, at least, and prompt. This is a comfort.

We take the carcass in the boot of the car to Benoît's farm. As we approach, black pigs run at us on both sides, charging to the fence and then galloping along with us, curious and noisy, hopeful for food, spraying mud and stones, nipping and barging in a flap of ears and tails. A racing drift of live pigs outside, a shrouded dead pig within.

Benoît and his butcher examine the carcass and the papers. *Oh yes, a good pig. Well done.* We leave it all with them. This pig will be different to the last: one pig butchered on a table in the garden for roasts and stews and barbecues; one processed here with more skill for delicate cuts, transformed into hams and *saucissons* and *charcuterie* treats.

And that's it, for now. It's done. Over. Two pigs, a big one and a little one, have lived well with us and died without pain. Is that all right? Is that enough?

We might as well have named them, of course. And I suppose we did – Big Pig; Little Pig. By those names we came to know them thoroughly, each of them, the same but different. Fond, friendly, curious animals with a taste for games and fruit, robust and wild and just a little fearful. Beautiful black pigs. Some days they were absorbing, and I spent long hours pottering with them in the woods; some weeks I just kept an eye on food and water and left them to themselves. They were independent in a way that a pet is not, and I liked that. But they responded, too, to attention and because I've grown close to them, they've changed my life: they've made me know this place and its pasts, really know it, as if instinctively; they've taught me new and practical skills and plunged me into the world of husbandry; they've shown me what it is to kill a living thing – and what it is not to kill it, but to delegate that task to a stranger to be done out of sight. They've been fun, frustrating, comforting, exhausting, provoking, and they've made me appreciate every single morsel of pork I eat, every time I eat it, because that's their gift to us in the end. Pigs

are fine animals, characterful and good-natured and sparky. I'm
pleased I've got to know them, a little. I miss my pigs.

And so that leaves the meat. The produce. That's what it's all been
about, after all. That was the point of it in the beginning, and the
purpose we tried to keep in mind. We did all this, in principle at least,
for the meat. So, was it worth it? We've raised two animals as
humanely as we possibly could, in the best conditions we could provide. We now know what it means to commit without compromise
to the welfare of our pigs, and the time and money this demands. Big
Pig and Little Pig were agricultural animals, but we had the luxury
of keeping them without the day-to-day worries and constraints of
running a farm. All these factors should come together to provide us
with the best meat ever. Good lives: good meat. We all know how
this works; it's a given, surely. But is that how it's turned out?

One thing I've become certain of is that raising animals humanely,
under free-range conditions, is not just a matter of food snobbery or
one-upmanship. It's not always possible for everyone, everywhere, I
appreciate that, but I've seen pig lives and deaths up close, very close,
and I've seen what it takes to produce a piece of meat on my plate. I
know what pigs are. It would be a betrayal of all this, of the entire
experiment, of Big Pig and Little Pig, to fall back on an industry that
denies the nature and instincts of such beautiful and sensitive animals. High-quality, free-range meat is expensive, but our pigs cost a
lot to raise. To all those struggling to make a living producing the
best pork from pigs living under the best conditions, I raise my
threadbare sun hat.

And our meat? When we return to Benoît's butchery at the farm,
the cuts are laid out for us on trays along the metal bench in the cool
workroom. A jigsaw pig: head to tail, skin to innards. There are
pieces missing. One of the large back legs has been salted for ham and
is already hanging in the curing room where it will stay for just under
two years, drying out. Most of the other leg, along with some portions of a shoulder and some pieces of breast, has been chopped and
peppered and stuffed into cases for *saucissons*. These will hang alongside the ham for several months and come down in the summer,

perfect for slow *apéritifs* and quick salads. There are a dozen of them: twelve fat *saucissons* hanging in a barn.

We wait, not entirely patiently, for the *jambon* and the *saucissons*, and it's worth it. The *saucissons* are dense and peppery and rich and moreish. The first of them has the soft bite of dark meat; by the end of the twelve, when they've dried out longer, they're deliciously leathery. And then, later, when the pigs are so long gone that the enclosure at the Mas de Maury is overgrown again with brambles and nettles, there is the ham. Our very own air-dried, acorn-fed, free-range ham, over 8kg of finished weight – about €500 worth of meat.

Think of the best ham you've ever had, and double it.

Wafery thin slices of dark, dry, salty-sweet meat cut from the pleasing rise of the leg, textured, marbled, unctuous. All those hours up and down the slope in the woods at La Graudie; all those mornings spent running after pears and chestnuts, building up dense, tasty muscles – well done, Little Pig.

The *charcuterie* is a delight that makes meal-planning easy and recalls hot sunny days hosing down the pigs in rainbows of spray. But it isn't just a case of sitting back, waiting and reminiscing. When Christmas has passed and the visitors have gone home, there is work to be done, too. We have another head, a second head, and this time we have no intention of dumping it in the communal bins. There are chunks of fatty meat, a cluster of trotters, some large joints from the shoulder – plenty of pork still to be processed and stored. We simmer the head in a stockpot; we boil the trotters; we make a wet cure of salty water and dunk slabs of pork in it, submerging them for days. We roast the kidneys and the heart. We render down strips of thick fat into fluffy, pure white lard; we fry skin into crackling; we stew bones for stock. The house is full of the warm, rich smell of pig.

Having accomplished the salting and freezing, we turn our attention to canning, the traditional staple of French preserving. We've seen it done by our neighbours: Solange has an old barn lined with shelves of jars packed with beans and peas, potatoes and carrots, *rapountchou*, walnuts, stews and casseroles, meat of several kinds. The local supermarkets and garden centres put on magnificent displays of Kilner and preserving jars, different shapes and sizes, different seals and lids, regimented and shiny. Several of the hardware shops in town allow you to take along huge quantities of pâtés or terrines and the like so that they can stuff it into tins for you; you come away with trolleys full of plain, orangey-bronze tins, completely sealed. Although most people have freezers, many still prefer to keep food in this way; we've often been invited for an impromptu meal with friends and eaten heartily from a selection of home-preserved meat and vegetables and fruit tipped out, there and then, from jars and tins.

From the complicated range of equipment on display we choose a canning machine, a large plain metal pan that looks just like a big saucepan except for the small round pressure dial on the lid. This will allow us to raise the temperature of the meat high enough to kill off any bacteria so that it's effectively sterilized, then to seal the jars with rubber seals. In this way, the food should last for years, if we want it to. It's a simple but effective process, but more labour intensive than just bagging up joints for the freezer, and so we begin chopping meat and liver with herbs and spices and experimenting with recipes; we fumble the slippery seals, juggle jars to stack them in the pan, fret over the moment when the steaming whistle stops and the pressure takes hold. It feels like a strange cross between country cooking and a chemistry experiment. But at the end of it we have four or five kinds of pâté, terrines and galantines, some casseroles and ragus, and a supply of lovely soft, gelatinous brawn all neatly packed into jars, safely kept.

We're proud of ourselves: we've made tricky, country-style conserves in the tradition of proper French farmhouses. Some of the products have the hallmarks of the beginner – one or two of the pâtés would have benefited from more fat in the mix – but everything is edible, and most things are delicious. Delighted with my new *savoir faire*, I take a small jar of terrine to Solange the next time I call by. She's sitting at the wooden table in her all-purpose front room, the *séjour* that acts as kitchen and living room and dining room. She takes the jar politely, without enthusiasm, holds it to the light, turns it, and places it back on the table. I presume she will never eat it. But on my following visit, she admits to having tried some. It was, she says, *pas mauvais*. Not bad. I take that, with pleasure, for the high praise it is.

Finally, there's the pork pie. A fitting finale. A happy ending.

For a start it's huge. This is not a little snack pie, or a pie you can slip into your pocket, or even a pie you can fit on a dinner plate. This is a statement of a pie, gluttonous, extravagant, ceremonious. It takes two days to make.

We make it as a challenge, to see whether we can. On the first day, Ed simmers two trotters and a few raggy bones to make a stock, and then simmers the stock to make a thicker, gelatinous goo – the pork-pie jelly. It cooks for hours in a steam of stomach-rumbling meaty smells and in the meantime we chop the pork we've set aside. This is mostly shoulder, dark and fatty, but there are strips of belly, too – the meat mustn't be too lean or the pie will be dry and gritty; you can't have an eye on the calorie counter. The filling needs to be rich and soft and plump. There's sage and thyme and savory in the mix, cut from the garden, some grated mace, a little white pepper and a lot of black. We knead it together by hand.

We also take the final wedges of dense back-fat from Big Pig's fine shapely back and render them down in a frying pan, slowly, slowly, pouring off the liquid fat as it melts until we have a bowl of shiny, downy lard.

That's it, then. Ready.

The next day we put the thing together. I soften the lard with hot water, boil it briefly and then mix it with flour to make the pie pastry. It's the first time I've tried working with hot-water pastry and

I'm taken aback by its slithery trickiness. Warm and slightly animal, it slides through my fingers as I attempt to mould it. It tears and slumps. I've got a cake tin as a kind of pork-pie mould, but the pastry simply sags off the sides into a heap. I give up on the tin.

By now the pastry is cooling. I can't afford to let it get cold or it will become brittle and unworkable, but this not-quite-cool dough is perfect. For a few minutes it becomes supple and pliable; I find I can mould it like clay with my fingers, stroking it with my thumb so that it stretches and shapes. I settle on using it in a single piece, wrapping the meat in a parcel as though wrapping it in cloth. I ease out a base and we place the meat on it in a mound; I work the pastry up the sides with both hands and pinch it closed at the top. I leave a little gap, enough to let out the steam. It's hefty; there's too much pastry frilling where I've drawn it together. But it looks as though it might hold up, which is all we can hope for. We bake it.

When we take it out of the oven, it's golden and crunchy and, better still, there's been no collapse or seepage or cracking. An intact pie. Ed warms the jelly stock and pours it carefully into a fat syringe so that we can squirt it into the hole at the top of the pastry. When the pie seems full we wait for it to ooze down into all the gaps and then squirt again. Drip, drip; every last drop into every last nook.

The pie cools. Handsome and homely.

I don't really like pork pie. I particularly don't like the slippery, rubbery jelly stuff that clings to the pastry; I'm not keen on the chewy meat. But this is not that kind of pork pie.

Everything about this pie is delicious, addictively pleasing: the crisp pastry, the tender, yielding meat and the amazing melt-in-the-mouth, utterly-pork jelly. It's a pie to savour and remember. We tuck in, revelling. We thank the pigs for allowing us this pleasure. On a bright, January day we take our pie into the sunshine on the top of the steps by the front door, and we let it ooze and crumble on to our plates. Somewhere at a distance a buzzard mewls; a robin flicks and fusses around the bowl of chicken food by the woodshed. The day is calm and very quiet.

It's almost exactly a year since we were preparing for the arrival of the weaners. At that point, I had very little idea about what to expect – it was just a couple of piglets, wasn't it, that we would pen into a field? But now I know. I know about Big Pig and Little Pig from snout to tail, from hairy black hide to glistening innards; I know about the effort and the commitment, the expense, the anxiety, the love. And was it worth all of this? Was it really worth raising pigs ourselves?

When I'm asked these questions I think of the pork pie. The stock, the lard, the meat – all ours, all from our own hearty black pigs. There's something special about this; it's an achievement I'm proud of. It feels an important thing to have done and I would not hesitate to do it again. The store of dark, firm, rich meat that we feast on for months is fantastic, a magnificent stash that makes every pork meal a treat. Each forkful of fine roast or ham or pâté answers the question unequivocally: yes, this was worth raising pigs for.

But Big Pig and Little Pig, my two life-affirming pigs – would I prefer the meat on the plate, the fat, juicy pork pie, or would I rather have them careering towards me up the slope in the woods?

Now that's a different question altogether.

Notes

1

pp. 12–13 'There is no savings bank . . . without seeming to have cost anything': Samuel Sidney, quoted in William Youatt, *The Pig* (London: Routledge, Warne and Routledge, 1860).

p. 15 I read about an experiment carried out at Cambridge University: Broom, D. M., Sena, H. and Moynihan, K. L. 2009. 'Pigs learn what a mirror image represents and use it to obtain information'. *Animal Behaviour*, 78 (5), 1037–41.

p. 19 'To kill a hog nicely . . . tear the carcass about': William Cobbett, quoted in Robert Malcolmson and Stephanos Mastoris, *The English Pig* (London: Hambledon, 2001), p. 95. This book offers a wealth of first-hand historical accounts of raising a cottage pig, the slaughter and butchering.

p. 27 'I have observed great sagacity': Erasmus Darwin, quoted in *The English Pig*, p. 14.

p. 29 In the fifteenth century: the story of the Abbot of Baigne is quoted in Bentley, Jr., G. E. 1982. 'The Freaks of Learning'. *Colby Quarterly*, 18 (2), 90.

p. 29 'squalling [. . .] in different keys or notes': quoted in Jan Bondeson, *The Feejee Mermaid and Other Essays in Natural and Unnatural History* (Ithaca, NY and London: Cornell University Press, 1999), p. 21.

p. 31 'but that, if he did not perform his lessons well': Robert Southey, *Letters from England*, 3rd edition, 3 volumes (London: Longmans, 1813), vol. iii, p. 19.

p. 31 'the most tractable . . . good natured as a spaniel': *Curiosities of Biography; Or, Memoirs of Remarkable Men* (Glasgow: Griffin, 1845), p. 190.

pp. 32–3   'Each pig you come across . . . pine for sympathy and company':
            Robert Morrison, quoted in *The English Pig*, p. 20.

                                      2

p. 54   'Don't fall on your food like a pig': Desiderius Erasmus, *De
            civilitate morum puerilium*, a handbook containing instructions
            for the moral and practical education of children, first
            published in Latin in 1530 and subsequently translated into
            many languages.

p. 58   'keeping the left arm round the body': George Borrow's
            account of pigs at Llangollen Fair is included in *Wild Wales*
            (first published in 1862), quoted in Edward Thomas, *George
            Borrow: The Man and His Books* (New York: Button, 1912),
            p. 278.

p. 58   A pig in boots: for an account of droving routes and traditions,
            including the wearing of boots, see Shirley Toulson, *The
            Drovers* (Buckinghamshire: Shire, 2005).   –

p. 59   'unwearied patience': from 'Bisset, the Animal Teacher' in *The
            People's Magazine* (Saturday, 1 June 1833).

p. 66   'neat garden cabinet for growing bacon . . . contents of the
            carpet sweeper': from a collection of cartoons in Heath
            Robinson and Cecil Hunt, *How to Make the Best of Things*
            (London: Hutchinson, 1940).

pp. 67–8   'I told you we were having a piggy salted . . . did not get hold
            of our piggy': Luc François, 'A Village and a World at War:
            Sister Joachim (1867–1956) and World War I in Ooigem', West
            Sussex Record Office, Chichester, Ad. Mus. 14478.

p. 75   'Poor injured Bisset': 'S. Bisset, A Singular Character' in *The
            Sporting Magazine*, volume 27 (London: Rogerson & Tuxford,
            1806), p. 240. This article recalls the stories of a number of
            eccentric sportsmen and hunters, some years after Bisset's
            unhappy experiences in Dublin.

p. 76   'in the practice of good manners': from 'Some Account of S.
            Bisset' in *Anthologia Hibernica* (January 1793).

p. 83   'During the Spring and Summer Months': William Marshall, *The Rural Economy of the Southern Counties*, 2 volumes (London: Nicol, Robinson and Debrett, 1798), vol. ii, p. 206.

p. 83   'all the small potatoes . . . and mash it': quoted in Robert Malcolmson and Stephanos Mastoris, *The English Pig* (London: Hambledon, 2001), p. 50.

p. 83   'an important member of the family . . . scratching piggy's back': see family pigs in Flora Thompson, *Lark Rise to Candleford* (Oxford: Oxford University Press, 1945), p. 22.

p. 83   Similarly, the French belle époque: for pigs and the belle-époque postcard, see Michael D. Garval. 2015. 'Visions of Pork Production, Past and Future, on French Belle Epoque Pig Postcards'. *Nineteenth Century Art Worldwide*, 14 (1), complete article and figs. 1–36.

p. 84   'To have a sty in the garden': Walter Rose, quoted in *The English Pig*, p. 47.

p. 88   I'm struck again by the brutality and trauma of the slaughter: the accounts of pig slaughter in this paragraph are taken from *The English Pig*, pp. 94–101.

3

pp. 91–2   One of those who see the show, for example, is Anna Seward: her impressions of the Sapient Pig, and Dr Johnson's response, are quoted in Bentley, Jr., G. E. 1982. 'The Freaks of Learning'. *Colby Quarterly*, 18 (2), 91.

p. 93   'for the Pig to be burnt': for a discussion of pigs and the black arts, see 'The Freaks of Learning', 91–2.

p. 93   'The Big Black Pig . . . people who played cards': Donald Mackenzie, *Scottish Folk-Lore and Folk Life: Studies in Race, Culture and Tradition* (Edinburgh: Blackie, 1935), p. 51.

p. 93   'lovers of the monstrous': from an untitled 1846 article about the Roxburghe Ballads, attributed to John Winter Jones, principal librarian at the British Library from 1866 to 1873, quoted in Patricia Fumerton and Anita Guerrini (eds), *Ballads and Broadsides in Britain 1500–1800* (Farnham and Burlington, VT: Ashgate Publishing, 2010), p. 106.

p. 95   'My brothers and I had to collect acorns': quoted in Robert Malcolmson and Stephanos Mastoris, *The English Pig* (London: Hambledon, 2001), p. 46.

pp. 99–100   'no two pigs are the same . . . in this county as elsewhere': John Boys and John Farey discussing pig breeds, quoted in Julian Wiseman, *The Pig: A British History*, 2nd edition (London: Duckworth, 2000), p. 29.

p. 100   'it is painful to see . . . in a fit state for breeding': the Derby show of 1881, reported in *The Pig: A British History*, p. 63.

pp. 100–101   'Lean bacon is the most wasteful thing . . . not well fatted': William Cobbett, *Cottage Economy* (London: Clement, 1821), pp. 148–9.

p. 102   For pigs raised in intensive conditions: for antibiotics used to treat animals and humans, see 'Cutting Antibiotics: Denmark Leads the Way in Healthier Pig Farming' in *Der Spiegel* (International Edition, 13 November 2013); figures from Thomas P. Van Boeckel et al. 2015. 'Global Trends in Antimicrobial Use in Food Animals'. *PNAS*, 112 (18), 5649–54.

p. 106   'what with the weather, and the concourse of visitors': an unnamed newspaper report quoted in Jan Bondeson, *The Feejee Mermaid and Other Essays in Natural and Unnatural History* (Ithaca, NY and London: Cornell University Press, 1999), pp. 23–4.

p. 107   'great torture must have been employed': Henry White, a clergyman, reported in James Boswell, *The Life of Samuel Johnson*, 2 volumes (London: J. Davis, n.d.), vol. ii, p. 911.

p. 107   'a plenitude in the belly': *London Unmask'd or The New Town Spy* (1785), quoted in Hannah Velten, *Beastly London: A History of Animals in the City* (London: Reaktion Books, 2013), p. 127.

p. 107   'You are not to beat him . . . appear to read your thoughts': American conjurer William Pinchbeck in *The Expositor or Many Mysteries Unravelled* (Boston: printed for the author, 1805), p. 23.

p. 107   'The creature was shewn': Sarah Trimmer, *Fabulous Histories Designed for the Instruction of Children, Respecting Their Treatment of Animals*, 5th edition (London: Longmans, 1793), p. 71.

p. 108   'some pigs have evinced . . . to converse with men?': *A Present for a Little Boy*, first published 1798 (London: Darton & Harvey, 1800), unpaginated.

p. 121   'the proprietor is rapidly amassing a fortune': *London Unmask'd; or The New Town Spy* (1786), quoted in Paul Keen, *Literature, Commerce and the Spectacle of Modernity, 1750–1800* (Cambridge: Cambridge University Press, 2012), p. 173.

p. 125   'When the appointed day came round . . . a few pork cuttings': Edwin Grey, *Cottage Life in a Hertfordshire Village: How the Agricultural Labourers Lived and Worked in the 1860s and '70s* (Harpenden and District Local History Society, 1935), p. 116.

4

p. 130   'while someone held the poleaxe on the pig's forehead': Beamish Museum Archives, quoted in Robert Malcolmson and Stephanos Mastoris, *The English Pig* (London: Hambledon, 2001), p. 98. The book has an extensive chapter on pig-killing, with some intriguing first-hand accounts.

p. 130   'upended, had their throats slit': Ralph Whitlock, *A Family and a Village* (London: John Baker, 1970), p. 96.

pp. 130–31 'A most barbarous and disgraceful way . . . like a cricket-bat)': William Gooch, *General View of the Agriculture of the County of Cambridge* (London: Richard Phillips, 1813), p. 284.

p. 135   In 1612, the significance of adding peas: Gervase Markham, *Cheap and Good Husbandry For the Well Ordering of All Beasts and Fowls* (London: George Sawbridge, 1668), pp. 105–7.

p. 136   'This bacon is raised here . . . thrown away': Daniel Defoe, *Tour through the Whole Island of Great Britain*, 4th edition (London: S. Birt and T. Osborne, 1748), p. 42.

p. 141   As far back as the 1690s: 'Instructions to Fatten Swine in Towns' in Adolphus Speed's *The Husbandman, Farmer and*

Grasier's Compleat Instructor (1697), p. 91, quoted in *The English Pig*, p. 41.

p. 141   'their condition and surrounding were filthy . . . winds carried far and wide': Medical Officer, St George the Martyr, Southwark, quoted in *The English Pig*, p. 43.

p. 142   'The houses of the poor': *Four Periods of Public Education as Reviewed in 1832-1839-1846-1862 in papers by James Kay-Shuttleworth* (London: Longmans, 1862), pp. 21–2.

p. 143   '"I have," said a lady who was present': Sarah Trimmer, *Fabulous Histories Designed for the Instruction of Children, Respecting Their Treatment of Animals*, 5th edition (London: Longmans, 1793), p. 71.

p. 143   'the learned pig was in his day a far greater object of admiration': Robert Southey, *Letters from England*, 3rd edition, 3 volumes (London: Longmans, 1813), vol. iii, p. 19.

p. 150   'hogs fattened with chestnuts': *The Journal of the Royal Agricultural Society of England* (London: John Murray, 1842), vol. 3, p. 82.

pp. 150–51 it's been estimated that a family would need to put in: for estimates of labour for chestnut gathering, see Kenneth F. Kiple and Kriemhild Coneè Ornelas (eds), *The Cambridge World History of Food*, 2 volumes (Cambridge: Cambridge University Press, 2000), vol. 1, p. 361.

p. 154   one card from 1905: for 'Lyon-vaise. The bleeding of pigs', see Michael D. Garval. 2015. 'Visions of Pork Production, Past and Future, on French Belle Epoque Pig Postcards'. *Nineteenth Century Art Worldwide*, 14 (1), fig. 21.

p. 161   'the Learned Pig of Charing Cross . . . Montreuil, &c., &c.': a newspaper report quoted in Jan Bondeson, *The Feejee Mermaid and Other Essays in Natural and Unnatural History* (Ithaca, NY and London: Cornell University Press, 1999), p. 25.

p. 162   Louis as a pig: for the pig-king career of Louis XVI, see Jacob Rogozinski, translated by Nicholas Newth, 'Revolution and Terror: or how Louis XVI was turned into a pig' in *Stasis* (2 July 2014).

p. 163   'strongly resembling England': see Arthur Young's journal
          entry for 15 May 1787 in *Travels during the Years 1787, 1788 and
          1789* (London: Richardson, 1792).

pp. 164–5 'Too much learning, we suppose, had driven the pig mad . . .
           such amusement in most parts of England': newspaper report
           quoted in *The Feejee Mermaid*, pp. 25–6.

p. 166   'At Banbury, Mr John Nicholson': marriage notice from the
          Monthly Magazine, or British Register (London: Richard Phillips,
          1812), vol. 33, p. 81.

5

p. 173   'The smiling countenance of my own grandmother's deceased
          pig . . . and slops': draft letter to the *Times* newspaper, in
          Beatrix Potter's Letters, edited by Judy Taylor (London:
          Frederick Warne, 1989), p. 191.

6

p. 196   'the doors of the exhibition room are daily thronged': the his-
          tory of Munito, the Learned Dog, is taken from a collection of
          newspaper clippings known as Lyson's *Collectanea*, quoted in
          Jan Bondeson, *Amazing Dogs, A Cabinet of Canine Curiosities*
          (Stroud: Amberley, 2012), p. 22.

p. 196   'not by any means competent': Scott Martin, *Cultural Change
          and the Market Revolution in America, 1789–1860* (Lanham, MD:
          Rowman and Littlefield, 2005), p. 203.

p. 196   'It was clear he chose by smell': Charles Dickens was examin-
          ing Munito's tricks when he made the comment about learned
          animals being trained by smell, quoted in *Amazing Dogs*, p. 32.

p. 197   'Acrobats in its drawing-rooms': a description of Savile House
          by George Sala in an article entitled 'Leicester Square' (19
          March 1853). *Household Words*, 7, 64–5.

p. 201   'ferocious and blood-thirsty . . . beating each other to death':
            Louis-Sébastien Mercier and descriptions of eighteenth-
            century Paris are quoted in Sydney Watts, *Meat Matters –
            Butchers, Politics, and Market Culture in Eighteenth-Century Paris*
            (Rochester, NY: University of Rochester Press, 2006),
            pp. 63–84.

p. 201   'drunkenness, confusion and riot . . . savage': Smithfield mar-
            ket as described by John Hogg, *London as it is, being a series of
            observations on the health, habits and amusements of the people*
            (London: John Macrone, 1837), pp. 218–20.

p. 207   In February, *The Times* carried an advertisement: classified
            advertisement 'For the attention of GENTLEMEN and
            LADIES', *The Times* (Thursday, 9 February 1815).

p. 207   'The Life and Adventures of Toby the Sapient Pig: with his
            Opinions on Men and Manners. Written by Himself': the
            quotations from Toby's 'autobiography' are taken from the
            edition republished by the British Library Historical Collection
            (London: British Library, 2011).